MW00342312

Special Privilege:

How the Monetary Elite Benefit at Your Expense

By

Vincent R. LoCascio

FAME

**The Foundation for the Advancement of
Monetary Education
New York, NY
www.fame.org**

Copyright © 2001 by Vincent LoCascio. All rights reserved

No part of this publication may be reproduced, stored in a retrieval system or transmitted in any form or by any means, electronic, mechanical, photocopying, recording, scanning or otherwise, except as permitted under Section 107 or 108 of the 1976 United States Copyright Act, without either the prior written permission of the Publisher, or authorization through payment of the appropriate per-copy fee to the Copyright Clearance Center, 222 Rosewood Drive, Danvers, MA 01923, (978) 750-8400, fax (978) 750-4744. Requests to the Publisher for permission should be addressed to the Permissions Department, the Foundation for the Advancement of Monetary Education, Box 625, FDR Station, New York, NY 10150-0625, (212) 818-1206, fax (212) 754-6543, E-mail: Permissions@FAME.ORG.

This publication is designed to provide accurate and authoritative information in regard to the subject matter covered. It is sold with the understanding that the publisher is not engaged in rendering professional services. If professional advice or other expert assistance is required, the services of a competent professional should be sought.

Library of Congress # 2001135577

LoCascio, Vincent
        Special Privilege: How the Monetary Elite
        Benefits at Your Expense

ISBN 0-9710380-3-1 (paper back)

Printed in the U.S. of America
10 9 8 7 6 5 4 3 2 1

In loving memory of my father, Vincent LoCascio
(1906 – 2000)

ACKNOWLEDGEMENTS

My initial inspiration came in 1990 when I read the late Murray Rothbard's *The Mystery of Banking*. Although I hold an MBA in Corporate Finance, with distinction, from NYU, and have studied the money issue intensively, I never truly understood the nature of banking until I read Murray Rothbard's book. Shortly, thereafter, I read Howard Katz's *The Paper Aristocracy,* which further inspired me to write *Root Causes*---the primary predecessor of *Special Privilege*. Thank you both for the inspiration to put my ideas on paper.

Dr. Lawrence Parks, Executive Director of the Foundation for the Advancement of Monetary Education, Ltd., thank you for the insights, observations, and subject matter edits you provided on my original *Root Causes* manuscript. Your comments helped me to sharpen my thoughts, be more precise in my language, and truly appreciate---if not fully adopt---the point of view that holds fiat money most responsible for our current circumstance.

Thank you, Vinny LoCascio, you never doubted my ability, son, to produce the original 1991 manuscript during a difficult and trying time in my life. Thank you, Serge Geacintov; several of your casual comments have impacted *Special Privilege* immeasurably. When you first suggested, for example, at 3am around the pool table, that I use fictional characters, I dismissed the idea out of hand. The next morning, when I awoke, I loved the idea. Your anthropological assessment of the financial situation seemed important to include---as the very last lines of the final chapter. Thank you, Jack Gargan, for giving *Special Privilege* a thorough "read" and providing your kind comments.

Thank you Doug Harvey, Roy Marden, Andrew Salmieri, Bob Grygo, Ed Goertzen, Jody Parker, Nick Andrews, Eric Schwartz, Wally Roberts, Joe LoCascio, Jacob Anodide, Steve Slate, Cheryl Worrell, Stefanie Mallia, Chris Aldanese, and Frank Peters for providing useful inputs at various stages of the project. Thank you Billy Thacket of Arcadia Studios for the superb cover design.

Thank you, Bette Jayne (BJ), for being the most understanding and supportive wife that I could have hoped for---not only throughout the production of my book---but always.

About Vincent R. LoCascio

Mr. LoCascio received his B.A. in Economics, *magna cum laude*, in 1966, from Hunter College and his M.B.A. in Corporate Finance, with distinction, from New York University, in 1969. Since that time he has had a diverse financial career as a consultant with two of the "Big 5" accounting firms, as a Wall Street trader and as a financial planner. Throughout this period, Mr. LoCascio has authored numerous articles, pamphlets, textbook chapters, and frequently lectured on and taught about monetary matters.

Vince has studied the monetary system since the early 1970's. *Special Privilege* is an important update, integration, and condensation of his previous writings on the monetary issue. Vince is semi-retired although he thoroughly enjoys working part-time teaching for Kaplan, Inc., the test prep subsidiary of *The Washington Post Company*. In this capacity, he is proud to have been named "Tri-State Teacher of the Year" in 2000. Vince is married, has two grown children, and lives with his wife, Bette Jayne, in Old Bridge, New Jersey.

To contact Vince, send email to: vinceloc@monmouth.com

Table of Contents

INTRODUCTION

Tick, Tock...Tick, Tock

"The study of money, above all other fields in economics, is one in which complexity is used to disguise truth or to evade truth, not to reveal it."

-John Kenneth Galbraith, 1975

Unless the United States of America substantially restructures its monetary system, a financial collapse of mammoth proportions is both foreseeable and inevitable. When this collapse will occur is impossible to predict. Why it will occur, however, is already abundantly clear. It can be summarized in two simple words: *Special Privilege*. The nature and implications of these special privileges are summarized later in this introduction and explored throughout the book. *Special Privilege* puts forth the following proposition: politicians grant special privileges to the monetary elite (bankers, central bankers, and, by proxy, their favored borrowers). These special privileges offend the very essence of both democracy and free enterprise. Furthermore, while these special privileges virtually guarantee a future monetary collapse, they temporarily put-off the timing of that collapse.

The proposition that only substantial reform can save us from dire financial consequences (the seeds of which have already been sown) admittedly requires significant evidence and support. *Special Privilege* will provide it. The proposition that immoral, unfair, and unwarranted special privileges exist and are antithetical to everything we believe in, requires nothing more than recognizing what undeniably does exist and pursuing the rather straight-forward implications thereof (currently, not 1 person in 100 has such knowledge---yet, virtually all will grasp it, upon reflection).

Special Privilege should appeal to a broad spectrum of concerned Americans---including those not normally drawn to financial books. It is, particularly, for those who want to educate themselves on important issues that are not widely understood or discussed; for those who already sense that something is wrong but want to pinpoint exactly what it is; for those who are not certain whether anything is wrong, but who are willing to suspend final judgment until they have read and evaluated a well thought out point of view.

THE NARCOTICS ANALOGY

The United States financial system can be instructively compared to a patient who is dying from narcotics addiction. One form of treatment is to provide larger and larger quantities of the narcotic. Under these conditions, the patient will temporarily function better but will face death or an even more painful cure in the future. Alternatively, the patient can kick the habit, cold turkey----knowing that the withdrawal may be long and require painful adjustments and reassessments. Many people, including the most powerful and influential, receive substantial benefits from the "patient" in his current addicted state. They recognize that the ill effects of increased addiction will not be felt until some undefined time in the future and that they will be forced to forego special privileges and/or benefits of continued addiction during the cure period. Under these conditions, these people favor a liberal, ultimately destructive, continued flow of narcotics.

In our financial system, the narcotic is money, and our banking system is the mechanism by which it is created and distributed. *Special Privilege* focuses on the perversions to our society that emanate from a fundamentally flawed banking infra-structure; flawed logic that equates money to wealth; and the flawed conclusion that confidence in the system is an end in itself, regardless of any rational basis for it.

Special Privilege presents a point of view that is irreverent toward current institutions. Both common sense logic and simple justice dictate that we substantially reform these institutions. Furthermore, the time to act is now. Festering root causes have been totally

2

ignored for too long. So far, we have watched passively as the system deteriorates. Now even reforms that address core issues will require significant dislocations in redefining institutions and policies.

Those who are complacently satisfied with the status quo may prefer to deny realities. Others who are blinded by the temporary nourishment they receive from the current system may be unaware that their actions are destroying it. Still others who recognize the situation for what it is may be content to enjoy the party while it lasts and to extend the curfew as late into the night as possible. Finally, those who are closest to the money-creation process have a vested interest in keeping things as they are for as long as they can. However, they will also be among the very first to know exactly when to bail out---leaving the rest of us "holding the bag."

THE HEART OF THE PROBLEM

The sales pitch of a bank boils down to this: "Bring us your money and we will pay you 5% annual interest for the right to use it. We can do this because we will lend it to borrowers at 10% annual interest. But any time you should want your money back, we will give it back to you, on demand, with accrued interest."

This is a misrepresentation. As soon as a bank makes such loans, it can no longer fulfill its stated obligation to return depositor's money on demand. Money that is out on loan, quite simply, is not available to be paid back to depositors on demand. No degree of added complexity can negate this simple fact. Sophisticated depositors realize that the money is not in the bank, yet they expect it to be there, if, and when, they wish to take it out. These expectations are, of course, self-contradictory. People accept this obviously unsound logic because they have been conditioned not to think about it. The Federal Reserve ("Fed") and the Federal Deposit Insurance Corporation ("FDIC") have made it unnecessary for them to have to think about it.

The above paragraphs make multiple references to "money." As important as money is, however, few people have a well-conceived, proper understanding of exactly what it is. Many people, for example, believe that the government issues our money. The truth, however, is that paper money is issued by the Fed, which is a private corporation (albeit, one that was theoretically incorporated to fulfill a public purpose). Originally, it was limited by the amount of gold in its vaults. Today, it can create (or destroy) as much money as it chooses, acting in secret, without restriction, and unaccountable to the American people. The second major component of our money supply consists of bank deposits (checking, savings, etc.), which are liabilities that banks create against themselves, limited only by their reserves at the Fed.

In other words, all money in our society is "issued" by private corporations as liabilities against themselves. It is the debt of the issuing organization. Money is debt. Unfortunately, many otherwise knowledgeable people are either unaware of this fact or are oblivious to its dire implications. One such implication is the self-perpetuating cycle: if money is created out of thin air and (mostly) lent out at interest, there will not be enough to repay all those debts unless still more is created out of thin air and lent out at interest!

Until the 20th century, money was generally not "issued" by anyone. It actually existed in physical form. It was valuable, in and of itself, and not subject to whimsical, arbitrary issuance by fiat. It did not derive its value from the creditworthiness of an issuer. Paper money, in those days, was viewed, essentially, as nothing more than a "warehouse receipt" for real money (typically, gold). Fiat money that the Fed creates without limit, together with the checkbook money that the banking system pyramids on top of this fiat money, is the heart of the problem. Indeed, the money-creating special privilege, alone (if not revoked or restricted), guarantees the future scenario this book predicts. The only open question is "when."

In the aftermath of the bank failures in the early 1930s, a vocal minority of respected academicians, including Irving Fisher of Yale and Frank Graham of Princeton, argued in favor of 100% reserve banking and/or similar reforms. Such reforms would have removed the important money-creating ability from banks and moved us in the right direction. Unfortunately, special interests seeking to maintain special privileges prevailed over these voices of reason. Simply put, the Fischer and Graham suggestions would have required that all demand deposits (checkbook money) be physically kept in the bank and not lent out. Today, however, banks are fractional reserve banks. They use a large portion of demand deposits to make loans;

and no matter how one looks at it or how much one tries to complicate it, fractional reserve banks inspire us to have confidence in something that we must know, deep down inside, is absolutely undeserving of confidence! Why do people accept such casual treatment of the most cherished of all commodities? Imagine, for example, this same process with regard to something as plentiful as water. Even then, depositors of water would have a natural tendency to want to know what the water borrowers are doing with it. Using the example above, everyone would realize that at the end of the process, if there were not at least 5% more water on hand than had been deposited, the depositors would be dissatisfied; and if there were not at least 10% more water than had been lent out, the bank would be dissatisfied.

That fractional reserve banks create and distribute money becomes clear upon basic analysis. If, for example, a depositor makes a $1,000 deposit in a bank by opening up a checking account, that $1,000 is part of the money supply. It is a medium of exchange that is immediately exchangeable in some quantity for any other good or service in the economy. When the bank lends, say, $800 to a borrower, that $800 also becomes part of the money supply. The original depositors' money, being available to him on demand, never ceased to be part of the money supply just because loans were made. Therefore, the loan has increased the money supply from $1,000 to $1,800. A fractional reserve bank, by virtue of merely making loans, increases the money supply. As John Kenneth Galbraith puts it, "the process by which banks create money is so simple that the mind is repelled. Where something so important is involved, a deeper mystery seems only decent."[1]

Actually, those who benefit from the system at everyone else's expense do go to great lengths to mystify the process. Early 21st century man is woefully uninformed about money and how it is created. Most think that the government creates our money. Ironically, people of the 19th century were far more knowledgeable. They were understandably distrustful of the money-creating activities of banks. In any event, is it possible that such institutions as the Fed and FDIC have, somehow, changed things? If so, is the change good, bad, or very bad?

THE LENDER OF LAST RESORT

The Fed was instituted as a lender of last resort in 1913. Its primary, original function was to provide liquidity to the system whenever it was needed. Providing liquidity may be thought of as creating bank money (reserves). During very troubled times, this newly created bank money may be used to meet depositor demands for currency. At all other times, it is used to make loans, which creates debt and creates money.

Before the existence of the Fed, financial panics developed every 15 to 20 years or so. Confidence in the system was, periodically, shaken and we required recessionary pullbacks from overheated economic activity. If no rational basis existed for these panics, the Fed's providing liquidity could have properly fended off recessionary consequences. Substantial historical evidence, however, supports the view that inappropriate speculative excesses were present in each case and, therefore, the panics were necessary and appropriate medicine.

Under conditions of speculative excess, pumping in liquidity only serves to encourage even more speculation. Increased speculation, quite understandably, leads to less and less confidence on the part of depositors. Over the last 20 years, there has been a veritable orgy of speculation and, indeed, fraud. However, the Fed, FDIC, and taxpayer bailouts have (so far) successfully avoided a major financial crisis.

Current wisdom argues that the Fed should virtually always provide liquidity to the system. Such reliable indicators of speculative excess as volatile financial markets, highly leveraged organizational structures, unstable currency relationships, complicated derivative products, frequent taxpayer bailouts, and other indicators of "irrational exuberance" argue in favor of caution. All too often, however, when caution is indicated, it is pushed to the side in pursuit of the big buck. History demonstrates that such behavior merely forestalls rather than avoids having to pay the price. To use a medical analogy, giving plasma to an anemic person will increase circulation, but it will not increase the all-important oxygen-carrying red blood cells that are required.[2]

The evidence suggests that providing more debt (money creation) in a speculative environment adds fuel to a fire that is already out of control. People have been conditioned to the view, however, that pumping more money into the system can solve all problems. Hardly anyone ever argues for less liquidity, higher interest rates, or debt contraction. Whenever trouble brews, a chorus of voices beseeches the Fed to ease, to accommodate, or to liquefy. "Ease," "accommodate," and "liquefy" are roughly equivalent terms. Each characterizes a set of policies whereby the Fed makes it easier for banks to lend. Often, people call for such a policy when the economy is suffering from strains of overextension. The policy says, in effect,

> *"Ignore the realities of overextension by overextending even further; rescue us from the natural adverse effects of past over-indulgences by giving us another needle in the arm."*

The Fed, playing its (pretended) role of tough taskmaster to the hilt, often refuses to budge until some other supposedly directly related problem is resolved. From this, the Fed may (incorrectly) appear to be delicately balancing its options to either restrain or expand the money supply. For example, the Fed will refuse to ease until Congress passes a "responsible" budget or until it is satisfied that inflation is in check. This, presumably, qualifies as restraint. If the budget has "only" a $150 billion deficit or if inflation is "only" 3%, this is not likely to be a *bona fide* reason to celebrate.

In any event, once a budget is finally passed, and in the absence of any other supposedly related issues to be resolved, the Fed submits. What a perfect way to instill confidence. After all, the Fed did not cave in for weeks to those urging earlier easing. Now that the budget crisis has supposedly been effectively resolved, however, even the intransigent Fed recognizes the benefits of more debt. This charade is part of an approach that has been going on since 1940 or so. The name of the game is to inflate problems away. And the Fed, together with the banking system, in general, is the engine of that inflation.

7

THEN AND NOW

It may come as a surprise to the casual observer under the age of 60 that inflation is not a natural and necessary phenomenon. After all, throughout that observer's lifetime he has known nothing else. He would probably be very surprised by the following fact: the purchasing power of a dollar in 1937 was roughly equal to the purchasing power of a dollar in 1802. Furthermore, throughout all the intervening years, the purchasing power swung back and forth---never rising above $1.75 and never falling below $.70. By 1960, that dollar was worth $.50, in 1937 terms; by 1976, it was worth $.25; in 1991, it was worth $.10; now, it is worth about $.08.

Until the mid 1970s, inflation was seemingly beneficial to the average homeowner. From roughly 1945 through 1975, the common man had the opportunity to borrow money for 30 years at a fixed low rate to buy a home. Under continuing and growing inflationary conditions, the value of his home went up at a rate that exceeded the interest rate he was paying. And all this time, commercial banks were making loans to productive enterprises. All in all, it was a prosperous, vital, growing America.

If a 20-year old skilled worker had only known in 1946 how the next 55 years would unfold, he would now be a 75-year-old multi-millionaire. All he had to do was work his trade and continually buy a bigger and bigger house every five years or so (each time taking the largest mortgage his circumstances and the bank would allow). If he was, then, smart enough to sell that house around 1987, invest the proceeds in the stock market, and rent whatever lavish home he could, this person would now be living, very comfortably, in the lap of luxury. It has been widely acknowledged that buying a house during this period was among the best investments a person could make. But this observation misses the point. The goodness of the investment had less to do with real estate, *per se*, than it had to do with the ability to borrow money on a long-term basis, at fixed low rates during a period of inflation. Had our hypothetical 20-year-old skilled worker been offered similar financing terms to buy collector comic books, he would have also achieved millionaire status.

The scene has changed dramatically over the last 25 years. Banks no longer make loans primarily to productive enterprises. Instead, from 1974 through 1982, roughly 50% of all money-center bank loans were made to lesser-developed countries (LDCs).[3] When the folly of these loans became apparent, funds poured into other speculative enterprises. These included adventuresome loans for speculative (or fraudulent) oil and gas projects, speculative (or fraudulent) securities speculators, leveraged corporate buyouts financed with junk bonds, opportunistic real estate developers, highly leveraged hedge funds, and "fad" loans to whatever corner of the world happens to be deemed the next "hot spot." During the 1980s and early 1990s one well known, high flyer---Donald Trump---was engaged, among other things, in building monuments to himself in both New York City and Atlantic City. Ironically, in the early 1990s during the height of Trump's own financial troubles, an electronic billboard at the entrance of his Taj Mahal casino in Atlantic City issued the following sage advice: "Bet with your head, not over it." Could the banks have been unaware that lending one man billions of dollars for risky elaborate real estate schemes was a risky business, or didn't they care? Actually, it was a little of both. Conspicuously absent in the orgy of bank speculation of the last 25 years, in any event, were good old-fashioned loans supporting productive enterprise.

BANK "PROFITABILITY"

Once upon a time, the capitalist system's central virtue was that it rewarded productivity. Those who produced value received value in return; those who produced very little received very little in return. Within that commendably moral framework, our limited resources were always efficiently allocated to the most productive available enterprises. All of this happened quite naturally. Everyone, wanting to receive as much as he could, produced as much as he could. Such was the way things were when productivity and profitability were compatible concepts.

Over the last 20 years, most particularly with regard to banking, "profitability" has become little more than sleight-of-hand accounting gimmickry. For example, if a bankrupt borrower is written-off by the bank, the bank's accounting profit is diminished (as, of course, it should be). But, if the bank chooses to lend more at higher and higher interest rates to the same bankrupt borrower, the bank's accounting profit is increased. What can be more perverse than this? The bank actually has a vested interest in not acknowledging a bad loan; and the only way to not acknowledge it is to make an even bigger loan to the bankrupt borrower. In this way, the bankrupt borrower can pay interest on the old loan and the bank can "book" profits rather than take losses writing off the bad loans. Reality is thus defined as whatever the banker chooses to recognize as reality. But, undoubtedly, somewhere beneath the recognized reality, there lurks a real reality with which we will have to reckon. Due to the level of reality denial over the past two decades, that day of reckoning may not be too far off.

This insane situation is truly mind-boggling. Aren't regulators, examiners, and independent accountants supposed to see that this doesn't happen? More often than not, these supposedly independent sources of assurance are nothing more than handmaidens to the bankers. In most cases, the latest audited financial statement of a recently failed bank bears little relation to the actual situation. How this can happen is best answered with the following rhetorical question:

"What possible motive can an independent auditor have for seeing things the way his client wants him to see things ---unless, of course, you consider the multi-million dollar annual audit fee?"

FDIC

In the 1930-33 period, several waves of bank runs and bank failures, together with a weakened economy, led to further government policies whose perverse effects are being felt to this day. One of the worst of these is the concept of federal deposit insurance. The most perverse element of deposit insurance is that it eliminates the very basis for investment decision-making. Investment should be made, first, where there is the least risk at a given rate of return. If there are alternative investments, each with the expectations of earning 5%, money should flow (first, if at all) into the one perceived to be the safest.

With regard to our banking system, however, federal deposit insurance tells a would-be depositor that, from his standpoint, he should view all banks as equally risky since any risk that does exist will be borne by the government.

Even if this were the only perversion brought about by federally insured deposits, it would lead, inexorably, to a gross inefficiency in the allocation of scarce resources. At some point, in the absence of regulations to the contrary, astute bankers will reason that by offering 6% to depositors while other banks are offering 5%, they can get most of the money flowing into their bank. With federally insured deposits, the depositors can't go wrong by putting the money in the 6% bank. From the depositor's individual perspective, of course, this is, absolutely, the right thing to do. But what does it do to the system? Generally, no one bothers to ask this pertinent question.

For one thing, it virtually guarantees that money will flow to the banks that offer the highest return. And which ones might that be? At first, they will "only" be the most speculative banks. They are willing to pay high rates because they charge still higher rates to speculative borrowers. That unleashes negative forces that ripple through the entire system. But it gets worse--- much worse. How much insight does it take to recognize that an outright fraudulent banking element will be right behind the speculative element? Historically, it has happened time and time again.

Investment, in a less speculative environment, takes place when there are reasonable assurances that productive gain will result. Debt capital, under such conditions, seeks not only assurances, but guarantees. Fraud in such a setting is easily detected. As investment becomes more speculative, there is a hope (not assurances or guarantees) that productive gain will result. A fertile breeding ground for fraud is thus established. Fraud flourishes in an atmosphere where victims can be told with feigned sorrow, "Gee, we were hoping that this would all work out; but, as you know, in life there are no guarantees." From a banker's perspective, reduced requirements for investment justification invite fraud. Fraudulent loans become the most convenient way to rip off a decaying system. By the late 1980s and early 1990s, the evidence grew larger with the arrival of each morning's paper that the fraudulent element had appeared, in full force, during the prior decade. In 1980, the rise in federal deposit insurance coverage from $40,000 to $100,000 per account indicated, in effect, that the system was promoting a government-insured pyramid scheme. While the banks were assessed for their participation in FDIC coverage, there was, initially, no attempt at all to equate risk to level of assessment. Most importantly, there was never a question that the federal government (i.e., the ordinary taxpayer) stood behind this coverage. The soundness of the system was no longer a real concern. All that mattered is that the Fed would rescue money-center banks and the FDIC would rescue depositors. The message to bankers was clear:

> *"Throw all caution to the wind. Offer whatever interest rate you must to attract funds into the bank. There will always be plenty of borrowers at higher interest rates under the prevailing mood. And, if not, your friends, relatives, and partners are ready to take a shot."*

AT THE CROSSROADS

Such is the nature of the current state of affairs. Real issues have been ignored and hidden while we become more and more creative (and dangerous) in our ability to deal with symptoms and our ability to banish negative effects by legislating and inflating them away. During the coming major financial crisis, everyone will become acutely aware of, and alarmed about, the state of our financial infrastructure. People will be forced to confront the fact that our system has severe problems. This book will have already explained where the real problems lie. The title begins to tell the tale: *Special Privilege*. If history is any guide, highly respected, powerful people who control our monetary system will put forth alternatives that do not remove their special privilege. They may deal, perhaps, with some of the worst excesses of the present system, but they will oppose the real, enduring solutions that a democratic, free enterprise society requires: removal of the special privileges enjoyed by a very small minority of 100,000 or so while the remaining 289 million of us are forced to accept the adverse consequences of these privileges. Without books like *Special Privilege*, there is virtually zero chance that appropriate solutions will be reached.

There is, of course, no question that real solutions will require substantial education and even re-education of those who are, essentially, complacent victims of the current system. Appropriate reform will require a groundswell of popular opinion that recognizes the immorality, unsoundness, and dangers of continuing on the current path. Maybe nothing will happen until the inherent weaknesses of the system become much more obvious. In that case, in the interim, the establishment will merely promote non-solutions that temporarily cover up the cracks in the decaying infrastructure. Once these cracks are sufficiently covered up, they will immediately begin to widen under the surface until the next crisis uncovers them again. The ultimate crisis will occur when the situation is so thoroughly perverted that the defenders of the status quo can no longer resurrect confidence in the system.

Throughout this book we explore the special privileges that politicians bestow upon bankers. Taken together, they are the root cause of the problems that exist within the monetary system and will ultimately cause it to collapse. They fall into six broad categories:

1. Money creation

2. Asset protection (discount privilege at the Fed)

3. Liability protection (FDIC coverage)

4. Rescue missions (bailouts and the like)

5. Accounting irregularities

6. Secrecy rules

This introduction has briefly touched upon some of these categories. The following pages describe each of them in greater detail, and the final chapter provides a concise summary. The List of Additional Resources presents a list of other resources that contain useful information about one or more of the special privileges information about one or more of the special privileges discussed enumerated above and discussed throughout this book.

At times, some of the material might be somewhat challenging to one who is taking a first serious look into this area. However, much of the mystery arises only because of the purposeful misdirection of those who would keep you in the dark about these issues. No less an authority than John Kenneth Galbraith explained it well in his 1975 classic entitled, *Money: Whence It Came; Where It Went*. He wrote:

> *"Much discussion of money involves a heavy overlay of priestly incantation. Some of this is deliberate. Those who talk of money and teach about it and make their living by it gain prestige, esteem, and pecuniary return, as does a doctor or a witch doctor, from cultivating the belief that they are in privileged association with the occult---that they have insights that are nowise available to the ordinary person. Though professionally rewarding and personally profitable, this too is a well-established form of fraud. There is nothing about money that cannot be understood by the person of reasonable curiosity, diligence and intelligence. There is nothing on the following pages that cannot be so understood. And whatever error of interpretation or of fact this history may contain, there are, the reader may be confident, none that proceed from simplification. The study of money, above all other fields in economics, is one in which complexity is used to disguise truth or to evade truth, not to reveal it."[4]*

Going one step beyond Mr. Galbraith's accurate assessment: you can virtually count on various self-serving vested interests telling you why the conclusions you have reached about money and banking are wrong. Don't listen to them: instead, follow your own heart and your own mind. These self-appointed experts will try to explain to you--- the supposedly "unsophisticated"---why there is nothing to worry about and nothing to fix. They will tell you that the conditions that have unerringly produced financial collapses in the past are now well understood and under their control. Don't believe them until you have at least looked at the evidence yourself. The issues are not nearly as complex as these people would have you believe. A new enlightened majority that recognizes the nature and scope of the problem in our monetary and financial system must seek real solutions to the root causes.

As other powerful constituencies (e.g. multi-national corporations) begin to recognize that the financial elite's activities adversely affect their own control of their own destinies, they will, hopefully, enlist in the reform effort. Chapter 6 discusses some of the ill effects that inter-currency volatility and derivative transactions can have on multi-national corporations. Since financial elites maintain their lofty position solely through the exercise of totally unnecessary special privileges, at some point, people and corporations will, presumably, step forward to object. After all, special privilege violates the basic tenets of a democratic, free enterprise society. To allow the current system and its institutions to continue is as immoral as it is dangerous. Furthermore, time is running out. There is no reason to wait. Tick, tock...tick,tock.

Chapter I

Early Casualties

"Whoever controls the volume of money in any country is absolute master of all industry and commerce."

-President James A. Garfield

During the mid-to-late 1980s, widespread Savings & Loan ("S&L") failures saddled American taxpayers with a $300-$500 billion bailout.[1] Among the assets found on the books of failed S&Ls were extensive collections of fine art, corporate jets, luxury yachts, and multi-million-dollar beachfront vacation homes that, primarily, enhanced the lifestyles of perpetrators of bank fraud. Where, then, was the public outrage and indignation? Why didn't we insist on retribution and, more importantly, on reforms to prevent future occurrences?

Had these crimes been committed by a band of traditional, gun-toting bank robbers, there would certainly have been a public outcry to put the criminals behind bars. This would have served to punish the perpetrators, to restrain them from doing it again, and to send a warning message to like-minded, would-be criminals. Under the actual circumstances, we could have done even better. Since the crimes were only made possible by a fundamentally flawed banking system, we could have set about to reform the system. Why, then, did this process not take place? Why, instead, did we leave ourselves exposed to even greater crises in the future?

The answers to the above questions are many-fold and will be answered in due course. In a nutshell, politicians would have had to admit serious errors and would have had to support reforms that lack a natural constituency; bankers would have had to forego enormous special privileges; all others, however, would have merely had to understand the issues. Once we understand the situation, the solutions more or less suggest themselves. The S&L crisis is a convenient and familiar point of departure. The problem, however, is endemic to the entire monetary and financial infrastructure, as we shall see.

Unfortunately, even avid newspaper readers only got bits and pieces of how the S&L crisis developed and how it grew to the proportions that it did. With literally hundreds of individual cases reported, it is often difficult to obtain a clear picture of how the sorry mess actually unfolded. A unified, fictionalized (but realistic) composite can provide a useful overview.

Y.B. Fehr and her brother, Will B. Fehr, had entered commercial banking as partners in 1968. Some of their trials and tribulations are chronicled in later chapters. Initially, Y.B. and Will had reasonably similar views on proper bank management. Y.B. was somewhat more willing to "play the game" with whatever new rules unfolded, whereas Will tended to stick to his own conception of prudence. Nonetheless, for 15 years, they worked side by side at the First National Bank of Fairfield, Texas, generally in agreement---or, at least, able to hammer out workable compromises.

In 1983, a billionaire from Louisiana named Manny Banks approached Y.B. with an opportunity that she couldn't pass up. Manny was well known within the Texas banking community. He was a silent partner in about 30 S&Ls---each one of which was growing at rates of 50% to 100% annually due to Manny's connections back East. At their first meeting, Manny laid out to Y.B. the kind of operation he envisioned.

"I am looking to buy the Smallville S&L in Smallville, Texas. It has about $25 million in deposits and $1 million in capital. Over the last few years, they have lost several million dollars. With your experience and the turn-around in the economy, I am sure you can improve upon current management's per-

formance regarding the existing loan portfolio. We can buy this bank for $1.5 million. I will lend you $700,000 over 5 years for your purchase of 49% of the stock. I will retain the other 51%. You will be completely free to run the bank as you see fit---as long as we can agree on some general principles. Your salary will be $300,000 plus performance bonuses---the details of which we can work out. How does that sound so far, Y.B.?"

"It sounds very workable so far, Manny. I know your reputation for having an aggressive, non-traditional operating posture. I have been trying for years to get my brother, Will, to see the advantages of moving in that direction in our bank, but he has been somewhat reluctant to come around to my way of thinking. Texas laws are now quite liberal on investment policy and I suspect I can be as aggressive as the next person in taking advantage of the opportunities that these liberalized regulations allow. I feel that the current portfolio should be invested, as it matures, in residential home mortgages, because, that is the justification for the S&L industry. We just won't make the mistake of not protecting ourselves from inflation as the industry has done in the past. Various adjustable-rate mortgage alternatives should do the trick. As for new funds, I am open to anything that makes good economic sense and doesn't violate the regulations."

"Great, Y.B. I think we are going to be able to work together profitably. Just to make sure we are on the same wavelength, let me sound you out on two key issues. As you know, brokered deposits are the wave of the future. We have contacts up in New York putting together brokered CD's. As long as we match the best rates offered elsewhere, we can easily bring in at least $25 million into Smallville within the next year. As a sign of good faith, however, the brokers with whom we work generally require that we lend at least

10% of the money to people that they designate. Do you have any problem with that?"

Y.B. hesitated. *"Well, Manny, if the designated borrowers are otherwise good risks, I certainly don't see anything wrong with that. However, by paying maybe 1/4% more on our CDs we can probably get our money from Merrill Lynch brokers who wouldn't have such strings attached to the money they broker. Wouldn't that make more sense?"*

"I don't think so, Y.B. We have established some pretty close ties to the people we deal with, and my banks have never objected to accommodating the wishes of our brokers. It really wouldn't be too good for our overall business to let our money brokers know that we are offering ¼% more for Merrill money in order to avoid their restrictions. Since they have only asked us to lend to some pretty solid projects, we have never had any problem in the past."

"You're probably right," Y.B. replied, not wanting to seem like she was going to be difficult to work with and thinking that she had probably been hanging around with Will too long. *"I can definitely live with your current procedures...You mentioned there were a couple of important points. What's the other one?"*

"We also have contacts with some people that deal in substantial amounts of cash. On a more or less continuing basis, they need to get this cash back into the banking system with as little fuss as possible. Now it would be illegal for us to take in cash deposits in the size that we are talking about, but there are ways around that which are perfectly legal. Our banks have always been willing to accommodate these contacts. The profitability on these funds is enormous. I estimate that Smallville can expect about $1 million per month of this money; and with the processing fees we charge, plus the interest earned on these funds for the period that they are in our bank, you would be looking at about $500,000 per year in clear profits from such activity.

Y.B. was somewhat uncomfortable but she tried not to show it too much. She was certainly aware of the widespread laundering of drug money and the prevalence of it even among otherwise respectable banks--- especially along the points of entry into the country. Smallville was only 5 miles from the Mexican border.

"One-half million is a pretty tidy sum to pass up if the bank can maintain its integrity with the community and its employees. I'm assuming that we are not talking about a stream of seedy looking characters with shopping carts of cash on a daily basis."

"If you are in general agreement, Y.B., I can show you how we handle these transactions at our other banks. They involve a minimum disruption to your day-to-day operations, I assure you. So what do you think? Do we have a basis to continue?"

"Well, of course, I want to mull it over, but...yes...I think we should be able to work together on this. I will get back to you in a few days with a definitive answer." Y.B. wanted to satisfy herself that she wasn't getting in over her head. She also wanted to consider how her brother might evaluate this opportunity, but, strangely, she didn't want to actually discuss it with him. It was almost as if she was ashamed that her decision was going to be to go ahead with the deal. She knew that Will would advise against both the brokered deposits with strings attached and the drug money laundering. But, then, again, he had opposed other ideas of hers in the past---most of which had worked out well when they did proceed with them. As far as the brokered deposits, she could always turn them down if they were conditioned on making loans that she viewed as imprudent. She was, therefore, still in control. As for the money laundering, that was a fact of life. After all, she had no involvement with how the money was earned. It wasn't her place to ask any depositors where their money came from. And if she didn't take this money in, some other bank would. Why should they earn the fees

when she could. No, on balance, this was an opportunity that she just couldn't allow to slip by.

The deal with Manny went through and within one year the bank tripled in size to $75 million in deposits. The traditional business from the existing portfolio did a little better than break even and between the cash business and $50 million in brokered funds, Smallville earned $2.5 million in the first year, all of which was sheltered by previous tax-loss carryforwards. By the following year, an additional $75 million in brokered deposits and a doubling of the cash business allowed the bank to grow to $150 million in deposits and $8 million in capital.

Over the two-year period, Y.B. and Manny had each taken out $1 million in dividends. Y.B. had already justified the move in her mind just on the basis of what she had already taken out in salary and dividends. She was somewhat concerned, however, with the current portfolio, which consisted of $30 million in home mortgages, $70 million primarily in real estate deals in the still booming Northeast, $15 million in junk bonds, and $20 million to some Texas land developers who were the designated borrowers from the money brokers.

It was the latter category of loans that worried her the most. Texas real estate was still in a slump yet the developers were actively building condos and shopping malls at a fast and feverish pace. The loans had been rolled over from project to project, and now she was getting word that $1 million in interest and principal coming due in a few days might not be paid. The developers were asking for a rescheduling of their loans. The security for the loans was appraised for $30 million, and Y.B. was unsure how to approach the rescheduling. Y.B. felt it would be prudent to dispatch her own trusted appraiser to take a look at these projects up in the Dallas area.

She was horrified when he reported back to her that while the real estate securing the loans had, in *fact, recently changed hands at around $30 million, it appears that these sales were sham transactions between related parties, solely for the purpose of documenting the value at $30 million. The appraiser indicated that the true value of the property was closer to $9 million, or, in other words, $11 million less than the outstanding balance of the loans. Even if Y.B. foreclosed on these properties, the loss would wipe out the entire net worth of the bank and leave it with a negative $3 million in net worth. The bank would be rendered insolvent. Y.B. recalled a comment she remembered having heard from Arthur Burns, former Fed Chairman, regarding the loans to the lesser-developed countries. He said that the money-center banks had made some pretty foolish loans, and that now, we can only hope that they make more of them. She and Will were stunned that Burns would say such a thing even if he believed it. Now, it seemed, she might be in a similar bind herself.*

She called Manny Banks to discuss the dilemma. Manny was surprisingly matter of fact about the report. "Our strategy, at this point is relatively clear," he began. "We obviously have to make whatever loans are necessary to keep these people afloat; we've got to keep the true situation hidden from the regulators for as long as possible; and, most importantly, we have to take as much money out of the bank as possible, consistent with maintaining the fiction that everything is fine. I will leave the details up to you. But I should mention that, on average, in similar situations, we have found that our banks can be kept open for about three more years. With your skills and my help on overall strategy, I think we should have no problem lasting into 1989."

Y.B. could do nothing but agree with Manny's analysis. There seemed to be no other choice. But even though she was likely to make a bundle in the process, she longed for the days when she and Will were legitimate bankers. As much sense as Manny's *suggestions made, Y.B. decided to speak to Will about her predicament. They had remained close since she moved to Smallville, although they had previously made it a strict rule never to discuss business. Y.B. called Will and described the situation to him. "Y.B., your strategy at this point is relatively clear," Will began---curiously, using the exact same opening words that Manny had used---,"You have to foreclose on the Dallas developers and take your lumps. From the figures you have just given me, you will still have a negative $3 million in capital on $150 million in deposits. FSLIC can, therefore, make the depositors whole at a relatively minor cost to them.*

Of course, your stock in the bank will be worthless, but you have, personally, done well over the last few years---better than you would have back here in Fairfield. I'm sure you realize that there is still a place here for you. I'm ready to retire and I can't think of a better banker to turn the reins over to than you."

"Will, I just don't know what to do. I'll have to think about it further. Thanks for your support. I want you to know--- regardless of what I decide---that I wish I had never left Fairfield, but to turn back now, under the current circumstances--- well, I just don't know. I'll just have to see. Will, one other thing---I love you." Y.B. hung up the phone, crawled into bed rolled up into an embryonic ball and cried. She knew what her decision would be---she just didn't know why.

With regard to the Texas developers, Y.B. knew that they were not going to be anything other than a cash drain on the bank. They and their partners were still tied into the money brokers who were providing her with fresh funds. These brokers were now requiring that 25% of the funds they provided be lent to their friends. The bigger these loans got, the more difficult it was going to be to keep the regulators from seeing through the obvious facade. Her outside auditors were also a problem.

First, she introduced the accounting partner in charge of the bank's audit to Manny who was looking for someone to run a new bank he was buying. Then, she used this as a reason to change CPA firms. In evaluating the successor CPA firms, her sole criterion was whether they seemed willing to look the other way regarding questionable loans and practices. Next, she offered the FSLIC regulator a job at the Smallville bank at twice his prior salary. She formed her own data services company to which she paid substantial fees for keeping the records of the bank. When the new FSLIC examiner called the data service company for the bank records that he needed for his supposedly surprise examination, Y.B. was alerted. By this time she had already established a practice of trading assets with some of Manny's other banks, ostensibly for the purpose of risk sharing. The actual reason, however, was to cover up the rash of transfers just before an examination, the purpose of which was to trade a large portion of her questionable loans for more suitable alternatives with the other banks.

Even with all the deception, however, by 1987, the FSLIC examiners were calling attention to the deteriorating condition of the bank's loans. Over the years, Y.B. had allowed key Congresspersons to use the jet, the beach house, and, particularly the yacht, which was moored in the Potomac. In addition, she contributed to several Senators' campaigns and gave a bundle in "soft money" to both major political parties. She requested that they get the overzealous bureaucrats off her back, and they were able to pull some strings for her.

Y.B. continued to lend to the development projects in the Northeast. By now, they suspected the true condition of the Smallville bank just from the way their new loans were structured. Specifically, the loans were offered at 2% below the current market rate but the developers were required to buy insurance from an offshore company that Y.B. and Manny had set up. The cost of the insurance was only 1.5% of the loan amount, so the borrowers were happy to go along. From Manny and Y.B.'s perspective, not only did they siphon off funds from the bank, they also avoided income taxes. Manny's people took care of these arrangements, so Y.B. justified it to herself on that basis. All she was doing was making loans below the market rate.

Y.B. developed various other devices for siphoning funds out of the bank. With a good friend of hers, she formed an art dealership in Houston. The bank lent the money for the venture, and the offshore insurance company provided the insurance. An added benefit was that Y.B.'s office was furnished with very attractive, expensive paintings and sculptures. Furthermore, fine art had been an excellent investment over the years and because of the illiquidity of the art market, it was difficult for examiners and auditors to challenge inflated market valuations.

Y.B. also formed a securities firm with Manny's good friend, Barbara Bonds. Barbara was a computer genius and was also very knowledgeable in the securities markets. Speculating in futures was fraught with risk but could also produce incredibly large profits. Initially, Y.B. had hoped (more in desperation than anything else) that maybe Barbara's operations would be so successful that they could, miraculously, rescue the bank. Barbara's operations soon became nothing more than a tool for overtly fraudulent activity. But by now Y.B. was in too deep. Again, she justified her participation because she was removed from these operations except for the financing of them.

Barbara was involved in significant wheeling and dealing with term repos and reverse repos. In simplified terms, the net effect of these esoteric techniques---in combination with Barbara's own fraudulent twist-

-- was to make one dollar do the work of five or six dollars. Specifically, she would begin by lending the Smallville S&L $1 million for which she received $3 million in government bonds as security. She would then borrow $2.5 million from each of two money managers, putting up the same $3 million in government securities to secure both transactions. A friend of Manny's, whom Barbara used as her clearing and transfer agent, would fraudulently confirm to each of the money managers that the securities had been properly credited to their accounts.

During the term of these loans, therefore, Barbara had $5 million to use speculating in interest-rate futures, foreign exchange, and stock market index options. Her genius in these markets had produced several million in profits between 1987 and 1989. On October 13, 1989, a day on which the stock market index futures dropped 7% in a period of 20 seconds, she lost $15 million---$13 million more than her $2 million in equity. Barbara knew, of course, that the big boys had manipulated the markets in their own self-interest. The shadiness of her own operations, however, made her the last person with a right to complain. Besides she lacked the clout to go up against the biggies.

On October 16th, rumors of Smallville S&Ls exposure to the losses of Bonds Investments, Inc. caused a run on the bank. On October 17th, the regulators closed the bank for good. At the time the bank closed, Smallville's books showed $250 million in deposits and $8 million in capital (before a $5 million loss from Barbara Bond's operation). Of its $220 million in loans and investments, $50 million was to the various Texas developers who had been the designated borrowers of Smallville's New York money brokers. There was, supposedly, $70 million in real estate securing these loans, but, upon closer inspection, it was found that the security was only worth about $15 million and none of the loans were any *good. One major condo project currently under construction by these developers had been built so shoddily that the units had to be torn down. Even if they had been allowed to stand however, the over-supply of condos in the area would have made them impossible to sell or rent.*

The $5 million loss on the securities operation and the $35 million loss on the development loans converted the $8 million in Smallville's book capital into a $32 million real deficit. Meanwhile Y.B. and Manny had managed to pull out about $10 million for themselves---a significant portion of which was in the Cayman Islands, the Netherland Antilles, and Switzerland. In other words, these funds were beyond the reach of the authorities. Investigations are now underway against Manny Banks, Y.B. Fehr, and the Texas developers---to date, however, only Barbara Bonds has been officially brought up on charges for securities fraud.

WIDESPREAD FRAUD: A SYMPTOM NOT A CAUSE

The above story is a composite, anecdotal portrayal of the kinds of activities that precipitated the S&L crisis. The activities included in the story were, of course, not all prominent features in each and every failed S&L. The use of drug money, for example, was a relatively minor and profitable activity. Its prevalence was, however, indicative of the moral decay that attended the S&L crisis and that has infected banking over the last two decades. Banks in and around the ports of entry, like Miami, were regularly involved with, indeed, fought for, the highly profitable money laundering business.[2]

Much of what was written about the S&L bailout addressed the issue of how it all happened and where all the money disappeared. People generally have a problem coming to grips with issues whose impact is measured in hundreds of millions of dollars, let alone billions of dollars. For that reason, seemingly precise accounts will often be accepted as plausible when, in fact, they are nothing more than thinly veiled attempts to cover up the true story. One of the more frequently quoted experts on this subject was Bert Ely, a consultant to (and apparently an apologist for) the banking industry. Mr. Ely was frequently quoted in the press and in magazine articles and appeared on many TV talk shows and call-in shows to explain to the lay public what caused the S&L crisis. Typical of what he put forth is presented in an article by Gary Hector in the September 10, 1990, issue of *Fortune* entitled, "S&Ls: Where Did All the Billions Go?" Mr. Hector characterized Mr. Ely's answer to his title question as "the most detailed breakdown yet." Mr. Ely estimated the cost of the bailout at $147 billion (not $145 or $150, but $147). His breakdown consisted of the following overlapping, double counting, double-talking mixed bag of items:

1. $43 billion: We didn't shut down failed institutions earlier.
2. $28 billion: New laws allowed riskier projects.
3. $25 billion: In the 1970s, inflation produced adverse effects.
4. $14 billion: Banks had increased operating costs.
5. $14 billion: The S&Ls offered above-market interest rates.
6. $12 billion: Government was inefficient in closing banks.
7. $6 billion: Banks made imprudent junk bond investments.
8. $5 billion: Crooked bankers stole this amount.

This list is so riddled with holes that it is difficult to figure out where to begin criticizing it. Perhaps the best way to demonstrate the sheer nonsense in Mr. Ely's list is by analogy. So, here is "the most detailed breakdown yet" of how $10 million disappeared (into notorious bank robber Willie Sutton's pockets) during the 1930s:

1. $3 million: He was not apprehended earlier.
2. $2 million: In the 1920s, inflation produced adverse effects.
3. $2 million: New laws allowed banks to have fewer guards.
4. $2 million: New laws made banks keep more vault cash.
5. $1/2 million: Banks engaged in unsafe practices.
6. $1/2 million: Mr. Sutton had a criminal mentality.

It appears as though the primary purpose of Mr. Ely's analysis is to assert that fraud was a relatively minor element in the crisis.

Virtually every other authoritative source alleges that fraud was in evidence, not only in the S&L crisis but in every banking scandal in history. As a graduate student, Raymond B. Vickers, a lawyer and chief bank regulator in Florida for a time, examined failures that occurred in the 1920s and found a similarity to the pattern in the 1980s. He concluded, "I haven't found a single bank failure that didn't involve a conscious conspiracy to defraud."[3] William K. Black, General Counsel for FSLIC, said in June 1987, that insider abuse and fraud along with growth in risky investments "are overwhelmingly responsible for virtually all recent failures."[4] In June, 1989, the GAO profiled a small sample of failed institutions. Among other things, they found that fraud was a significant element in each of the 26 sampled failed S&Ls.[5] The U.S. News & World Report reported that "Attorney General Richard Thornburgh, FBI Director William Sessions, and FDIC boss William Seidman say that up to a third of the losses are based on fraud."[6]

Most recently, Alan Greenspan, in a speech on September 18, 2000, to the American Bankers Association in Washington D.C., alluded to the long-held notion that banks and bankers do, indeed, succumb to temptation and abuse their special privileges:

> *"Perhaps Hugh McCulloch, our first Comptroller of the Currency, may have been a little over the edge, in this regard, when in 1863 he proposed that the National Bank Act 'be so amended that the failure of a national bank be declared prima facie fraudulent, and that the officers and directors, under whose administration such insolvency shall occur, be made personally liable for the debts of the bank, and be punished criminally, unless it shall appear, upon investigation, that its affairs were honestly administered.'"*

The focus on fraud as a cause, however, is somewhat misplaced. Fraud can be considered as a possible cause when an isolated incident of bank failure occurs in which fraud is clearly present. This is not as true for widespread fraud, however. Hundreds of bankers don't simultaneously decide to be fraudulent unless there are underlying reasons for this behavior. There is no question that fraud and insider abuse have been around since the beginning of banking and are more prevalent in financial institutions than elsewhere. Such activity does not rise to the level we experienced during the S&L crisis, however, if the system is sound, the legislative and regulatory environment is restrictive, the economic climate is stable, and morality is high.

The banking system must be based on self-sustaining, economically sound principles. A fundamental principle that applies to every industry except banking is that the maturities of assets should match the maturities of liabilities. If an industrial company modernizes its plant over a multi-year period in order to reap benefits over an even longer time period, it does not finance the modernization with 30-day commercial paper. Instead, it finances with equity capital or long-term bonds.

Commercial banks and S&Ls, on the other hand, mismatch assets and liabilities with reckless abandon. The liabilities of a banking institution are deposits ---many of which are due on demand---while their assets consist of loans and investments of longer terms. The S&Ls, in particular, historically made 30-year fixed mortgage loans. As long as they could continue to pay 4% on deposits and receive 7% on the mortgages, everything was fine. When inflation, and therefore interest rates, went into double digits after the banks were already committed to outstanding 30-year assets earning 7%, they were in a hopelessly unsound predicament.

Instead of acknowledging economic realities, bankers traditionally rely upon governmental favors and special privileges that, in effect, allow them to defy reality. From 1933 through the early 1970s, the regulatory and legislative environment protected banks from competition. During this period, laws protected banks from competition across state lines; protected them from interest-rate competition; and, above all, guaranteed their deposits through a so-called "insurance" program. Banks have been accurately described during this period as groups of regionalized, government-supported cartels. However, when non-bank financial institutions found ways to compete with banks for deposits---through such products, for example, as money market funds that paid higher interest rates under the inflationary conditions of the 1970s---the politicians came to the rescue once again.

In the late 1970s, the administration removed the ceilings on interest rates and allowed banks to invest in riskier projects. But instead of also eliminating the protection of federally insured deposits, the government raised the coverage, first, from $20,000 to $40,000 in 1974, and, then, in 1980, to $100,000. The protection was liberally interpreted to apply to each account rather than to each person. These increases became law without debate, without public pressure in support of them, and without any official public statement defending them. Henry Gonzalez, a former Chairman of the House Banking Committee, said that his predecessor, Ferdinand St. Germain, asked in 1980 for unanimous consent to amendments proposed in conference to the Depository Institutions Regulatory and Monetary Control Act. One such amendment was the increase in deposit coverage from 40,000 to $100,000. According to Gonzales, no copies were made available, and there was never one minute's consideration or hearing on that increase---there was no debate. In fact, only about 10 members were on the floor at the time.[7]

By the early 1980s, then, all the conditions necessary to facilitate widespread fraud had been put in place. First, legislative and regulatory special privileges had protected banks from the realities of free enterprise for 40 years, and banks continued to borrow short-term while lending long-term. Then, when the inflationary 1970s exposed the folly of such a policy, the banks were not forced to pay the consequences (as free enterprise requires). Instead, politicians granted banks a new set of special privileges that allowed them to continue to defy economic reality. From a banker's perspective, economic reality amounted to the creative exploitation of special privilege in order to maximize his own and his institution's best interest. This, then, added the last element required for fraud to become inevitable: a loosened morality. The new set of special privileges was more conducive to exploitation by bankers than by banks. Under these conditions, bankers acted predictably. They merely used the new set of privileges to help themselves rather than their institutions. The very essence of special privilege encourages those who receive it to view themselves as above the rules that apply to others.

The loosened standards of morality were therefore encouraged by the mere existence of special privilege. In a U.S. News and World Report editorial entitled, "The Bad Guys of the S&L Fiasco,"

Mortimer B. Zuckerman, Editor-in Chief, stated, "These were men temperamentally and morally suited to exploit financial privileges without financial responsibility who engaged in mismanagement and outright fraud."[8] In addition, from the early 1970s to the early 1980s, money---the very standard of value---was permitted to lose over 50% of its value. Ayn Rand has accurately stated, "Money is the barometer of a society's virtue."[9] When that barometer was in a state of free-fall, virtue fell right along with it. The ensuing fraud, then, was not the cause of the S&L crisis; it was the predictable result of supporting an unsound system with special privilege within an environment of declining morality. In a moral system without special privilege, fraud is indeed the aberration. The perpetrator does not accept the standards and values of a moral society. Until we address root causes, fraud will be the rule rather than the exception. Don't blame fraud as the cause, however; blame the elements of society that make it inevitable---particularly, special privilege.

Morality and spirituality (more precisely the lack thereof) is at the very heart of the problem. It cannot be ignored. In 1941, an otherwise forgettable film, "Here Comes Mr. Jordan," makes this point succinctly. The plot involves the death of a boxer due to a heavenly mistake. (He was mistakenly killed before his time.) Mr. Jordan, who is essentially the boxer's guardian angel, brings him back to life by putting his soul and spirit into a new body. The new body is that of an ultra rich, immoral banker named Bruce Farnsworth. When Joe (the boxer) professes that he knows nothing about finance, Mr. Jordan counsels him to "just follow your heart." As the plot develops, Joe, as Farnsworth, rectifies some of the evil deeds and swindles perpetrated by the original Farnsworth.

In a 1979 remake of this film starring Warren Beatty entitled "Heaven Can Wait," the original plot is replicated almost scene for scene---even keeping the names of most of the characters. Curiously, however, the 1979 version significantly downplayed the financial subplot. There is a message here that starkly portrays what had changed from 1941 to 1979, in reality, as well as in this story. Still a third version of this film, starring Chris Rock, was released early in 2001.

A BREAKDOWN IN MORALITY IS CONTAGIOUS

In the absence of FDIC guarantees and the increase in the amount of coverage, brokered deposits would not have grown from $1 billion in 1984 to $46 billion in 1986 to over $80 billion at the height of the market in 1988.[10] Money would, therefore, not have been coaxed out of relatively sound institutions paying relatively sustainable interest rates on deposits, into banks paying unsustainable interest rates that encouraged bankers, first, to speculate and, then, to steal the money as the situation deteriorated. To the extent that we would have had an S&L crisis at all without FDIC guarantees, it would have been substantially reduced. The cost of whatever reduced crisis we may have experienced would have been borne by the depositors who went chasing after ever higher returns on their money and who were willing to place their confidence in S&Ls that were attempting to defy reality. The crisis would have only been a crisis for the people that had only themselves to blame.

Instead, we not only had a larger crisis, we had a taxpayer bailout. People who collectively had billions to lose and who, individually, in many cases, had millions to deposit, were bailed out of their folly by taxpayers---many of whom had little or no money in banks. How is this anything other than a welfare transfer from the relatively poor to the relatively wealthy? How is this fair or proper? How is this moral?

Free enterprise is the most moral economic system yet devised. In its pure form, it gives each individual the greatest freedom to reach his or her fullest potential. It suffers, however, from the same problem that every system suffers from---namely, that those in a position of power can, and do, pervert the system. They use their power to grant themselves special privileges in order to perpetuate their superior position. Welfare is, indeed, a conceptual departure from the strict capitalism model. It may or may not be a justifiable departure when used to guarantee a certain minimum standard to the poor, the disadvantaged, the aged, and the weak, but that is outside the scope of the current debate. However, welfare paid to the relatively rich by the relatively poor is entirely counter to the morality and spirit of free enterprise. Yet, this perversion permeates our society---it is particularly characteristic of our monetary and banking infrastructure.

It seems that people will tolerate the widespread granting of special privileges as long as they are given a few crumbs of their own. Therefore, although a significant number of bankers are now known to have abused the special privilege of FDIC deposit guarantees by using it to rip off their banks and society, people will resist the simple solution: abolish these perverse guarantees! People resist giving up the security of insured deposits---even while knowing that bankers have used the device to rip them (and others) off. Chapter 5 addresses this issue in greater detail.

Under our current banking system, banks are very different from every other business. As the fictionalized account portrayed, failing banks do not face the same fate as other failing businesses. Other failing businesses must contract, face more restrictive credit conditions, tighten their belts, and turn adverse results around as quickly as possible if they want to be viable. Failing banks, on the other hand, can ignore the reality of their situation. They can double or triple in size merely by offering a slightly higher interest rate than their competitors. They can, then, use these deposits to try to speculate themselves out of trouble. If and when that fails, bankers can bleed (and have bled) their banks dry for their own personal enrichment. If banks and bankers did not have all the special privileges they enjoy and were forced, instead, to recognize the same realities as everyone else, they would not be able to produce the kind of devastation that they did during the S&L fiasco.

Virtually every failed S&L and failed commercial bank grew at phenomenal rates just prior to its downfall. The regulatory and legislative environment---supposedly designed to help banks survive---succeeded, instead, in producing more costly failures. Banks that abuse their special privilege of creating and distributing money generally use additional special privileges to cover-up and extend their folly. Often, special privileges work better for the bankers than they do for the banks; they always work better for the bankers than they do for society, in general. Those bankers who don't cross the line into fraud and abuse generally prosper; some (but not all) of those who don't abide by even a lax code of ethics face criminal charges. The perpetrators who go to jail, however, are usually the ones whose crimes are easiest to understand---those who take kickbacks or forge documents, for example. The more sophisticated, higher-level scams---no matter how heinous---prove too complex for juries or even prosecutors to understand. Besides, smart defense lawyers point out that the CPAs, in effect, put their seal of approval on many of these deals---so how fraudulent can they really be. This raises reasonable doubt in the minds of jury members and judges, alike.

The breakdown in morality went well beyond the S&L crooks, however. The S&L industry was "ripped off" by a wide-ranging cast of characters. Builders, appraisers, accountants, lawyers, politicians, and Wall Street firms all took advantage of an illogical set of regulations in an atmosphere reeking of moral decay. The builders and the appraisers benefited because real estate was an area of investment that left plenty of room for sharp practices to replace moral behavior. The lawyers and accountants found the loopholes in the regulations and the legal environment and were more than happy to help S&L owners exploit these loopholes. Politicians who were in a position to grant favors and exert political pressures on behalf of the industry in return for money and other favors were, apparently, all too willing to do so.

The major benefactors, by far, however, were the Wall Street firms. They brokered deposits into the insolvent thrifts and then sold the relatively unsophisticated S&L managements on sophisticated investments such as junk bonds, collateralized mortgage obligations, Eurodollar market underwritings, interest-rate futures, and options programs.

Yes, indeed. Wall Street collected on the brokered deposits going and coming. After all, it is no secret that the best and the brightest financial, mathematical and scientific minds coming out of graduate school in the late 70s and early 80s were finding their way to the "Street." The term "rocket scientists" was coined on Wall Street-- not at NASA. The same guys who, in the 1960s, worked at NASA to send men to the moon were working at investment banking firms. These guys never met clients and didn't have fancy offices. They wore orange sports jackets, shared offices with other "techies," ate lunch at their computers, and, oh yes, were paid $500,000 per year salaries for their efforts. To the slick financial sales types, the techies were well worth their salaries. The wheeler-dealers harnessed all this analytical computer expertise and earned $10s of millions themselves.

The ads in the New York Times back in the 70s would read: "Mathematicians, scientific programmers, PhD's preferred to work on Wall Street. No financial knowledge necessary. We will teach you all you have to know. $50,000-$100,000 plus bonuses of 100% to 300%." Nowadays, there is a cadre of such people who even have the financial background. These positions---at investment banks or hedge funds, for example---pay even more handsome salaries, today. Under the circumstances, it is surprising that we still had "rocket scientists" left over to program the software for Patriot missiles, Star Wars, and the like. Undoubtedly, the Texas developers walked off with millions--but, clearly, the slick, Wall Street, financial types who harnessed the rocket scientists walked off with the real money.

FIRST CASUALTIES

The S&Ls were merely the most visible early casualties of our faulty, banking system. Problems went beyond the S&Ls. In August of 1990, on ABC's Nightline program, Dan Brumbaugh, then a Stanford University banking expert, called attention to the fact that "the accounting data in use at the moment obscures the extreme deterioration [in our money-center banks]. If more realistic values are assigned, you will find that they are near or at insolvency." When William Seidman, another guest on the program, chided him for being irresponsible, Brumbaugh backed off slightly.

Many (if not all) of those who labeled Brumbaugh's statement "irresponsible" must have known that his analysis was right on target. He caused enough of a stir, that various other experts were immediately solicited for contrary comments. Brumbaugh's statement was irresponsible only in so far as he shared the view with a lay audience. The implication is that the general public cannot be told the truth no matter how obvious the facts are to knowledgeable analysts---or even to lay people who bother to give the subject serious thought.

Any realistic view of the numbers (i.e., using the rules that apply to everyone else such as marking to market) demonstrates that both banks and S&Ls have virtually all been insolvent (or nearly so), most of the time, since at least the early 1980s. The supreme flaw in our system has been that confidence must, above all, be maintained. Hopefully, this flawed logic will someday be replaced with a reality-based view that calls attention to the root cause of every banking calamity throughout the ages: abuse of special privilege. Until then, we will not develop enduring solutions. Just because many banks have operated in an insolvent state for 20 years does not mean that they can (or should) do so forever or that there are not significant societal costs associated with such a practice. These costs include more fraud, more special privileges for the few at everyone else's expense, a declining morality, and---if we don't institute *bona fide* reforms soon---the collapse of the system itself.

Around the same time that Brumbaugh made his Nightline comments, a McKinsey & Company banking expert, Lowell Bryan, estimated that there was as much as $600 billion in bad loans including highly leveraged transactions (HLTs), LDC loans, and loans to commercial real estate ventures. Bryan pointed out that this represented 2.5 times the total capital of the entire banking industry![11]

Since banks are highly leveraged institutions, even a mere 5% overstatement of assets translates into an 80% overstatement of capital. Because banks are allowed to carry assets at acquisition costs rather than market value, they can easily be insolvent at any time and no one would even realize it. Why are they allowed to do this? No one else is. The first step to a reality-based approach to money and banking requires that banks value their assets at current market values rather than at acquisition costs. We can then at least weed out hopelessly insolvent institutions before they cost the rest of us too much. Even Bert Ely should, presumably, favor this approach since he listed not closing S&Ls earlier as the number-one element of cost in the S&L bailout. While the AICPA has, for years, supposedly considered requiring banks to "mark to market," it has never seriously taken this eminently fair and reasonable idea beyond the "thinking" stage (see Chapter 8, "Who's Watching the Watchdogs?")

The system, it seems, does require reforms. Some merely favor removing the government-imposed cartel and requiring full disclosure. Others believe that fractional reserve banking is inherently unsound, and that we should eliminate it. These differences are partially practical in nature, and partially reflective of different points of view. Each alternative, however, recognizes that we must remove special privileges. The guiding principles are those that underlie our most fundamental institutions and concepts: free enterprise, democracy, and justice.

Chapter II

The Seeds of Perversion

"The bankers own the world. Take it away from them, but leave them the power to create money and control credit, with a flick of the pen they will create enough money to buy it back again."

Josiah Stamp, President, Bank of England, 1920s .

Major man-made change takes place, primarily, when innovative solutions purport to eliminate widely recognized inadequacies of some aspect of our existence. Usually, these innovations lead to an overall improvement to the human condition. In some instances, however, the perceived inadequacies are more imagined than real and/or the innovative solutions, contain, within themselves, the seeds of even graver future consequences. FDIC deposit guarantees, for example, fall into this latter category (see Chapter 5). Man-made change may also occur when powerful people and powerful institutions---acting in their own best interests---promote ostensibly beneficial innovations without regard to whether they truly advance the general interest. The historical developments leading up to the invention of bank money creation and distribution fall into this category.

BARTER YIELDS TO MONEY

Early trade took place by barter. Money was then conceived as a useful artifact that substantially enhanced trade. Much later, money lending was conceived as a useful activity whereby the use of money could be transferred, at a price, from those who had more than their current needs to those who had less than their current needs. Later still, we discovered the benefits of money depositories where people could store money. Each of these developments was a positive, forward step that generally facilitated the creation of wealth and overall economic activity. Then, in the 17th century, the two distinctly different and not necessarily connected functions of money lending and money depositing were combined in a manner that was unsound. Its conception benefited its promoters but did more harm than good for virtually everybody else. With this development, fractional reserve banking was born. The origins of most financial disruptions of any kind can be traced to this 17th century development. A short history of European money and banking clarifies these developments.

Barter trade is a primitive yet civilized economic activity, whereby people peacefully exchange ownership of goods for mutual benefit. It merely requires the coming together of two (or more) independent traders who recognize the benefit of exchanging surplus quantities of goods they have for other goods that they want. Conceptually, therefore, trade is inherently good in that it adds, in some measure, to the wealth of each of the participants. Unfortunately barter as a method of trade, has severe and obvious limitations. The chief limitation of barter trade, very simply, is that the concept of buying is not separated from the concept of selling. In order for any transactions to take place, each party must be both a buyer and a seller.

This inadequacy of barter can be avoided if we devise some standard of value ---any standard of value--- that is universally accepted as the unit by which we measure all commercial transactions. Such a standard, by definition, is money. The monetary unit then becomes one side of every transaction and the concept of buying and selling is established. In order for money to gain widespread acceptance it must have certain important characteristics. Among other things, money must be: easily divisible without losing its value; not subject to physical deterioration or decay; easily transportable; in predictable and limited supply; standardized; and stable in value. The extent to which any commodity or "thing" has the above-listed characteristics---in practice as well as in theory---is the extent to which such commodity or thing is an effective form of money.

Even though money is conceptually easy to understand and its benefits are undeniable, there have been unresolved problems from the very beginning. These problems continue to this very day. They relate, primarily, to the fact that we have not developed money that is permanently and universally accepted. Throughout history, whenever money was unable to measure up, sufficiently, to one or more of the prerequisite characteristics, people instituted changes to rectify the situation. Unfortunately, more often than not, those who understood money the best and were in the best position to institute changes chose reforms that benefited themselves rather than the general interest. The temptation to do this when it comes to something as vital as money is virtually always too great a temptation to overcome.

MONEY HAS ITS PROBLEMS TOO

By the Middle Ages, for example, barriers to the transportability of gold and silver led to innovative solutions. The city-states of Italy were, then, in their heyday as the center of commerce. When merchants in these city-states engaged in trade with others, it became necessary to ship substantial quantities of precious metal from buyer to seller. Such transports were costly and subject to attacks by marauders. Depository banks permitted such transfers to take place with the stroke of a pen. Merchants "warehoused" their money in depository banks just as they stored surplus quantities of other commodities in a warehouse. When commercial transactions took place, the buyer's and seller's respective accounts were updated. Certainly, this was a big improvement over shipping large quantities of precious metal over vast geographic areas.

Another limitation of early money was its general lack of standardization. While everyone accepted the general notion of money, coins of ostensibly identical value were not always accorded such status. The problems of lack of standardization were many-fold in the 16th and 17th centuries. For one thing, money existed in both minted and un-minted form. In minted form, one could never be certain whether the composition was pure or the weight was proper.

The brand of inflation that existed, then, is best described by anecdote:

> *In 1590, King Vincent II of Coinland had just succeeded King Vincent I to the throne. All the coins of Coinland had been minted with the likeness of Vincent I emblazoned on their face. Vincent II called in all the coins to be re-minted with his likeness to replace the former monarch. In this process, Vincent II decided to mix some cheaper metal into the coin and to mint a slightly lighter coin. Vincent II then used the excess precious metal from this process to fatten the coffers of the Royal Treasury of Coinland. Since this procedure was followed, to a greater or lesser extent, by every mint, a lack of standardization was a certainty.*

Particularly at the international level, lack of standardization exists to this very day. For example, in 1990, Brazil owed approximately $100 billion. At that time, one dollar was theoretically equal to 160 Brazilian cruzieros. But could Brazil have paid off its entire debt by delivering 16 trillion cruzieros to its creditors? Brazil's central bank could have created 16 trillion cruzieros easily and effortlessly with a few keystrokes and been instantly out of debt! Unfortunately (for Brazil) and fortunately (for Brazil's creditors) this would not have been acceptable. Brazil's debt was denominated, primarily, in dollars and, to a lesser extent, in other "hard" currencies. In 1994, even Brazil gave up on the cruziero and revised its monetary system. The official currency of Brazil is now the Real, which has (so far) been relatively stable---compared to the cruziero and the cruziero's predecessor, the cruzado.

By the early 17th century, Amsterdam had replaced the Italian city-states as the hub of European commerce. In 1609, the Bank of Amsterdam was formed in order to deal with the lack of standardization in coins. Its basic function was to accept coins from anywhere in Europe and to credit to the depositor's account, the fair value based on weight and composition. The bank, therefore, served as an institution that standardized money. The bank's excellent record and reputation as a depository and exchange bank, led to imitation by others.

SEEDS OF PERVERSION

Unfortunately, the Bank of Amsterdam soon noticed that few depositors ever seemed to want to withdraw money on deposit. The directors, therefore, decided to lend out some of the money on deposit at interest. The concept of lending money at interest dates back to before the time of Christ. The money that was lent, however, was not other people's money on deposit, but rather, the capital of the lender. At the same time as these developments were taking place in Amsterdam, goldsmiths in England were operating as precious metal depositories. They, too, were finding that they could issue more receipts (by making loans) than they actually had in gold on deposit. The seeds of perversion were thus sown.

These early examples of fractional reserve banking were, indeed, quite modest by today's standards. Today, a bank will typically have about $1 in cash for every $8 on deposit. In the 17th century, a ratio of $1 in metal for every $8 in paper would not have been tried by even the boldest of practitioners. In some cases, such as in the case of the Bank of Amsterdam, the practice was in violation of its legal function. In other cases, the loans were made with the full knowledge of depositors who participated through interest payments on their deposits.

At the end of the 17th century, in 1694, the Bank of England was formed primarily to make loans to the crown. These loans were secured by the government's promise to repay with interest. The philosophical basis for such procedures has set the standard for the funding of public debt to this day. The only security is the confidence of creditors in the government's ability and willingness to repay. The chief function of the bank was, quite unabashedly, to be the financing arm of the government. Approximately 1.2 million pounds were raised through the sale of bank stock. The money was then lent to the government, secured by the government's (interest bearing) word to repay. The bankers now took these promises to repay and lent them out at interest. In other words, interest-bearing debt obligations were lent out as money! In addition, the stockholders of the bank put their stock up as security to take out loans for themselves. These dangerous precedents set by the Bank of England can best be demonstrated by a current day analogy.

BANK MONEY CREATION

The example below parallels specific actions that principals of the Bank of England took when they formed the bank. It involves, among other things, such practices as borrowing money from the bank in order to buy the bank stock. But the most perverse aspect of the transactions, as we shall shortly see, is the effect that these transactions had on the money supply.

1. John Doe forms the Doe Bank and capitalizes it with $500 million in gold bullion.

2. The Doe Bank buys $500 million of government bonds. The government opens up a checking account with the proceeds of the loan, thereby putting the $500 million right back in the bank.

3. Doe borrows $400 million in gold from the Doe Bank, using $500 million of bank stock as collateral for the loan.

4. Jim Smith borrows the $500 million in government bonds by putting up $750 in land as collateral.

5. Jim Smith borrows $400 million from the Jones Bank, putting up the government bonds as collateral.

The net effect of the five steps above is to increase the money supply by $800 million. Specifically, Doe, initially, gives up $500 million in gold in order to capitalize the bank but then borrows back $400 million of it, thereby only reducing his personal money supply by $100 million. The government's money supply increases by the proceeds of the bond sale---$500 million. Smith's money supply increases by the amount of his loan at the Jones Bank where he "monetized" the government bonds. Therefore, the money supply increases by $800 million. After all five steps, the Doe bank's assets are $100 million in gold, $400 in loans to Doe, and $500 million in loans to Smith. Therefore, total assets equal $1 billion ($1,000 million). On the other side of its balance sheet, it has a $500 million liability to the government in the form of a checking account balance and $500 million of paid-in-capital, also totaling $1 billion. The Doe Bank creates $400 million of the increased money supply because it only has $100 million in gold as reserves against the government's $500 million deposit. The Jones Bank creates the other $400 million when it monetizes the government bonds in step 5.

If the newly created money is used for consumption, those who don't receive any of it will be disadvantaged to the full extent of the effect of the increased supply of money "chasing" the same amount of goods. If the newly created money is used for productive investment that would not have otherwise taken place, the analysis is seemingly more complex but ultimately identical: those who receive none of it will be disadvantaged relative to those who receive it first or early--- at least until sufficient new production is created. In any event, the people who receive the newly created money first or early are big winners in this process. The bank that earns interest on money it creates from nothing is, of course, a big winner in the process. In a society such as ours where every single penny of money in circulation has been created by the banking system, there will be many borrowers who cannot repay both principal and interest unless still more money is created for that purpose.

Under these circumstances, then, bankers and their favored clients benefit at everyone else's expense. There is, however, a banking structure that does not suffer from these drawbacks. In fact, as long as banks create no new money, the lending process will not disadvantage some for the benefit of others. Such an alternative system is not only possible, it is sound, logical, moral and fair. If, for example, the Bank of England did not lend out the government's promises to pay and the bank's stockholders did not borrow from the bank (in other words, stopping at step 2 in the analogy above), then, the bank's stockholders would have merely given up their own use of money in exchange for an interest bearing asset. No change in the overall money supply would have ensued. The stockholders' money supply would have gone down by exactly the amount by which the government's money supply rose. Under such conditions, the institution would have been perfectly sound. Banks would not have received a special privilege to create money granted by government force and the government would not have benefited by receiving newly created money. Others would have been unaffected by the transaction.

In tracing out the history from a barter economy to 18th century European banking, one sees that certain innovations properly sprang forth in response to the inadequacies of prior institutions: money, money lending, depository banking, and exchange banking all fit this mold. Each of these developments substantially enhanced trade. Then, in the 17th and 18th centuries, innovative banking techniques were directed at changing the amount and distribution of money. These innovations were largely motivated by the desire of an opportunistic privileged class to circumvent an essential characteristic of money-- its limited supply. Large, powerful borrowers (e.g., governments) conspired with powerful potential creditors to rig the system to their mutual benefit. From then to today, similarly inclined governments and powerful special interests have continued to act in this manner. Hopefully, the social and political atmosphere of the early 21st century can play a role in abolishing these self-serving practices.

COLONIAL GOVERNMENT MONEY CREATION

The colonists sought various solutions to their chronic shortage of specie---real money. For a time, tobacco and corn (called "country pay") were used as money. Limitations of transportability, standardization, durability, and instability, however, prevented country pay from achieving widespread acceptance as money. Nonetheless, the colonists generally recognized that bank paper money was nothing more than a bank's promise to pay that which it did not have. People had little confidence that bank money would be redeemed in "real money." Then, beginning with Massachusetts, the colonial governments began to print paper money that was redeemable in real money upon the collection of taxes. By the 18th century, most of the other colonies had followed suit. The rationale for such paper was the shortage of specie---real money.

Late 20th and early 21st century men and women may have a block to real understanding of these matters because, today, there is a total and complete acceptance of paper money. But in the 18th century, paper money was viewed as a claim to money and not money, itself. Whenever governments (or private banks) create money, its "realness" or lack thereof is almost of secondary importance. The effect that such creation has on the value of money, in general, should be the paramount issue. Whether it is described as real or fake, if it maintains its value, that's good; if it doesn't maintain its value that is not good.

Presumably, the colonists would have (incorrectly) not objected to the discovery of a cheap process for converting sand to gold. But just as certainly as paper money would have become worthless if created in abundance, gold would have similarly become worthless if it became available in abundance. Sand to gold conversion benefits the original discoverer at everyone else's expense. Most importantly, it would not have added one whit of wealth to the society. The same, of course, would be true today, if, somehow, by some magical procedure, someone were to discover how to make money grow, for example, by planting it. Obviously, the first person to discover the process and everyone who became aware of its existence early would benefit at the expense of everyone else by buying up assets and thereby "getting out of cash." Sellers of these assets, as well as those who "stayed in cash" would, of course, be the losers, when, inevitably, money became worthless.

In less dramatic terms, that is how our society operates. The money supply grows, but at a rate perceived to be relatively undramatic. Therefore, the recognition that money is becoming worthless is not universally acknowledged. The biggest benefactors from this process, of course, are the banks that begin the process by costlessly creating the money in the first place and then lending it out at interest. Additionally, the favored borrowers benefit by converting the continuously depreciating currency into real assets. Growth in the money supply, certainly in excess of whatever growth in production it engenders, and by whatever means accomplished, perverts the very essence of money. In the past, both governments and banks (usually in conjunction with each other) have been the primary offenders. It is no different today, except that banks have become an increasingly greater and more troublesome factor. When bankers lend out newly created money, everyone's purchasing power is reduced for the benefit of the borrowers. When government borrows the newly created money, the result is a form of taxation. When individuals or corporations borrow the newly created money, it redistributes wealth as well.

FRACTIONAL RESERVE BANKING

The Bank of Amsterdam and the English goldsmiths were the precursors of fractional reserve banking. In the U.S., these banking concepts did not become full blown until the early 19th century. The Bank of England set the standard for how creative monetary concepts could be used, big time, to create money. It monetized the national debt by lending it out as money, and then monetized bank capital by allowing stockholders to borrow against their bank stock. The effect of both was to create money out of thin air and to distribute it based on self-interest.

In the 1920s, a Boston businessman named Ponzi promised investors he would give them a significant portion of the 400% he was supposedly able to make in an international postal coupon redemption scheme. While there is some evidence he was engaged in some such activity, he made little, if any, profit from it. Furthermore, he had neither the intent nor the expectation of satisfying investor redemptions out of profits. From the beginning, Ponzi intended to pay early investors with the capital contribution of later investors. As long as more and more money flowed in relative to the maturing notes of earlier investors, Ponzi stayed in business. When redemptions exceeded new inflows, Ponzi knew it was time to close up shop. Ultimately, he was arrested and convicted of fraud.

The fraud in this transparent scheme is twofold. First, Ponzi offered guaranteed returns in an investment program that could not guarantee anything close to the results he promised. Second, and more sinister, he never had any intention of achieving the promised results for investors. The first element of fraud differs in no significant way from the promises made by every fractional reserve bank.

This was well recognized by many of the early leaders of our country---including five of the first twelve U.S. Presidents (see Chapter 3). Fractional reserve banks cannot guarantee the promises of cash on demand to depositors any more that Ponzi could guarantee such claims. In the absence of substantial special privileges stemming from the Fed's ability to create unlimited money out of thin air (see Chapter 4), banks could not fulfill their promise of cash on demand to depositors from the very first loan! Furthermore, the special privilege of FDIC deposit guarantees has the effect of inducing depositors not to worry about the bank's clear inability to fulfill its promise (see Chapter 5).

When banks are failing, bankers commonly use their special privileges to create money to loot their banks leaving taxpayers holding the bag. In other words, failing fractional reserve banks, more often than not, become overtly fraudulent.

A bank's ability to honor its obligation to depositors depends on its making loans and investments that earn at least the promised return to depositors and that mature before its deposits mature. To guarantee the availability of deposited funds on a timely basis, in other words, requires that loans and investments be matched, by maturity, with the duration of the deposits. An obvious corollary is that deposits that are due on demand (e.g., checking account balances) can only be guaranteed if the funds are not lent at all. The very act of lending out these funds, amounts to a representation that is no less fraudulent than Ponzi's empty promises. Ponzi's activity, at least, only had an adverse impact on participants in his schemes. When banks lend out demand deposits, they are creating money and thereby impacting society in general. Many people who have not given the process much thought probably believe there is actually paper money behind their checkbook balances.

That, of course, would be true if banks were not allowed to lend out these funds. Allowing banks to lend out these funds is the absolute equivalent to allowing banks to create money. The process proceeds along these lines. Depositor A deposits $100 in a checking account at bank X; bank X lends out, say, $85 to customer B who deposits it in bank Y (or customer B buys a product from a company that deposits it in bank Y- it doesn't really matter); bank Y, now, lends, say, $70 to customer C who deposits it in bank Z, who lends $55 to customer D, etc.

The original $100 in our example will ultimately grow to $700-$800. Except for the original $100, banks created all of the money. If this process were performed with cash rather than checking accounts the banks would have had to print paper money. The effect, regardless of the method, is that banks create and distribute money. Measuring the money supply is complicated by the fact that there are different definitions of money in common use. The most prominent are M1, M2, and M3, which we discuss in later chapters. In the last decade alone, however, banks have created almost $3 trillion by this process as measured by M3, which has grown from just over $4.1 trillion to over $7.1 trillion. The distribution of this money was certainly uneven, often wasteful, and sometimes fraudulent.

One used to hear the comment about our foreign aid that had we just dropped the money out of an airplane, the people would have benefited more than they actually did when we distributed it through corrupt third world dictators. Similarly, had banks indiscriminately lent $2000 to every man woman and child in the country, the banks, the country, and most of the citizens would be better off. Offsetting this is that bankers and favored borrowers would have had to endure a lower standard of living.

Banks, then, create claims to money they do not have and which they cannot guarantee will exist when presented for redemption. In essence, they operate like chain letters or multi-level marketing schemes that seem to promise something for everybody but which, in reality, only tend to enrich promoters and insiders. A chain letter, for example, works as follows:

> *You receive a letter with twenty names on it. You send $1 to the person on the top of the list, cross his or her name off, and add your own name to the bottom of the list and move all the other names up one spot. You, then, make two copies and convince two other people to go through the same process. You will be the 20th name on 2 lists; the 19th name on 4 lists; the 18th name on 8 lists....and ultimately the 1st name on 524,288 lists. For a $1 investment, you end up making over $1/2 million---not a bad return.*

In order for you to collect, of course, 1/2 million people have to get on line behind you. The last of these people requires 275 billion people to get in line behind him. Since this is many times the entire world's population, it is a safe bet that the only winners will be the people who started near the top of the very first list. The people who take the money out, in other words, are not the people who put it in. In our current banking system, the people who take out big loans are the big winners. All others (including innocent bystanders) lose. Donald Trump, for example, understands the process and has succeeded in selling people on the idea of joining his "lists."

The self-serving conventional wisdom, today, is that economic growth and prosperity for all is contingent on banks making loans to the supposed creators of wealth---the large borrowers who are supposedly building the productive capacity of the country. The only germ of truth to this position is that wealth is indeed created by investment. The loans that were made over the last several decades to lesser-developed countries, to leveraged buyout takeover artists, to builders of garish structures, to highly leveraged hedge funds, etc. were actually destructive of wealth and served only to enrich the few at the expense of the many.

Since fractional reserve banking is inherently unsound, why has the system not already collapsed? Answers are provided throughout this book (and summarized in its two-word title). Until the 20th century, natural checks on the system prevented it from getting too far out of hand. Then, early in the 20th century, we got cocky. We treated symptoms and effects and ignored root causes. So-called solutions that not only do not address root causes but, in effect, obscure them are doomed to fail. But before they do, the specially privileged purveyors of fiat money will first get the ordinary citizen and taxpayer to bail them out of their folly. When 100s of billions of losses are "socialized" over 100s of millions of ordinary taxpayer "victims," the cost per person is hardly noticeable and is easily obscured. When that money is borrowed so that only interest need be paid (albeit, forever), the cost is even further obscured. Ironically, the money for the rescue is, essentially, borrowed, at interest, from the very institutions that are being rescued!

Chapter III

The Recurring Nightmare

"If the people only understood the rank injustice of our money and banking system there would be a revolution before morning."

-President Andrew Jackson

It is often said that those who don't learn from history are doomed to repeat it. Nothing makes this point better than the almost eerie recurrence of financial panics that struck the United States during the 19th and early 20th centuries. In some (but not all) cases severe recessions or depressions followed; in some (but not all) cases major frauds or swindles helped to touch off the panic; in some (but not all) cases, a stock market decline was a contributing factor. In some instances, the government helped to create the antecedent conditions; in other instances, the government played a role in precipitating the panic, itself. In each and every case, however, liberal extension of credit for speculative purposes preceded the panic. Also, in every single case, banks failed. Without irresponsible credit expansion, these panics would not have occurred at all. Without fractional reserve banking, irresponsible credit expansion could not have occurred in the first place.

Why did we establish a banking infrastructure so powerful that its actions were a significant element of every single panic we have ever experienced? And having thus established this infrastructure, why did those at the helm of these powerful institutions become irresponsible, excessive, abusive and even fraudulent time and time again? A short, cynical answer to the first question is that powerful monied interests conspired with the government to construct banking institutions that served their own mutual interests with little regard for the general welfare. A short, cynical answer to the second question is that power corrupts, and absolute power corrupts absolutely. History confirms that this cynicism is merited.

IN THE BEGINNING

Alexander Hamilton was Secretary of the Treasury under George Washington. While he lacked the broad based liberal arts intellectualism of Benjamin Franklin, Thomas Jefferson and John Adams, Hamilton was undeniably masterful in the fields of law, finance, and government. His policies, which shaped the emerging Republic's financial infrastructure, were supported by commercial and financial interests and were opposed, primarily, by agricultural interests. Among other things, his program called for the formation of a nationally chartered bank called the First United States Bank.

Each of Washington's other cabinet members---Jefferson, Adams, and Edmund Randolph---vigorously opposed the bank on constitutional and other grounds. Ultimately, however, Hamilton prevailed by making various concessions to Jefferson and James Madison on unrelated matters. Until this compromise was struck, Washington was prepared to veto the legislation chartering the bank. The strength of the language with which Jefferson and Adams denounced fractional reserve banking is informative. For example, in a letter to John Taylor in 1816, Jefferson said, "I sincerely believe that banking establishments are more dangerous than standing armies and the principle of spending money to be paid by posterity in the name of funding is but swindling futurity on a large scale."[1]

In 1799, President Adams said, "Banks have done more harm to the religion, morality, tranquillity, prosperity and even the wealth of the nation than they ever have done, or ever will do, good."[2] As flowery statements of a point of view, these statements are as true today as they were then. A less flowery, straight to the point offering from Adams was that bank note issuance in excess of gold and silver on hand "represents nothing and is, therefore, a cheat upon somebody."[3]

THE PANIC OF 1819

When the 20-year charter for the First United States Bank had run its course, the charter came up for renewal. Hard money advocates (opponents of bank money creation), and their strange bedfellows, state chartered banking interests that favored easy money (very liberal bank money creation), opposed renewal. In 1811, Congress narrowly defeated renewal of the charter. From 1811 to 1815 the number of state banks grew from 88 to 208 and, between 1812 and 1817, notes in circulation increased from $45 million to $100 million.[4]

Throughout its existence, the First United States Bank implemented a policy of presenting state bank notes for redemption in specie. This forced the state banks to follow relatively conservative banking practices. When the First U.S. Bank's charter was not renewed in 1811 this set the stage for liberal bank note issuances by the state banks. Bankers make loans when they receive what they perceive to be good security; borrowers seek loans when they see opportunity for profit---particularly, a quick profit. Such an opportunity seemed to exist in the form of buying public land for resale.

The Land Act of 1804 provided for the sale of public lands at $2 per acre in lot sizes no smaller than 160 acres. The Louisiana Purchase one year earlier had substantially increased the amount of publicly owned land. Actually, however, only the eastern most fringes of these lands were salable, as our frontier, only slowly, expanded westward. The initial intention of the 1804 Act was to sell land to farmers. Instead, in the 1813-18 period, land speculators were buying up vast quantities of these lands by borrowing from state banks and/or buying on credit directly from the government. The government was a very tolerant creditor and happily accepted state bank notes in payment. By 1815, large speculators, aided by their state banking allies, were already bidding up the price of these lands to ridiculous and unsustainable levels.

When the Second United States Bank was chartered in 1816, it did nothing initially to stop the wild speculation; if anything, it encouraged it. There was speculation in the stock of the bank, and officers and directors borrowed on their stock to capitalize on the wild speculation in public lands. In 1818, when a change in management attempted to put an end to the speculation, the boom came to a sudden halt. The volume of state bank notes declined, and the values of the notes fell below par. The Panic of 1819 had many victims as the following historically accurate, but fictionalized anecdote demonstrates.

In 1816, Gary Gambler, a would-be land speculator migrated to Missouri from neighboring Tennessee. Among the first people Gary met was Eldridge Banker who had been in Missouri since 1812, having emigrated there from Philadelphia where he had served as the able assistant to a director of the First United States Bank. Shortly after his arrival in Missouri, Banker and several other gentlemen formed the St. Louis Bank, which was one of only two banks in the entire Missouri Territory. Gambler was impressed with Banker's success in bankrolling several land speculators over the prior few years. They had bought up substantial quantities of undeveloped land that were now already thriving little towns on the outskirts of St. Louis.

When Banker agreed to go into partnership with Gambler on land purchases, Gambler thought his ship was about to come in. The St Louis Bank would provide the capital in the form of bank notes and Gambler would be involved in the resale and promotion of the acquired land. How could anything go wrong. After all, tracts that had sold for $2 per acre several years earlier were being resold for $10, $20 and $30 per acre as farmers and merchants continued to stream into the territory. In fact, real estate in highly developed areas in St. Louis was going for over $70 per acre.

Gambler and Banker bought two tracts. For one, they paid $20 per acre. It was just on the outskirts of the booming town of Mississippiville. They paid the entire purchase price in the form of St Louis Bank notes. The second tract, was more distant from any existing town but promised to be the site for a new town. For this tract they received excellent credit *terms from the government. They bought 50,000 acres for $2 per acre with only a 25% down payment. Within a few months, they had sold the first tract to about 50 farmers who paid an average price of $30 per acre. The second tract was sold to 10 smaller speculators at $3 per acre. These speculators paid partially in bank notes from banks in Tennessee and Kentucky and financed the balance with the St. Louis Bank. Gambler and Banker repeated this process with bigger and bigger deals.*

In 1818, when the Second United States Bank began to present notes to state banks for redemption, the roof caved in. Both the St Louis Bank and the other Missouri bank failed; state banks in the neighboring states withdrew whatever liquidity they could from Missouri; land prices tumbled; the flow of migration screeched to a halt; all banks ceased redemption in specie; and farmers could no longer sell their produce.

The farmers who had bought land from Gambler and Banker in their first land deal typically paid about $500 in specie---often their life savings---and financed the rest with the bank. In 1819, they still had mortgage balances of over $4,000. Meanwhile, from 1816 to 1819, these farmers had converted the raw land into fertile farmland, and, yet, their land wasn't even worth half of what they had paid for it. Foreclosure by the bank would not have even covered the outstanding balance on their debt. Money, which had been so plentiful just a few months earlier, had simply disappeared.

A substantial public outcry made debt relief and liberalized bankruptcy laws major political issues in the depression that followed the Panic of 1819. What caused land values to go from $2 in 1810 to $80 in 1818 and back to under $2 by 1820? Clearly, it had nothing to do with the productivity of land or any other concept of real wealth. It happened, quite simply, because money had been created by banks specifically for speculating in these lands and then was destroyed even quicker when the Second Bank attempted to bring the rampant speculation back under control.

The stringent measures taken by the Second United States Bank clearly caused the euphoria to come to an abrupt halt in 1819. Its reputation as the "monster" whose heartless directors had transformed the institution into a servant of Eastern business interests, however, was hardly deserved. Had the euphoria been allowed to go on, the ultimate reckoning would have only been worse. If the bank's actions could have, somehow, taught the lesson of why panics are the inevitable conclusion to wild speculation brought on by the wanton extension of bank credit, it certainly would have been worth the price. Unfortunately, within barely a decade of the depression of the early 1820s, speculative fever---in public lands, again, no less--- set the stage for the Panic of 1837.

THE BANK WARS

For much of the period between the Panic of 1819 and the Panic of 1837, objections to banking, in general, and the Second United States Bank, in particular, marked the political landscape. The most conspicuous personal battle within this framework took place between Nicholas Biddle---head of the Second United States Bank---and President Andrew Jackson (1828-36). Jackson was so blinded by his hatred for all banks that he failed to recognize that the Second Bank may have been the lesser of two evils when compared to the state chartered banks. "Everyone who knows me," he told James Knox Polk in 1833, "does know that I have always been opposed to the United States Bank, nay all banks."[5]

In his veto message to Congress on the Second Bank, Jackson lashed out at those who sought the special privilege that the Second Bank bestowed on them. His words apply to similar special privileges enjoyed by banks, particularly money-center banks, today:

> *"When the laws undertake to make the rich richer and the potent more powerful, the humble members of society...who have neither the time nor the means of securing like favors for themselves, have a right to*

complain of the injustice of their government...There are no necessary evils in government. Its evils exist only in its abuses. If it would confine itself to equal protection...it would be an unqualified blessing...Many of our rich men have not been content with equal protection and equal benefits, but have besought us to make them richer by act of Congress...It is time to pause in our career to review our principles."[6]

Roger Taney, Attorney General under Jackson and co-drafter of the above quoted veto message, scored Biddle for his attitude toward the power he wielded. It could easily apply to the Federal Reserve System today:

"It is this power concentrated in the hands of a few individuals---exercised in secret and unseen although constantly felt--- that is sufficient to awaken any man in the country if the danger is brought distinctly to his view."[7]

An 1829 committee of Jacksonian economists, journalists, lawyers, labor leaders, and businessmen had this to report:

"That banks are useful as offices of deposit and transfer, we readily admit; but we cannot see that the benefits they confer...are so great as to compensate for the evils they produce, in...laying the foundation of artificial inequality of wealth and power. If the present system of banking and paper money be extended and perpetuated, the great body of the working people must give up all hopes of ever acquiring any property."[8]

Senator Thomas Hart Benton, on the floor of the Senate in 1831, in opposition to the renewal of the charter for the Second Bank, said:

"I look upon the bank as an institution too great and powerful to be tolerated in a Government in free and equal laws...its tendencies are dangerous and pernicious to the Government and the people...it aggravate(s) the inequality of fortunes,....make(s) the rich richer and the poor poorer ...I [also] object [to it] on account of the exclusive privileges...it gives to the stockholders."[9]

Andrew Jackson, after his presidency, summed up the position of his faction of the Democratic Party as follows:

"The planter, the farmer, the mechanic, and the laborer...form the great body of the people...Yet, they are in constant danger of losing their fair influence in the Government...The mischief springs from the power which money interest derives from a paper currency which they are able to control..."[10]

The above quotes reflect the views of respected political leaders during the founding and early years of our nation. Five of our first twelve presidents (Jefferson, Adams, Jackson, Polk and Van Buren) spoke out strongly against banks. The sentiments they have expressed have resurfaced since then as well. Each time, they inspired fiery support from responsible men of vision. Perhaps, their inability to have ever succeeded is best summed up by the most unlikely of all sources, Walter Wriston, who, in 1975, as Chairman of Citibank, quite candidly said: "Our banking system grew up by accident; and whenever something happens by accident, it becomes a religion."[11] It may be time for a new religion.

THE PANIC OF 1837

As intellectually sophisticated as the anti-banking establishment was between the 1819 and 1837 Panics, it again was marred by the same strange bedfellow syndrome that afflicted the opposition to the First Bank. Namely, these hard money advocates opposed to all

fractional reserve banking and paper money creation by private institutions were politically aligned with easy money state banking
interests who opposed the Second Bank for exactly the opposite reasons. When skirmishes were won by this coalition, the ultimate vic-
tors, by (Wriston's) historical accident, were the easy money state
banking interests.

Ironically, upon Jackson's re-election in 1832, the Second
Bank lost political clout well before the end of its charter. The state
banks were, of course, quick to move in to fill the void. In 1833, for
example, there were about $10 million in state bank notes in circula-
tion; four years later, at the height of the speculative frenzy, $150
million in state bank notes were in circulation. This represents a
whopping 72% annual compound growth rate (by 1843, the amount
had declined to $58 million).[12] Land speculation became a national
pastime. In 1830, less than $2 million of public land was sold; in
1837, over $20 million was sold; by 1843, sales had declined, again,
to below $1 million. Could there really have been any question that
a financial panic would ultimately ensue? The increase in circulating
bank notes from 1833-37 was even greater than the 1813-18 increase and caused an even more violent panic.

*Gary Gambler, Jr. was 19 years old in 1833. His
father's stories of those few good years from 1816-18
were his only memories of the days when the family
was relatively wealthy. The quality of life for the
Gamblers had, changed quite dramatically for the
worse during the 1820s. Gary Jr. was not content
with farming the 80 acres that he, his father, his
mother, and his five younger brothers and sisters
struggled to keep afloat. He wanted a better life for
himself and thought the time was right to strike out
on his own.*

*He moved to Chicago in the belief that it was des-
tined to become a large and prosperous city. Although he had little money, he was very ambitious
and had voraciously read everything he could about
banking and finance. His vision was to connect with
monied people who would recognize his talents and
help him realize his goals.*

Shortly after his arrival in Chicago, Gary met John Rich, a wealthy recent émigré from Boston whose family had been in banking for years and who were happy to provide capital to the profitable enterprises that Gary had so aptly and confidently described to John. Gary had become convinced that his father and Eldridge Banker had made a big mistake by not diversifying their interests.

He had promised himself not to make the mistake of investing only in land. By late 1833, Gary and Rich had formed the Chicago State Bank. By 1836, only 15% of the bank's loans were involved with land speculation although that was the most booming fast money action in town. Instead, Gary had taken on various partners in numerous other ventures---all of which were financed with his bank's notes.

For example, with Bill Rivers, he constructed canals and built ships; with Jim Overland, he established wagon routes into the hinterlands of Illinois and down into Missouri and built railroads extending out from Chicago in each direction.

In recognizing the importance of eastern markets, Gary and others in Chicago helped to insure that Chicago would be the cheapest route to the Northeast for the products of both the Northwest and the Southwest. Furthermore, his financial interests in these ventures diversified his portfolio of investments and increased the value of his land holdings, which were almost exclusively in Chicago.

By the time of the Specie Circular in December of 1836, Gary was among the richest men in Chicago. The Panic of 1837 hit like a ton of bricks. Every bank in the country suspended specie payments---the Chicago State bank was no exception; land speculators were crushed; several of Chicago State Bank's competitors failed.

While Gary's opportunities were abruptly curtailed by the panic, for the most part, his assets were kept in tact. Over the ensuing depression years, Chicago's trade actually continued to grow---largely due to the links created by Gary from the East to Chicago and from Chicago out to the wilderness. The simple strategies of diversification and conservatism regarding speculative markets allowed both Gary and the Chicago State Bank to weather the storm of the late 30s and early 40s.

THE PANIC OF 1857

In 1840, there were 800 banks in the country; ten years later, in 1850, there were still only about 800 banks; but by 1857, the number had grown to over 1400. These banks were operating under different state laws and were issuing over 10,000 different bank notes---all of which, together with specie, made up the nation's currency. Counterfeiting became a major problem as non-existent banks were circulating bank notes.

Leading up to the Panic of 1857, there was a major shift in the predominant form of speculative investment: railroads had replaced land as the investment rage. Within the lifetime of a fifty-year-old man, the trip from, say, New York to St. Louis had changed from a one-month horseback ride through the wilderness to a two-day, $20 train trip.

Life had been good to Gary Gambler, Jr. He was at peace with himself and the world about him. Substantial early financial success assured that neither Gary nor his family would ever want for material things. Being financially secure afforded Gary the opportunity to indulge, most fully, his deepest passions: to read, to learn, and, especially, to teach. For five years now, Professor G's classes in philosophy, history and finance were among the most popular at Northwestern University.

In mid September 1857, Paul Eager, an enterprising and able student, approached Gary after class. "Professor G.," he began, "last year, I was fortunate to make a $2,000 profit on a land speculation. I'm now thinking of investing it in Cicero State Bank stock and then using the bank stock to secure a loan so that I can invest it in the Reading Railroad. What do you think?"

"Well, Cicero State Bank's stock will either go higher or lower over the next year and I'm pretty sure I can say the same for the Reading," Gary replied.

"I'm not sure I understand what you're saying, Professor G. But didn't you do very well in that kind of investment in the 30s?"

"Well, yes, Paul. But then was then and now is now."

"O.K. I think I'm getting your point. But I have done a good deal of research that indicates Reading has earned increasingly more per mile of track in each of the last five years, and it is currently constructing another 1000 miles of track. Also, its stock has risen from $20 a share to $70 a share over the last year alone, and I've heard rumors of a possible stock split."

"Well, Paul, its difficult for me to evaluate this on the spot, but something is telling me that this may not be the right time. I get uncomfortable when interest rates exceed 20% and people are more than willing to pay it to speculate on land, stock, pork, wheat, or whatever. I'm also concerned about the failure of the Ohio Life and Trust Company last month."

"I admit there are some signs of speculative excess over the last two years, Professor G., but in 1819 and 1837, according to your lectures, such forces were building for almost five years before the bubble burst. Even if there is no long-term merit to the investment, it may be a good idea for a short-term speculation. But, you are probably right. I think I'll wait." The following week, the Reading had risen to $96 a share. Paul pointed out to the professor that he had missed out on a 30% profit in just one week's time.

"Paul, if you are interested, I will share with you, a bit more about my current concerns." Paul nodded in the affirmative. "First of all, my thesis is that liberal credit extension is the prime cause of speculative bubbles. It's still too early to tell, but based on my studies of 1819, 1837 and similar European experiences, panics are always deepest and occur without prior warning, when all of the money goes into a single area of investment. This is particularly true, when the investment goal is capital gains rather than dividends or earnings. When I began to build what is now the Central Illinois back in '35, there was only about 800 miles of track in the country. The tracks we laid, then, in conjunction with our Great Lakes transportation system, was unarguably the cheapest way to connect fertile Illinois and Missouri farmland to markets back East. As you know, New York, Philadelphia, and Boston were major importers of pork, beef, and wheat.

Up until 1850, there were still only 8,000 miles of track in the country. In the last seven years, however, we have tripled that to over 24,000 miles. This may prove justified but my analysis tells me that we may very well have temporarily overbuilt. The banking situation also concerns me. Loans have increased by over 60% since '52. My work shows that such growth has never been sustainable in the past. In the end, I feel you should follow your own instincts, but for what it's worth, my instincts are telling me to avoid these investments like the plague!"

Four days later, Reading had fallen to $36 a share and 150 banks, including Cicero State Bank, had suspended specie payment. By the end of the following month, every bank in the country had suspended specie payment. Overnight interest rates in New York were being quoted in the 60% to 100% range. Paul Eager was thankful he had listened to the professor.

THE PANIC OF 1873

By June 1858, the economy had pretty much recovered from the financial panic of 1857. It was business as usual until the strains of the Civil War created a need for government financing beyond the capabilities of the state chartered banking system. The Banking Acts of 1863 and 1864 created, for the first time in our history, a national banking system. The system remained in place, without modification for 50 years, when the Federal Reserve System replaced it in 1913. A significant aspect of the National Banking System was that it created a standardized national currency to replace the thousands of state bank issues.

Legislation during the Civil War provided for liberal federal loans to railroads. The government made outright grants of 175 million acres of land to the railroads, over 50% of which went to Northern Pacific, Southern Pacific, Union Pacific and Sante Fe. It has been estimated that lands granted to the Northern Pacific were sold for twice the entire construction costs on those lands.[13]

Critics have charged that liberal government credit and land grants, in particular, caused railroads to build well beyond the needs of the economy at the time of construction. As always when large sums of money are involved, graft, corruption, insider dealings and fraud were commonplace. Historical accounts abound, well into the present century, that relate financial shenanigans, stock manipulation, and fleecing of the unsuspecting investment public by the likes of J. P. Morgan, Cornelius Vanderbilt, Jay Gould, National City Bank, et al.

It was the first day of the Fall Semester, 1873, and Professor G's class in Financial History was even more packed than usual. It had been rumored that the professor was preparing to reveal his findings on a study he began over 30 years earlier.

"As most of you are aware," he began, "I have devoted much of my time collecting and examining data in an attempt to isolate the root causes of financial panics. In my lecture, today, I will lay out my overall conclusions. The data in support of these conclusions will be left for subsequent lectures. In addition, I wish

to make some comments on the current state of the economy and give my prognosis for the future..."

"....So to summarize, then, the following factors appear, in some combination, to have caused every financial panic:

- *liberal extension of bank credit to finance a narrow base of ventures, particularly, when the borrowers were motivated by considerations of resale rather than long-term investment.*

- *major government policies and/or legislative initiatives that were used to stimulate areas of investment viewed as important for public policy purposes.*

- *the existence of high interest rates on short-term funds, often accompanied by acceleration of inflationary forces.*

"Unfortunately, I see each of the panic-causing agents at work in our economy today. The government's land grants and liberal government and bank credit policies have induced railroad construction to unparalleled speculative levels. The government, by making loans per mile of track laid, is inadvertently encouraging speed over quality, cost saving coolie labor over domestic labor, and, above all, construction without regard to our current needs.

In 35 years, from 1830 to 1865, we built 30,000 miles of track. In the last seven years, we have doubled the amount of tracks and bank credit has even more than doubled from $600 million to $1.4 billion. Furthermore, the government's purchase of railroad bonds has added additional leverage to the system. Seven years ago, 35% of railroad capital was debt capital. Today, it's 50%, even if one accepts official statistics at face value. A further element of concern, however, is that construction companies are often be-

ing paid in stocks and bonds whose market value is 4-5 times the cash price of construction. Our leading bankers and investment bankers have watered down the capital base in the name of creative financing. To my mind, it is junk financing.

I predict we will, unfortunately, see a financial blow off of these excesses within the next 12 months. Afterwards, we could be in for some real rough sledding. On a more optimistic note, I believe government will institute policies over the next 20 years or so, to deal with these problems of speculative excess. They will do so, when they recognize the factors I mentioned as the root causes of financial distress and develop institutions to keep these natural tendencies in check."

As it turned out, Professor G. was very right in his short-term economic prognostications and wrong, in the extreme with regard to his long-term predictions. Government action was not forthcoming within 20 years. When the government did act, after the Panics of 1907 and 1929, it treated symptoms and effects. Root causes were concealed rather than remedied.

On September 18, 1873, Jay Cooke and Company---the largest investment banking firm in the country---filed for bankruptcy protection. It had made short-term loans to the Northern Pacific Railroad with a plan to refinance through sales of long-term bonds to foreign investors. When those sales did not materialize and nervous depositors withdrew deposits Jay Cooke was forced to close up shop. Other smaller houses were also brought down, banks failed, and the stock market closed for 10 days. The subsequent depression produced over 30,000 business failures over the next 3 years. These failures escalated the tendencies for wealth to become concentrated in the hands of a few ultra rich families and trusts. This process continued for 40-50 years.

THE PANIC OF 1893

Professor G founded the Northwestern University Finance Club just before his retirement in 1878. At its January 4, 1894 meeting, the four current members were honored to have the club's founder joining them in a roundtable discussion of current financial matters concentrating on panics and their causes. The members were all honors students---each with strong but differing views on financial issues. Robert Barrons was the first to speak.

"First of all, I'd like to express, for all of us, our appreciation for your joining us today, Professor G. We are all familiar with your work, and, I am sure, have all incorporated it into our own thinking. Your careful analysis that shows how unbridled credit expansion has led, time and time again, to speculative blow-offs seems to be re-proved every 20 years or so. You may have also observed, as I have, that while many people get crushed by these panics, others seem to become all the more powerful because of them. Over the last 20 years, in particular, a few families have amassed fortunes that were unthinkable not too long ago. The tool they have used, in every instance, is the coordination of economic power---whether one calls it combination, pool, or trust. Those who join them become members of the trust; those who don't seem to get periodically crushed by panics and depressions which merely seem to serve the will of the monopolists. These monopolists build shoddy railroads, shoddy products, pay political graft, mistreat their laborers, exploit the nation's natural resources and cheat unsuspecting investors. And when some competitors can still compete, they create panics to get rid of them. I am firmly convinced that panics occur because these people want them to occur and cause them to occur in order to further their own best interests."

Professor G., ever the diplomat, wished to find what he could in this analysis to commend. "Mr. Barons, I must agree with you that the concentration of economic power is indeed a fact. And while I must give further thought to your belief that men of great wealth purposely engineer periodic panics, I can certainly agree that the concentration of wealth is typical in the euphoric speculative build-ups, which ultimately result in panics. Over the last seven years, the level of outstanding loans and the money supply have both doubled. And yet, prices have, on balance, declined.

Certainly, had this newly created money been more evenly distributed, we would have seen a rise in prices. But having gone into the hands of speculators, instead, the only price rises we've seen are in stock prices and real estate. But without a consuming public, the products of industry and the railroads that move those products cannot go up forever. The panics seem to occur when the speculators see signs that the upward momentum of stock prices has been arrested."

Phillip Cash, another of the club's member, interjected. "I couldn't agree with you more, Professor G. The money supply is growing as it should to stimulate growth but it is going into the wrong hands. If instead of liberal credit extension, the government would intervene in the economy by spending more, it would trickle down to the workers, the farmers and the consuming public, in general. I can't understand why President Cleveland is so opposed to the Sherman Silver Purchase Act. The government's coinage of silver would tend to bring things back into balance. It would have to be a better economic stimulus than bank's extending liberal credit to speculators."

"Well, you have a good point, Mr. Cash," Professor G. replied. "In the 20 years between the '73 Panic and the one we just experienced last year, loans have tripled while currency in circulation has

not even doubled. I don't doubt for a minute that had we been more restrictive in the extension of bank credit and achieved the same growth in the money supply by liberal coinage of gold and silver or issued more greenbacks as the Greenback Party had urged, we would not have had the sort of panic we have just had. That does not necessarily mean, however, that people, in general, would have been better off had we done so. For example, we may not have grown in the interim as much as we did. On the other hand, if the money supply were controlled by the government instead of banking interests we may well have been able to achieve balanced growth without the panics."

Ken Lendall, having listened intently to the conversation, decided it was time to jump in. "Professor G. has really got a good point there. We need a central banking system that can respond in ways that the National Banking System can't. Our current system is incapable of responding with needed liquidity for several reasons. First, the banks are required to keep a portion of their reserves in government bonds and are therefore limited in what they can do by the amount of government debt. When the government uses surpluses to retire debt, it has the effect of restricting banks' ability to issue notes at the very time it is needed most. In addition, when interest rates are low, business investment is attractive, but the banks have to bid up the value of government bonds--- producing even lower returns---in order to meet the demands of business. Perhaps, this is why---as you've pointed out Professor G.---that loans are being made more and more by deposit creation rather than note creation.

My biggest problem with the system, however, is the inelasticity of the reserve system we have established. National banks keep substantial portions of their reserves as balances in the New York banks in order to take advantage of the call loan market, for example. These reserves allow the New York banks to provide greater liquidity to these markets. However, during the spring and fall, when the country banks want to make agricultural loans to their farming customers, they draw down these reserves and cause an artificial contraction in the money-centers. As far as I can see, this type of situation is a prime cause for the most recent panic conditions. This could be easily avoided if the federal government established a centralized reserve system that could be more responsive to legitimate credit needs."

Before Professor G. could comment on Ken Lendall's suggestions the last of the club's members, Frank Speaker, seized the floor. "Ken, as usual, you seem to have taken indisputable facts and somehow come to the exact opposite conclusions than I do. I am sure if we both witnessed a party taking place on a frozen portion of Lake Michigan next March you would be seeking ways to artificially freeze the ice over the summer and developing plans for light weight transport to re-supply the beer and pretzels. I, on the other hand, would be looking for ways to gently coax the revelers back to shore and developing ways to erect barriers to prevent the party from venturing too far forth next winter.

Now, we all agree, I trust, that institutions that foster liberal extension of credit for speculative purposes do our society no service. Why, then, do we have an institutional structure that encourages this in the first place. Ken, has alluded to the practice of country banks keeping a portion of their reserve balances as deposits with the money-center banks during the winter and summer. The New York banks, as we all know, are allowed to treat these deposits as part of their own reserves. The only purpose this serves is to allow banks that are already pre-disposed to over-extend themselves to gain even more leverage in this pursuit.

Does it really surprise anyone that every fall and spring, when country banks draw down their deposits at the reserve city banks, that a liquidity crisis oc- curs? Last year 496 banks failed. That is more than the total number that failed in the previous 12 years. That amounts to 1 out of every 19 banks in the coun- try. The panic last year was caused---as were others through the years---primarily, because the value of loan security fell below the balance on the loans. But never before in history did so many banks fail be- cause of it. It appears to me that the failures, this time, resulted, in part, because depositors are becom- ing more sophisticated. They are beginning to realize that fractional reserve banks are unstable and that deposits are not safe in them. And until we move to another system whereby demand deposits must be re- served 100% such problems will continue. And fur- thermore..."

As Professor G. left the Finance Club meeting he thought back on his prediction back in '73 that gov- ernment will soon recognize the causes of panics and will establish machinery to eliminate them. He thought of the insightful Frank Speaker and hoped that he and others who saw things as clearly as he did would soon institute change. On the other hand, brilliant people like Ken Lendall---should they hold sway--- could exacerbate future panics by applying their creative genius to help extend euphoria to dan- gerous limits. Professor G. shuddered as he walked off into the cold Evanston night.

The Panic of 1893 resulted in substantial business failures. In that year alone, over 15,000 industrial and commercial businesses went bankrupt. Such leading names in railroads as the Philadelphia and Reading, Sante Fe, and the Northern Pacific all went into re- ceivership. In fact, it has been estimated that railroads representing 1/4 of the total miles in the country went into receivership that year.

THE PANIC OF 1907

The origins of the Panic of 1907 can be traced to an attempt to corner the copper market. The primary players in this drama--- Augustus Heinze and Charles Morse---were also involved in banking activities in New York City. Although the established New York financial community largely regarded them as outsiders, Morse did have connections to the third largest banking establishment: the Knickerbocker Trust Company. Morse had borrowed heavily from Knickerbocker for the purpose of speculating in both copper and the stock of United Copper.[14]

In October of 1907, a run on Knickerbocker caused it to fail when J. P. Morgan ignored pleas for assistance from Knickerbocker's president. The growth of trusts over the prior decade had been quite astounding due to loopholes in the Trust Company Act that allowed them to engage in banking activities without having to be concerned with reserve requirements or investment restrictions. From 1898 to 1906 deposits in trusts grew from $200 million to $800 million. J. P. Morgan, himself, had established Banker's Trust Company to capitalize on these loopholes. In the absence of any regulatory control of the trusts, the risk level of their assets and their overly leveraged financial structure made them particularly vulnerable to upheavals in the system.

A book by Wilbur Aldrich published in 1903 entitled "Money and Credit" makes it clear that the dangers of huge financial trusts were already quite apparent at that time. Aldrich quotes from Philip King, a financial journalist for the New York Sun: "Many of these institutions [trusts] are now organized frankly to act as sponsors for speculations, flotations, and promotions." He goes on to add that trusts are banks that may lend on real estate and their own stock, that do not have to meet reserve requirements or capital requirements, and that have accounted for more than 50% of Wall Street speculation from 1895 to 1901.[15]

The inability of money-center banks to avert the Panic of 1907 re-ignited talk among banking interests regarding revisions to the National Banking Act to make the system more responsive to temporary crises. It had long been recognized that when country banks withdrew reserves from the money-center banks liquidity crises of varying magnitudes ensued. In an attempt to avert the 1907 crisis, the Secretary of the Treasury made large deposits in the New York banks, but this proved to be insufficient and widespread restriction on redemption of specie followed. As a temporary measure, Congress passed the Aldrich-Vernally Act to provide emergency relief. In addition, we created a National Monetary Commission to recommend permanent reform. This led to the introduction of a bill sponsored by Representative Carter Glass, Chairman of the House Banking and Currency Committee, that was signed into law by President Wilson in 1913 as the Federal Reserve Act.

ISN'T THERE A LESSON HERE?

The 19th century and early 20th century panics were so uniformly accompanied by the liberal extension of credit for speculative purposes that any serious reviewer of these events could not possibly fail to hypothesize a likely causative relationship. Little if any attention, however, was focused on the role that the prior euphoria played in causing the resulting panic. Rather, attention was focused on the panics, themselves, and the virtually unanimous conclusion by those in a position to bring about reform, was that greater elasticity of currency and credit would ameliorate, if not eliminate, the panics.

During the 50 years of the National Banking System, currency had increased from roughly $1 billion to $3 billion--or, by a factor of 3. Bank loans, on the other hand, grew from roughly $.5 billion to almost $13 billion--or, by a factor of 25. This provides a rough numerical measure of the tendency (which continues to this day) that money creation has been tied to debt creation by banks. This process redistributes money from savers to borrowers and redistributes wealth from ordinary citizens to banks, bankers, and their powerful favored clients. In the last half of the 19th century, the advent of the industrial age hastened this process. As it gained momentum, a relatively small number of families, corporations, and trusts came to own a growing share of the proverbial pie. By historical accident and the desire of powerful forces, the banking system became a primary vehicle by which this redistribution was accomplished.

This shouldn't be and doesn't have to be the case. Reforms that replace the fractional reserve banking system with a 100% reserve banking system will benefit virtually everyone by merely removing an inappropriate special privilege of the banking system. Recommendations along these lines were last made during the Great Depression. Even then, while they were supported and promoted by key members of the intellectual community, they lacked a power base (as they still do). But while a power base may be lacking, there is a natural constituency: the vast majority of American citizens.

The bank wars fought by the Jacksonian Democrats stated quite eloquently why ordinary people should oppose special privileges that are bestowed upon the banking community. The situation is many times worse today. The Federal Reserve System protects money-center banks (temporarily) from reality; The Federal Deposit Insurance Corporation acts as a government sponsored marketing program for all banks; secular inflation created by the Fed and the banks continue to erode the value of our money; creative accounting allows banks to "produce" fictitious profits from real losses; taxpayer bailouts encourage banks to ignore normal standards of prudence.

Why do so few voices cry out for the justice that is so lacking in the current banking system? It's as if we have succumbed to the view that some members of society should always be privileged and our goal should be to obtain as many of these privileges for ourselves. Hopefully, instead, there will be a rejuvenation of Jacksonian principles. If it doesn't happen soon there may be very little left to save.

Chapter IV

Building (False) Confidence

"We have in this country one of the most corrupt institutions the world has ever known. I refer to the Federal Reserve Board and the Federal Reserve Banks...This evil institution has impoverished and ruined the people of the United States ...Some people think the Federal Reserve Banks are United States Government institutions. They are private credit monopolies which prey upon the people of the United States for the benefit of themselves and their foreign customers..."

-Congressman Louis T. McFadden

Political, social and economic reforms that significantly alter the distribution of power rarely occur without bloodshed. Even in a democracy in which the status quo clearly contains gross inequities (e.g. slavery), this principle applies. Even if the overwhelming majority favors effective reform, powerful interests will resist and, probably, defeat any reform efforts. At a minimum, relevant reform of our banking system will only occur if a majority recognizes the inequities of the current system and/or if powerful counter-forces oppose the established power structure. These bases for reform are pursued in the final chapter.

What masqueraded as bank reform in the early 20th century, however, was nothing more than the desire of banking interests to become even more powerful than they already were. They (successfully) sought to enhance their ability to create and distribute money. In 1910, the following group of men met at Jekyll Island to hammer out bank "reform": Henry Davison (J. P. Morgan interests), Charles Norton (J. P. Morgan interests), Frank Vanderlip (Rockerfeller interests), Paul Warburg (Kuhn-Loeb interests), and Nelson Aldrich (Rhode Island congressman, and father-in-law to a Rockerfeller). With a group of this composition all pulling together in the same direction, it is difficult to imagine a result other than that we would soon have a central bank along the lines they favored. But, what if....

Frank Speaker, Ken Lendall, Phil Cash, and Robert Barrons arrived on Jekyll Island with an important mission. As financial leaders and theorists, each had been asked by Congress to help develop the basic structure for bank reform. Although they had all attended the same University, they represented a cross section of viewpoints. Phil Cash, ever the populist, was now a bank president in his native Louisiana; Ken Lendall was an Under Secretary of the Treasury and was still a fervent believer that the Federal government could and should direct, control and support the natural impulses of banks and bankers in providing for the nation's economic growth; Frank Speaker, with his penchant for teaching, headed up the Finance Department at the University of Chicago; Robert Barrons, having changed the most since college, was Sr. Vice President at Banker's Trust and now was as passionately in favor of the concentration of economic power as he had once opposed it. After exchanging greetings and catching up with each other they set out to attack the monumental task facing them.

Phil Cash: Let me begin by quoting from Thomas Edison who, while not an economist, seems to have recognized the problem we face under the current National Banking System. Edison pointed out that "it's absurd to say that our country can issue $30 million in bonds but not $30 million in currency. Both are promises to pay. But one fattens the usurers and the other helps the people." Clearly we must all agree that the National Banking System's principle *failure has been its inability to provide us with an elastic currency.*

Frank Speaker: I certainly don't disagree with the fact of inelasticity, but I am not so sure that an elastic currency is what we need. The primary characteristic of a rubber band seems to be that when it gets stretched too far it breaks and when tension is released, it contracts violently. Perhaps, instead, our goal should be to prevent the system from becoming stretched to begin with.

Phil Cash: The problem with your analogy, Frank, is that the rubber band only breaks when stretched because it ceases to be elastic at that point. A sufficiently elastic structure to our banking system would prevent random events from causing it to break down.

Robert Barrons: If we are to make any headway here, I think we have to steer clear of nit picking on small points and concentrate on the important issues. As you all know, our recommendations do not have to be unanimous. All we should be attempting to do is come up with something that treats all constituencies fairly. And, except for Frank, I am pretty sure we all agree that an elastic currency and, indeed, an elastic money and credit structure is a desirable element to any reform we recommend. Toward that end, I suggest we discuss the specifics of how that elasticity can best be accomplished.

Frank Speaker: I will yield to the general consensus but not before I say my piece. It is clear, at the outset that the positions each of you will take, will be closer to each other's than to mine. But I would, at least, like a chance to change your minds or to at least, give you some food for thought. The natural constituency for the positions I hold is the vast majority of the

American people. For their sake alone, if for no other reason, I'd like to state my views as clearly as I can.

Our money supply, today, consists of approximately $1.7 billion in currency and about $12.8[1] billion in checkbook money. The former has a physical existence. It can be seen, felt, and freely used by the bearer of that currency. It clearly states, on its face, to "pay the bearer on demand" the denomination indicated. The $12.8 billion in checkbook money, as we all know, does not exist in physical form waiting to be reclaimed. Instead, it is just numbers recorded on bank account statements without specie in the bank's vault to back it up. In fact, from initial deposits of approximately $2 billion, the banks created the other $10.8 billion. This money, in effect, is merely the banks' promises to furnish money on request---a promise which they can not fulfill but which, nonetheless, passes as money, itself, in our society.

In effect, a bank is allowed to create money and lend it out in return for promises to repay by the borrowers. And, as we all know, bankers have found ingenious ways in the past to choose the borrowers that serve their own interests rather than society's interest. Bankers and their favored borrowers benefit from the bankers' ability to create and distribute money. This is some advantage in the land of equality. The only restriction is that the banks can only continue this process until the amount of currency in their vaults is 15% of the money they have created (assuming a 15% reserve ratio). I submit this process is dangerous to the depositors (only 15% of their money exists) and dangerous to the innocent, bystanding general public (due primarily to inflation, but also to the debilitating effects of potential deflation).

So, here is my solution.[2] Establish a Federal Currency Commission to turn into cash enough of the safest and most liquid investments of each bank to increase their cash reserve to 100% of their demand deposits (checkbook money). This procedure would give an all cash backing to demand deposits but will neither increase nor decrease the money supply. Cash will be defined for these purposes as a general obligation of the United States Treasury. Banks will, then, be required to permanently maintain a 100% reserve of demand deposits. If this procedure deprives banks of earning assets, they will be reimbursed through service charges to depositors. Depositors would be inclined under these conditions to put more of their idle funds into deposits of longer maturity. We could call these deposits certificates of deposit.

These reforms would provide many advantages. For example, the system I propose would reduce: the frequency of bank runs; the number of bank failures; the amount of government debt (many of the assets converted to cash will be government debt instruments); the frequency of inflations and deflations (due to absence of bank money creation and destruction); the occurrence of business cycles, panics, and depressions; and the control of industry by banks. In the process, we would also streamline both our banking system and our monetary system.

Ken Lendall: Strangely, Frank, I actually see some merit in your proposal. I assume, the Federal Currency Commission would have the obligation to establish an appropriate money supply? That would be quite a responsibility, but certainly one that the government can perform better than individual banks acting, primarily, in their own best interests.

Frank Speaker: Yes, it would--but all that is really required in order to maintain a stable price level is to grow the money supply at the long-term growth in productivity. The commission, of course, would be required to select the appropriate assets to purchase for accomplishing that purpose. Asset purchase is the *logical way to achieve the money supply growth because it has predictable results. Specifically, the purchase of $1 million in assets (e.g. government bonds) will increase the money supply by exactly that amount. In times of war, however, the commission would also be a lender of last resort to the government.*

Robert Barrons: Can we bring this conversation back to reality? I don't see any possibility for such a scheme to work and, in any event, it would not be acceptable to my bank. We and our corporate clients have been responsible for a significant portion of the industrial growth of our nation. There is no way we will tolerate reform which essentially converts us into a depository whose sole function is to be a warehouse for money.

Phil Cash: As I recall from our days at the university, you believed the people with whom you are now allied were responsible for bankruptcies of untold numbers of industrial, railroad and small banks throughout the country.

Robert Barrons: My views from 20 years ago, Phil, are somewhat irrelevant to my current views. Are you really ready to accept a harebrained scheme that allows the government to usurp a function that has always been the proper concern of banking in this country?

Phil Cash: From what I understand of Frank's proposal, and I admit I have to hear more in order to be convinced, we bankers would share in the general benefits that would accrue to the country as a whole from a sounder monetary policy; we will be free from the worry of future bank failures or bank runs, and would only be ceding to the government control over money not the primary function of banking which is to channel loans from bona fide savers to bona fide investors. After all, as I understand it, we will still employ our own capital plus the capital of bondholders plus the capital from these holders of what Frank calls certificates of deposit to make loans.

Robert Barrons: What you have just described, Phil, still has the effect of substantially reducing our collective abilities, as bankers, to shape the future of this nation. Furthermore, these radical proposals go well beyond what we have been asked to do and go well beyond what is necessary to achieve our goals.

Frank Speaker: What, then, would you suggest Robert?

Robert Barrons: The only problem with our current banking system is as Phil suggested at the outset. Namely, the inelasticity of the system in responding to legitimate random and seasonal liquidity needs and the attendant problems--such as panics and disturbances that arise when everybody in the system seeks to liquefy simultaneously.

All that is required is to establish a system that serves--in the words of the Englishman, Walter Bagehot-- as a lender of last resort. This can be accomplished, very simply, by having a central bank standing ready to turn into cash the investment and commercial paper holdings of its member banks by rediscounting them. In a sense, this central bank will provide a means for liquefying assets in the same way as Frank's Currency Commission-- but with an important difference: it will only be done to the extent necessary to meet market conditions and it will be done at the initiation of the member banks. To the extent that the central bank wishes to encourage and discourage member bank rediscounting activities, it can raise and lower the rate at which it is willing to perform this function. Furthermore, the central bank

*will have the right to raise or lower reserve require-
ments to the extent that major policy shifts in the de-
sired levels of reserves is warranted. What can be
simpler than that?*

*Phil Cash: For one thing, I am worried that the
money-center banks will control the system in their
own interests.*

*Robert Barrons: So we will establish regional banks
that will form the central system and play an active
role in it.*

*Ken Lendall: What restrictions will there be on the
types of assets that can be rediscounted at the central
bank?*

*Robert Barrons: Only self-liquidating, short-term
loans will be eligible for discount. In other words, the
system will lend liberally to all who show good
credit, but it will not be committed to bolster weak
and failing institutions.*

*Ken Lendall: Well what would prevent aggressive in-
stitutions from using this procedure to convert all of
their riskless investments into reserves to provide the
basis for relatively speculative enterprises?*

*Robert Barrons: We will make the ability to borrow
from the central bank a privilege rather than a right.
In that way, the central bank can deny any member
the ability to increase reserves for speculative purposes if it deems such denials appropriate.*

*Frank Speaker: What if depositors seek redemption
requiring members to liquefy, thereby, turning all
their good assets into cash while the shakier assets
remain on their books? And, on an unrelated issue,*

will the central bank have an unlimited ability to in-fuse new reserves?

Robert Barrons: I think the solvent, well-managed banks will be able to take care of themselves. And, as I mentioned earlier, weak and speculative banks will be allowed to fail. As far as the ability of the central bank to expand reserves--that will be limited by the amount of gold they have. I recommend that member reserves not be allowed to exceed 35%-40% of the gold supply....

Phil Cash: Well we've made good progress for one day. Let's resume our discussions tomorrow.

Well, of course, in reality, there was no Frank Speaker, and, in fact, no advocates of anything but central banking at Jekyll Island. The system ultimately passed by Congress and signed into law by President Woodrow Wilson was pretty much what we have today with a handful of relatively minor exceptions and one major exception. The major difference is that initially we were on a modified gold standard. Federal reserve notes and member reserves required 40% and 35% backing, respectively, in gold. Initially, then, the Fed was a lender of last resort that, itself, had limits on how much it could lend. In the 1930s we went off the gold standard, domestically, and in 1971, we defaulted on our international promises of gold redemption, as well. Holders of dollars--both domestic and foreign--have no claim to gold and the Fed has no limits on its ability to create "reserves." Our currency, today, is a fiat currency that can be created in unlimited supply, by decree, by the issuing authority: the Fed. As the French philosopher, historian, and essayist Francois Marie Arouet (pen name Voltaire) noted, succinctly over 200 years ago, "paper money always returns to its intrinsic value, zero." The thesis of *Special Privilege*, then, is actually not all that daring: it merely states that if we don't reform the system, Voltaire will once again be proved right.

To date, Japan and Europe have been content to acquire and hold dollars even though the United States government went from the world's largest creditor to its largest debtor in the early 1980s and has maintained that status ever since. One reason that the dollar has held its value is that the United States is the world's only military super power. As such, it gets to dictate the "rules of engagement" in the financial realm as well.

THE FED IN A NUTSHELL

Second only, perhaps, to the agencies involved in counterintelligence and espionage, the Fed is shrouded in secrecy. There appears to be an intentional effort to describe its activities using terms that hinder rather than aid in understanding this most powerful body's operations. Yet when stripped down to their essence, these operations are quite easily understood.

One function of the Fed is to clear checks for the banking system. While you may legitimately wonder why it takes up to 5 business days to perform, this function is non-controversial, perfunctory, and useful. It does not require further consideration here.

All of the important activities of the Fed can be instructively understood as a single function: to enhance or restrict the ability of the banking system to create money (debt). As we all now know, money creation and debt creation are identical in our society. In a nutshell, then, that is what the Fed does. Having said that and keeping it squarely in mind, it is useful to further categorize these activities as the lender of last resort function and monetary policy. For expository purposes (even though not technically correct) the terms "funds" and "reserves" are used interchangeably in the explanations below.

As lender of last resort, the Fed provides "funds" to a single bank or some broader segment of the system when it is "needed." Whether this is described as providing liquidity or increasing reserves or any of a host of other terms of art, it adds very little to understanding the concept, process, or purpose. The Fed increases funds available to banks primarily by standing ready to buy the bank's assets. If the Fed, for example, bought a car from a bank, then the bank would have more "cash." Instead, however, the Fed buys financial assets from the bank, such as T-Bills. When the T-Bill matures it will be worth its face value. The Fed buys it from the bank at a price lower than its face value that reflects the discount rate. This is nothing more than an implied interest rate. The Fed can raise or lower the inclination of a bank to discount its assets with the Fed by raising and lowering the discount rate. A very low rate encourages a bank to engage in this process, thereby, increasing its funds for other purposes. Conversely, a high discount rate, discourages a bank from discounting its assets with the Fed.

Monetary policy is a broader concept than lender of last resort in that it includes all methods whereby the Fed controls the money supply. Euphemistically, it is called "controlling credit conditions" rather than the money supply. In addition to the discount rate, the Fed controls the so-called reserve requirement. This is the percent of each deposit in a bank that must be kept in the bank. Raising the required ratio, inhibits a bank's ability to create money; conversely, lowering the rate, enhances the bank's ability to create money. While reserve requirements can be used to compel a reduction in the money supply, neither the discount policy nor reserve requirements can be used to compel money creation. Furthermore, if the reserve ratio were set to, and frozen at, 100% on demand deposits, money would no longer be created and destroyed by banks.

Today, the primary monetary tool, and by far the most flexible one, is open market operations. When the Fed buys assets (generally, U.S. government securities) in the open market, it increases funds available to banks; when it sells assets in the open market, it reduces funds available to banks. If the Fed buys in the open market and, say, a pension fund is the seller, then it is the pension fund's bank account that is increased. This does, indeed, increase the funds available to (technically, the reserves of) the pension fund's bank. The common, everyday interpretation of the term "increased reserves" tends to imply that the bank is somehow safer by having more of them.

Coming back to basics, then, whether the Fed is described as having accommodated, eased, loosened, liquefied, etc. and regardless of what particular tool it happened to use to accomplish these purposes, the essence and effect is that it has acted to enable banks to expand the money supply. Conversely, when it is said to have followed a tight or restrictive policy, it has acted to inhibit the banking system's ability to increase the money supply. In the discussion that follows, therefore, these various equivalent terms are liberally interchanged. They merely translate into raise or lower, increase or decrease, up or down, etc. depending on the context.

RECORD OF THE FED---MONETARY POLICY

As an institution, the Fed is generally characterized as powerful, independent, respected, revered, and august. It is the unquestioned, preeminent authority on monetary matters. Its policy, shrouded in secrecy, is constantly being anticipated, second-guessed and debated by knowledgeable outsiders.

"Fed watchers" continually attempt to anticipate when the Fed will ease or tighten. When the Fed does act, for example, to raise the discount rate, commentators will suggest that the Fed raised rates because of this or because of that. People invariably ask "What can we do to get the Fed to ease monetary policy"---as if easy money is always the natural, appropriate desirable state. We must, however, earn the right to easy money by pleasing the Fed. This situation is somewhat akin to the son who says to his parents, "if I do the dishes, can I have the car?" Occasionally, however, Fed watchers will grow impatient: "What more does the Fed want before it will agree to ease?" Rarely, if ever, do you hear, "The Fed is wrong!"

From this, one might infer that the Fed has a long record of achievement; that its past wisdom has been demonstrated over and over. The astonishing fact, however, is that the Fed's record in monetary policy is absolutely abysmal! Virtually every account of monetary policy, especially when evaluated with hindsight, has concluded that the Fed is wrong much more often than it is right. Had it flipped a coin to decide monetary policy we would be better off. A statement attributed to Milton Friedman is that the Fed is always too loose---except when it's too tight. Maxwell Newton, in his book, "The Fed" published in 1983 states that the Fed is:

> *"the most powerful single force for economic and financial destruction this nation has ever seen, and over the last decade it has been the principle creator of waste, destroyer of wealth, disrupter of markets, discourager of investment, and underminer of corpo-*

rations. Single handedly, it has brought economic growth in the United States to a halt[3]

The Fed's record is so awful that it is a wonder it still exists---and yet, it is not only alive and well, but also revered. We can gain a reasonable impression of the Fed's less than sterling record of achievement by looking at major periods in its existence:

1. The Fed was instituted in 1913 to help avoid panics. Within 16 years of its founding---in 1921 and again in 1929---we suffered severe panics. The evidence suggests the Fed did not help to avoid the panics; if anything, it actually helped create and prolong them.

2. The Great Depression of the 1930s was the worst ever in our history. Again the Fed did not get us out of it; instead it was widely criticized for having significantly worsened it.

3. From 1945-1969, America was the unquestioned superior world power. During that period, the United States GNP was 1/3 to 1/2 of the world's total. Nonetheless, our currency was debased throughout this period---nationally and internationally. The blame rests primarily with the Fed.

4. From 1970-78, Arthur Burns presided over the worst prolonged period of inflation we have ever experienced. Burns would have had us believe that the all-powerful Fed had nothing to do with it.

5. From 1979-1982, after an abbreviated stint with Chairman Wm. G. Miller, Paul Volcker presided over and has been credited with ending, the worst stagflation this country has ever seen. Chairman Volcker, however, contributed to Fed disasters in its role as lender of last resort.

6. From 1982-1991, Chairmen Volcker and, then, Alan Greenspan brought inflation "down" to what became viewed as an acceptable annual rate. In the process, we went from being the world's largest creditor nation to being the world's largest debtor nation.

7. From 1992-present, we have experienced regular bailouts of the specially privileged bankers by ordinary taxpayers. These are disguised as bailouts of the poor unfortunate debtors.

These periods bear closer scrutiny.

Monetary Policy (1913-1929)- At the outset of the Federal Reserve System, the discount rate was the prime instrument of control. However, the Fed also manipulated the reserve ratio as well. From 1913-17, the Fed lowered reserve requirements from 21% to 10%. By 1919-20, there was substantial speculation in both commodities and land, yet the Fed kept its discount rate low. Banks borrowed from it, liberally---not as a last resort, but as a first resort. When the Fed finally acted to raise the rate, it overdid it. That the Fed made the 1921 Panic worse by easy money in 1919-20 and then by hitting the brakes in 1921 is not disputed. Milton Friedman points out the lack of smoothness: in 1919 and 1920, the money supply grew by 25%; in 1921, it was cut back by 10%--- the largest one year decline since 1879.[4]

So within 7 years of its inception, the institution formed to help us avoid panics, instead, helped us to have a severe one. All of this took place without the Fed using what is now its major tool: open market operations. Open market operations came into prominent use in earnest during the 1920s. Benjamin Strong, President of the New York Federal Reserve Bank and the strongest figure within the system at the time, recognized the flexibility of open market operations. They can deal incrementally in ways that are not possible with either reserve requirements or discount policy.

Leading up to the 1929 crash, broker loans were growing at a breakneck pace. In the 22 months from 1927 year-end and the stock market crash in October of 1929, these loans grew from $4.4 billion to $8.5 billion. Interestingly, at the beginning of 1928, 1/3 of these broker loans were held by money-center banks, but 20 months later at the time of the 1929 crash, only about 1/8 of them were held by the money-center banks.[5] Perhaps, this is a classic case of what Wall Street euphemistically calls "distribution"---the process whereby insiders sell to outsiders while maintaining that everything is fine! In any event, the banks orchestrated both ends of the stock market speculation: they underwrote the new issues and then financed the retail sales.

Another monetary development of the 1920s was the substantial reduction in reserve requirements for time (savings) deposits from 21% to 5% and later to 3%. As a consequence, banks had a vested interest in encouraging depositors to put money in such accounts rather than into demand deposits. In 1914, time deposits were less than 1/3 of total deposits; by 1929, they were approaching 50% of total deposits.[6]

Monetary Policy (Great Depression)- In view of the fact that the Fed was established to avoid financial panics, one might have expected by 1929 it would have been clear to everyone that the Fed was a colossal failure. Could it now redeem itself by providing the leadership for getting us out of the depression? Milton Friedman (among others) has concluded that the Fed actually made the Great Depression worse. Virtually no one suggests that the Fed was a positive force.

Keynesian economists (named after English economist, John Maynard Keynes) favored fiscal policy (managing the government's revenues and expenditures) not monetary policy as the tool needed for fighting the depression. Monetary policy in a depression has been described as similar to pushing on a string. All it does is increase excess reserves. Lowering interest rates during a business contraction won't necessarily get people to invest. Government deficits, on the other hand, induce investment. Entrepreneurs will not borrow and invest unless someone has the money to buy their products.

In 1934, Mariner Eccles became the first "Chairman" of the Fed. Until this time, the Fed had been properly seen as a private collection of 12 regional reserve banks that acted on behalf of banking needs not social policy. While it remains such, since Eccles, it has cleverly established a more public policy image. Eccles accepted fiscal policy as the primary weapon against depression. He favored the centralization of the Fed in order to use its monetary policy in concert with the government's fiscal policy. Banking interests generally opposed this philosophical shift.

Monetary Policy (1945-69)- Mariner Eccles was chairman of the Fed until 1948. He had favored an easy money policy during the depression and had agreed to one during the war. After the war, however, he felt that easy money should no longer be automatic. But, by now, the Fed was more or less tied to the Treasury Department and the latter favored a continuation of easy money. From 1945-51, first under Eccles and later under Thomas B. McCabe, the Fed fought for its independence from the Treasury. An accord was reached in 1951.

Independence, which had been established on paper since the Fed's inception, was formalized again, in this accord. William McChesney Martin, who succeeded McCabe in 1951, operated reasonably appropriately for most of his tenure. Specifically, the Fed operated as a counter-cyclical force by tightening credit during boom periods. Moderate counter-cyclical activity is the best guarantee against an overheating economy. The Fed pays lip service to such a policy, but is almost always too loose rather than too tight.

Martin pursued a counter-cyclical policy until the later years of his tenure. In 1965-1966, however, he incurred the wrath of President Johnson, whose "guns and butter" fiscal policy sought accommodation from the Fed on monetary policy. In keeping with the tradition of any central bank in times of war, Martin attempted to accommodate. From the inception of the Fed until 1968, the yield on U.S. T-bills rose above 5% only once (1920). After 1968, the yield continually stayed above 5% until the late 1990s.

The late 1960s was arguably a major turning point in United States history. The book, *Blood in the Streets*, by James Dale Davison and William Rees-Moog puts forth the theory that world events are primarily shaped by the super power's ability to project its military superiority. Using the rise and fall of the British empire as their model, the authors argue that the failure of the United States to assert its military superiority in the Vietnam War may have marked the turning point between the rise and fall of America. They examine political, social, technological, economic, and financial evidence to evaluate this proposition. Most of the evidence points to decline. However, on the other side, the United States remains the world's only *bona fide* military super power. The absence of another super power to replace us may allow us to avert decline. Our victory in the Gulf, for example, may have helped to relegate Vietnam to a curious random deviation from the still operative realities of U.S. military power.

Monetary Policy (1970-78)- On March 14, 1980, after his tenure as Fed Chairman, Arthur Burns addressed the American Institute of Public Policy Research on the causes of inflation. (He should have been embarrassed to speak on the subject.) First, he dismissed what he felt others think are the causes of inflation. Then, he shared with the group what causes inflation according to Burns:[7]

1. Government's bias toward economic stimulation.
2. Interference with free market competition.
3. Environmental and safety legislation.

Could Burns have really believed these were the three prime causes of inflation? Not likely. In September, 1979, also after his tenure, he asserted that: "...The Federal Reserve System had the power to abort inflation at its incipient stage fifteen years ago, or at any later point, and it has the power to do so today...It did not do so because the Federal Reserve was, itself, caught up in the philosophical and political currents that were transforming American life and culture."[8] In other words, he knew what should be done, had the power to do it, but his hands were tied by "philosophical and political currents." Paul Volcker, too, acknowledged the sheer power of the Fed when he said: "The truly unique power of a central bank, after all, is the power to create money, and ultimately the power to create is the power to destroy."[9]

Monetary Policy (1979-1982)---For years, Milton Friedman and other monetarists promoted the concept that monetary policy should control money--- not interest rates. Furthermore, said Friedman, the Fed should merely grow the money supply at a relatively constant rate equal to the long-term growth in productivity. Yet, until October of 1979, the Fed had resisted this approach. For one thing, it took much of the mystery out of monetary policy; for another, it took the discretionary power of the Fed out of monetary policy; and finally, it gave us an observable criterion by which to measure Fed performance.

In October 1979, however, Volcker agreed to try it even though he wasn't a 100% believer in it. By 1982, ultra high inflation was ultimately arrested at the cost of the 1981-1982 recession. During the process, interest rates ran up to over 20%. The Fed was reportedly amazed. But why? An all-too-late abrupt change of policy is obviously going to create dislocations. In the 19th century panics, short-term rates went through the roof when the supply of money was suddenly choked off. The Fed was also amazed that in the six months following its decision to control the money supply, it continued to gyrate up and down like a yo-yo.[10] What they forgot to consider was the banking community's bag of tricks: Eurodollars, money market funds and the like. For example, a foreign subsidiary could borrow Eurodollars overseas from a U.S. or foreign bank and then make an internal transfer to its domestic parent.[11]

Monetary Policy (1982 to 1991)- In Volcker's second term and continuing with Alan Greenspan, the Fed moved away from reliance on monetary aggregates as the sole aspect of monetary policy. During this period, the Fed presumably addressed multiple concerns such as interest rates, exchange rates, commodities prices, and the overall quantity and quality of debt. The underlying rationale during this period was that neither the price of money approach (1913-1979) or the quantity approach (1979-1982) had proved to be entirely satisfactory. First of all, the failure of the price approach had been demonstrated over a 66-year period and never had much of a theoretical basis for support. The quantity approach, on the other hand, had a theoretical basis and was only tried for a short period. The problems that did arise occurred because banks circumvented the policy.

In 1989, two bills were introduced in Congress to exercise some control over the Fed. One bill, introduced by Representative Steve Neal of North Carolina required the Fed to aim for a 0% inflation rate. Since the bill did not provide guidance with regard to how the objective should be achieved, its laudable intent was somewhat irrelevant. The other bill, co-sponsored by Representatives Lee Hamilton of Indiana and Byron Dorgan of North Dakota reinstalled the Secretary of the Treasury as a member of the Federal Reserve Board (this was the case until 1935), allowed new presidents to select a new chairman, eliminated the six week secrecy rule regarding decisions of the open market committee, and increased Congressional control over the Fed. Each of these bills---on balance--- provided positive steps in the right direction. In any event, neither bill succeeded.

Much better, perhaps, was the Milton Friedman approach of freezing the monetary base, deregulating banking, and allowing interest rates to be determined by market forces. The net result would effectively eliminate the Fed as a powerful force since all of its functions other than check clearing would be eliminated or made perfunctory. As long as we are willing to freeze the aggregate monetary base, why not go one step further and move to 100% reserve banking on demand deposits?

Monetary Policy (1992 to 2001)- Chairman Greenspan's greatest contribution to innovation at the Fed comes in the lender of last resort area. This former stalwart of the free market now promotes his own brand of reverse welfare: one shameless bailout of the specially privileged by the ordinary taxpayer after another. Meanwhile, he has also presided over a long economic expansion and is generally credited with much of the success. Nonetheless, over the last five years or so, during a period where the Fed's M3 monetary targets were in the 2%-6% range, the actual results have been in the high single digits and even low double digits. In other words, since 1995 we haven't even come close to reaching our stated monetary targets. However, because the newly created money is being distributed to people on the upper end of the income spectrum, the consumer price index has (so far) been growing at under 3% per year during this period.

THE FED AS LENDER OF LAST RESORT

At its inception, the Fed's primary function and sole justification was as lender of last resort. Its role, over the years has been expanded to entail all aspects of monetary policy. It is more difficult to evaluate the Fed's performance in this area than in the monetary control area. One has to first accept the premise that having a lender of last resort is good in the first instance. If so, one must evaluate, in any given case, whether the function should be provided. The policy now seems to be that whenever any crisis hits---regardless of the cause or nature of that crisis---the Fed should provide liquidity. The second element of the policy holds that some institutions are "too big to fail." This policy is presumably based on the belief that if a large institution fails other institutions will be brought down in a sort of domino effect. "Too big to fail" has, at times, been extended to non-bank financial institutions and industrial corporations.

The first opportunity the Fed had to be a lender of last resort occurred during the 1920s. In 1920, there were 23,000 banks in America. In 1929, there were only 18,000. In the interim 5700 banks failed and less than 1000 new ones were formed. In other words, about one out of every four banks failed during the 20s---the first full decade after we instituted the lender of last resort! During the 50 years of the reputedly ineffective National Banking System, only in 1893, a panic year, did more than 300 banks fail in a single year. From 1921 through 1929, during supposedly good times, an average of over 600 banks per year failed. Even in the best of those years (1922) 367 banks failed. From 1930-33, over 9100 more banks failed, producing a 50% reduction in the number of banks in a four-year period. As lender of last resort, the Fed was an even more miserable failure than as a source of monetary stability.

In 1933, Congress created the Federal Deposit Insurance Corporation. To the extent that the lender of last resort function was partially to protect depositors or to alleviate bank runs, FDIC made it less necessary. Besides, the Fed had already demonstrated from 1921-33 that it was incredibly ineffective in this role. By 1970 or so, the lender of last resort function was taking on a new role. Specifically, the Fed's powers to infuse liquidity would be used to rescue any bank as long as it was big enough--regardless of any greed, stupidity, or callous disregard for the national interest that the bank might have demonstrated.

The "too big to fail" syndrome is certainly not exclusive to the Federal Reserve System. The Fed has, however, made its fair share contribution to rescuing institutions that should not have been rescued. These rescues deviated substantially from the initially intended procedures that at least had technical merit. Specifically, the initial intent was to allow institutions facing liquidity problems to rediscount (sell) relatively riskless, short-term investments to the

Fed. Appropriate investments include short-term government obligations, commercial paper and, perhaps, other corporate obligations consistent with the "real bills" doctrine. This doctrine states that business loans made by banks should be limited to short-term, self-liquidating loans. Unfortunately, even in the best of times, banks have honored this doctrine more in the breach than in the keeping.

In 1956, for example, back when banks were not the boldly speculative institutions that they have since become, a study performed by the 4th District of the Federal Reserve revealed that fully 2/3 of the dollar volume of loans in the district did not conform to the real bills doctrine.[12] The study went on to candidly admit that even a strict adherence to the real bills standard requires non-crisis conditions to work and that "any wholesale attempt [by banks]...to meet deposit withdrawals...is bound to fail."[13]

In late 1979, 10% of all excess reserves went to finance the Hunt brothers' attempt to corner the silver market.[14] Incredibly, in a nation of 250 million people, 10% of all lending went to two brothers for a wild and potentially dangerous speculation of worldwide proportions. In March of 1980, silver fell from $50 to $10 per ounce even more quickly than it had previously risen to such heights. As a result, Bache, Citibank, Chase, et al were stuck with under-secured outstanding loans in the amount of $1.7 billion. Only specially privileged institutions that can count on being rescued when things go wrong can possibly be that irresponsible. In October 1979, the Fed had stated publicly that banks should "avoid loans that support speculative activity in gold, commodities, and foreign exchange markets." Nonetheless, when they did exactly that with the Hunt brothers, the Fed, itself, arranged the $1.1 billion bailout. As *Business Week* put it, apparently Volcker had modified his position: he was opposed to such behavior---unless they all do it.[15]

When institutions are bailed out from the consequences of their irresponsible behavior, it shifts the burden of any disaster from those who create it to the ordinary American citizen. For example, to rescue Citibank, Chase et al from their incredible escapade with loans to the LDCs, the Fed bought Brazilian bonds to help Brazil make interest payments to American banks. Whenever the Fed buys any asset--even a good one—it increases the money supply and it therefore damages everybody who holds dollars. When it purchases Brazilian bonds you can virtually count on the inflationary effect.

And as the St. Louis Federal Reserve Bank points out in its own literature, "the decrease in purchasing power incurred by holders of money due to inflation imparts gains to the issuers of money."[16] The Brazilian loan purchase had been made possible because, at Volcker's urging, a six-line addition to the 85-page Depository Institutions Deregulation and Monetary Control Act of 1980 permitted the Fed to buy foreign as well as U.S. government bonds. Thus, the Fed's ability to create unlimited amounts of money out of thin air and its willingness to do so in order to bail out the money-center banks provides a safety net to these banks.

In 1989, when a sprinkling of bank runs were touched off by the S&L mess, the Fed was ready to make liberal loans secured by whatever security was available as long as the loans were guaranteed by FSLIC. As James Ring Adams put it, "the Fed was willing to take an IOU from an insolvent thrift backed by a guarantee from an insolvent FSLIC."[17] This is certainly a long way from anything even remotely resembling the real bills doctrine.

How did the "too big to fail" theory become conventional wisdom? There is not a single historical event or a single shred of historical evidence that demonstrates the likelihood (let alone the inevitability) of national disaster if a large bank fails. In the past, even widespread bank failures have not led to the kind of disaster conjured up by proponents of the "too big to fail" doctrine. True, the U.S. economy contracted by 40% in the 1930-33 period while, at the same time, one half of the nation's banks were failing; but Canada and England, did not experienced the widespread bank failures that the United States did, and they also contracted substantially during 1930-33 period. "Too big to fail" appears to be no more than another excuse to provide welfare to the largest and most powerful institutions. The most generous motive one could ascribe to such welfare is that it maintains the status quo and/or it maintains confidence in the system.

The most repugnant aspect of the "too big to fail" theory is the stark acknowledgment that in a land of free enterprise, some institutions are so privileged that they are to be rescued from their own folly---no matter how irresponsibly they behave. They are above the rules and regulations that govern the rest of us. They are the nobility---the aristocracy of our society. Young men and woman who are sent off to war---perhaps to die for principles we believe in---are not too big to fail or too important to die. But one of the principles for which they must stand ready to die is that Citigroup (for example) is too big to die, even when, by any realistic standard, it is already dead.

The myth that confidence is an end in itself---to be nurtured and promoted at all cost---is patently illogical. Yet, the emotional appeal of this flawed argument allows "confidence men" to mollify a public that is, above all, yearning for everything to "be O.K." But, clearly, con men who engender false confidence can only succeed in putting off the day of reckoning; they will be powerless to do anything other than admit they were wrong when that day of reckoning arrives. Alternatively, we can reform the system so that even those in a position of power are forced to observe the discipline of the free-markets. Capitalism requires it.

Chairman Greenspan's tenure is now longer than any other chairman except William McChesney Martin in the 50s and 60s. Greenspan, who spoke out against the Chrysler bailout in 1979 as a private citizen, has become the (selective) undisputed taxpayer bailout champion. The early 1990s brought us the S&L bailout; in the mid 1990s we had the Mexican bailout; later in the 1990s we had the Russian bailout and the South East Asian bailout. In 1998, when Greenspan (and Treasury Secretary, Robert Rubin), each hit the airwaves within minutes of each other to promote the bailout of a hedge fund euphemistically named Long Term Capital Management ("LTCM"), they both proudly called attention to the fact that no taxpayer money would be used in the effort---this time. We discuss these bailouts and their implications, more fully, in Chapter 7.

THE ULTIMATE DRUG DEALER

The passage of the Federal Reserve Act in 1913 was the first in a series of 20th century "reforms" and remedies that has brought about the current sorry state of our banking system. We did not act to prevent excesses and abuses perpetrated by our banking system throughout the 19th century, but instead legislated away the natural consequences of these acts. The Fed would have been easily seen as a non-solution if the problem had been more correctly identified: the natural tendency of banks toward excess and abuse. Instead, powerful vested interests that proposed and designed the Fed had to redefine the problem. They invented systemic inelasticity of money and credit as the problem to which the Fed was the solution.

The same kind of logic if applied, for example, to the problem of drug abuse would require, first, that the problem be redefined to be one of drug withdrawal. Then, a solution that proposes a free flow of drugs would appear to be exactly what is needed. While the drug analogy is perfect, it is, unfortunately, not altogether apparent to everybody. First, people have to see the problem as the inherent unsoundness of fractional reserve banking rather than as the unfortunate periodic drying up of credit that culminates in "credit crunches." Second, they have to see that banking excesses and abuses sap the vitality from the financial condition of the country even if, superficially, some of these excesses (e.g., liberal credit extension) appear, at first, to improve the financial condition. This is analogous to the drug situation. If one observes two drug addicts, side by side---one who has just had a fix and another who is in dire need of one---the observer might conclude that the one who has just had a fix is in better shape. In looking at the history of financial panics in the United States, one sees a recurring cycle of fixes and cold turkey withdrawals. Every single panic was preceded by an over-extension of speculative credit by the banking system that started out slowly and built to a crescendo.

When the first time narcotics user experiences that first euphoria, he or she craves more and then becomes physically addicted; when the banking system expands the money supply (especially for speculation), it causes a similar euphoria. The first receivers crave more and others want a taste. In these early stages of euphoria, no one recognizes that the liberal flow of newly created money ultimately leads to no good. Later, when everybody is strung out, a plan to re-supply the drugs appeals more than retrenchment does.

The Fed almost always appears to agree to monetary easing only after the economy has become sluggish---when it is, supposedly, absolutely necessary. But the facts are contrary to this impression. After all, the Fed's initial role was lender of last resort. This function, by its very nature, keeps the money flowing and the party in full swing. Now if this were, in fact its true purpose, many would favor it even though it might be shortsighted to do so. Since more banks failed in the 20s---let alone the 30s---than ever before in history, one has to wonder whether lender of last resort was truly the Fed's planned role. Maybe it's function was to act as agent for the money-center banks.

Today, most people think the Fed's primary purpose is to control the money supply. If that were its true purpose and it actually accomplished such a purpose, it would be a worthwhile institution. After all, control of the money supply is needed. The Fed, however, has not controlled the money supply by any stretch of the imagination. Instead, it has presided over a long and persistent inflation. So either control of the money supply is not the Fed's true purpose, or it has failed miserably to accomplish it.

The single most important factor affecting our economy is monetary policy. What is the appropriate money supply and how should it be distributed? The real answer to the first part of the question is that it doesn't matter how large the money supply is. It could be halved or doubled across the board without any important effect whatsoever in the amount or distribution of wealth. The perversions are only caused by the distribution of that money. Monetary policy decides how much to inject, but banks get to decide how it is distributed throughout the economy. The Fed, therefore, only enables the perverse process. The banks are the progenitors of the all important money distribution process. (See Chapter 6).

THE FED: AGENT TO THE POWERFUL

The Fed has demonstrated an uncanny ability to bungle monetary policy throughout its history, and yet, has managed to increase its power and prestige over an almost 90-year period. One has to wonder why previous institutions such as the First and Second United States Banks and the National Banking System were ultimately scrapped while the Fed rolls merrily along. Could it have something to do with the fact that the Fed is the convenient agent of the most powerful economic and political forces in the country: the money-center banks and the U.S. Government Treasury? There is ample support for such a suspicion.

The Fed was formed because the most powerful of monied interests in America wanted it: the Morgans, the Rockerfellers, the Kuhn-Loebs. Early on, Morgan's close ties to the Bank of England led to U.S. support of England in WWI and ultimately to U.S. entry into the war. This allowed the Fed to pick up the most powerful of clients: the U.S. government---which needed to finance the war effort. Throughout the 1920s and 1930s, the Fed allowed thousands of banks to fail---not a single one of which was a large money-center bank. Sure, it allowed the relatively large Bank of the United States in New York's garment center to fail, but that was a "Jewish" bank, an outsider, and not a full-fledged member of the club.

By the 1980s, when the elite banking giants got themselves into trouble, the Fed was there to lend a helping hand. First (to come to public attention) was how two crap shooting brothers, trying to corner the silver market, managed, in the process, to get Bache, Citibank, Chase et al into trouble. Not that they would have failed, but why should they lose money if they can avoid it by breaking the rules that apply to everyone else.

Next there was the rescue mission to save these same banks from their colossal over-extension of credits to the LDCs. Meanwhile, the 1980s, like the 1920s, witnessed an extremely high number of failures among the smaller banks---the banks that are not "too big to fail," and, therefore, not full-fledged members of the club. In February, 1990, when Drexel Burnham Lambert failed, Greenspan indicated he was powerless to help even if he wanted to do so. Sure, Drexel was an upstart selling junk bonds and taking action away from Greenspan's clients, the money-center banks. Furthermore, the elite club members were not overly exposed to Drexel.

Years later, in 1998, when LTCM with its highly leveraged $100 billion portfolio was in trouble, the same Alan Greenspan who, supposedly, could do nothing for Drexel Burnham---even if he wanted to---was apparently again in a position to lend a helping hand. The degree to which money-center banks are exposed to a particular financial fiasco appears to be the degree to which the Fed's hands "are" or "are not" tied.

The Fed, therefore, has been effective in its apparent objective to wield power as agent for the money-center banks. Its lack of achievement in the monetary policy area stands in stark contrast to its ability to change rules and otherwise intervene on behalf of its client banks. Indeed, it earns high marks for its political achievements. After all, for almost 90 years it has acted as the engine of inflation unlike any we have ever seen, and yet managed to maintain its reputation as an effective monetary manager. Being able---through adept political ploys---to appear effective and responsible is the worst of all possible cases. It would be best, of course, if the Fed did not exist at all. If the Fed were truly effective---that would be second best. Failing that, it would be better if it were widely recognized as being ineffective and irresponsible. We could then replace it as an institution that isn't working out. Instead, it continues to inspire (undeserved, false) confidence through political maneuvers shrouded in mystery.

Meanwhile, there is no basis for the confidence. The Fed continues to debase the dollar in the service of the shortsighted self-interest of one client (the U.S. Government) and the greedy, callous self-interest and ineptitude of its other clients (the money-center banks). We have now come to the point where both "clients" are at important crossroads. The Fed's support has merely pushed reality into the future. But that future will all too soon become the present. The country needs to institute a system that rewards productive enterprise, discourages reckless speculative banking activity, maintains the value of the dollar, and provides opportunities for all to benefit according to his or her abilities. That's not what we now have.

Because a significant redistribution of power never occurs without bloodshed, any practical reforms will undoubtedly give the financial elite more than it deserves. If the financial elite loses its special privileges, that's the most we can hope for. Maybe the proper proposal can be made at a point when the elite is vulnerable. In the words of Irving Fisher in his plea for 100% reserve banking:

> *"If our bankers wish to retain the strictly banking function---loaning--- which they can perform better than the government, they should be ready to give back the strictly monetary function which they cannot perform as well as government. If they will see this and, for once, say, "yes" instead of "no" to what may seem to them as a new proposal, there will probably be no other important opposition."*[18]

Chapter V

"Nothing to Fear, But...."

"We are completely dependent on the commercial banks. Someone has to borrow every dollar we have in circulation, cash or credit. If the banks create ample synthetic money, we are prosperous; if not, we starve.... The tragic absurdity of our hopeless position is almost incredible, but there it is.... It is so important that our present civilization may collapse, unless it becomes widely understood, and the defects remedied very soon."

-R. Hemphill, Federal Reserve Bank, Atlanta, 1938

It was Good Friday, 1933, as Frank Speaker and his wife Abigail Bearsford Speaker boarded the plane for New York. They were invited to their daughter, Cecelia's house for the Easter holiday.

Ceci had married Jim Fehr, a prominent physician, over 13 years ago. They lived in Bronxville, New York, a small community in Westchester County with their 12-year-old son, Will Bearsford Fehr and their newborn daughter, Yolanda Bearsford Fehr. Frank was particularly looking forward to seeing his grandson, Will, (named after Will Rogers), who was as precocious as a child of his age could be. When the flight arrived at Idyllwild Airport, Ceci and Will were waiting to pick Frank and Abigail up. Will, who was as anxious to see his grandfather as Frank was to see him, immediately, began to "monopolize" Grandpa's time.

"Grandpa, you won't believe this. Since I saw you at Christmas, I have been spending all my free time reading books on money and banking."

"Don't tell me that you've already finished studying calculus. At Christmas, you amazed me with the way you had mastered algebra by yourself, and you told me you were thinking of doing the same with calculus."

"Algebra was fun, Grandpa, but I'm already way ahead of the other kids in math, so there is plenty of time to pick up calculus later. But, the way things are going in the financial system, I figured I'd better learn something about money and banking pretty fast."

Ceci rolled her eyes toward her Mother as if to say "Isn't he something else!" Neither Ceci nor Abigail had much interest in these matters, and they found it humorous that a boy of 12 could become so involved with it. "Dad, I'm really glad you're here. Will is so fascinated with money and banking, and yet neither Jim nor I have much knowledge on the subject. It's embarrassing when your 12 year old son asks apparently basic questions and a PhD in Philosophy and a medical doctor have to both admit that his knowledge of these subjects has already exceeded their own. Maybe, we can all use a little refresher course this weekend. With this Bank Holiday Roosevelt has called, it seems that everybody is talking about it, and those of us who are fortunate to have money in the bank are wondering just how safe it is."

Frank, never one to pass up an opportunity to discuss his favorite subject, readily agreed. That evening, after dinner, the entire family (except the baby) sat down in the large family room to discuss the banking situation in the country and banking, in general. "I must admit," Ceci began, "I have read that over the last few years thousands of banks have failed, and I know that significant new legislation is under discussion in Congress, but I don't know if I really understand how and why all this is happening."

"Let me answer that, Grandpa," Will quickly chimed in eager to demonstrate to Frank how much he knew. "You have to realize, Mom, that when you put money in the bank, the bankers don't just let it sit there, they invest it in interest-bearing government securities, or make short-term corporate loans with it. So when people come, all at once, to get their money out, it isn't there waiting to be reclaimed. Here's where I get a little hazy though. From what I understand, we set up the Federal Reserve System to handle just this kind of situation. When banks need to convert their assets into cash for any reason, they are supposed to be able to sell their best assets to the Fed to raise the cash they need. So why doesn't the Fed do that and everybody can get his money?"

"That's very impressive, Will," Frank began, "It seems as if you have learned quite a bit about banking. I can even understand why you are confused because, from what you would have read in the available literature, you should be perplexed. There are two things you should know. First, the description you gave of a bank's investments is theoretically what conservative bankers do. Unfortunately, during the 1920s an alarmingly large portion of bank loans were being secured by real estate and financial assets whose value have fallen below the outstanding balance on the loans. Secondly, the Fed doesn't necessarily want all the banks to meet depositors' withdrawals. It is not necessarily unhappy when the overextended banks--particularly some of the smaller ones--fail under the current circumstances."

"If I'm reading between the lines correctly, Dad, what you are saying is that the Fed is biased toward the larger money-center banks," said Jim, questioningly.

"That's right, Jim. I can't prove it for certain because Fed operations are shrouded in secrecy due to

the supposedly sensitive nature of its activities. But you will notice that as soon as money-center banks appear to be in trouble, the Fed moves quickly to infuse liquidity directly into these banks. Usually, the Fed infuses liquidity, primarily, through activities called open market operations, which increase overall liquidity but do not direct the liquidity, specifically, to banks with the most severe liquidity problems."

"So what you are saying, Dad, is that the Fed, to some extent, is a tool of the large money-center banks. I must say that is somewhat comforting to me on a personal level since all of Ceci's and my money is in Chase National and National City. It's nice to know that the Fed is particularly looking after the very banks in which we have our money."

"How can you say that, Dad," Will quickly countered, "It's just not fair that an organization incorporated to advance public policy like the Fed is just a tool for the richest, most powerful members of society, allowing them to maintain their advantages over everybody else by raw power rather than by superior abilities. Now, I'm even more in favor of the proposed federal deposit insurance that is being considered by Congress. At least that treats the smaller banks the same as the big banks."

"Will, I must say, every time you open your mouth, I am more amazed at your grasp of complex issues. Everything you have said is a reasonable conclusion to draw from the current situation. The only thing I would ask you to consider is this: just because some have a privileged position in our society, does that mean that giving others a special privilege improves things? Let me suggest that it does not. It..." At that point, Frank realized from the look on everybody's face that the conversation was only holding his and Will's interest. "Well, let's not try to solve all of the world's problems tonight; we have a whole weekend for that. I'm kind of tired from the trip and am ready

to retire." All agreed that it was late and time to go to bed.

"Grandpa. Grandpa. Wake up, I want to talk to you!" Frank slowly opened his eyes to see the eager expressive look on Will's face. *"Grandpa, I want to continue our conversation from last night. Why don't you get up."*

Frank tiredly, but happily, dragged himself out of bed at Will's suggestion. *"O.K. Will. I'm as anxious to pick up on last night's conversation as you are. Just give me 20 minutes to shower and have a few cups of coffee. Then, I will be more than happy to pick up where we left off."* After his shower and coffee, Frank went to the family room to relax and collect his thoughts. Traces of cobwebs stubbornly lingered in his not quite fully awake brain. Within seconds Will entered the room.

"Grandpa, I don't want to get bogged down in conjecture and theory, but I do want to understand the ramifications of what's going on in our society." Frank, as always, was impressed with Will's vocabulary. He not only knew the meanings of words like 'conjecture' or 'ramification' but also used them in his normal expression.

"Will, I'm ready to discuss anything you want. Shoot."

"What you said last night, Grandpa, about the Fed's apparent bias in favor of the large versus small banks disturbs me a little because it shouldn't show such favoritism. But right now, I'm more interested in evaluating plans currently under consideration for preventing these problems from happening again. In that regard, while I don't see anything dramatically wrong with it, the Glass-Steagall bill currently before the Congress does not seem to be addressing the root causes of the problem."

"Again, Will, you're right on target. The only way we are going to prevent this from happening again and again is to deal with the root causes. And legisla-

tion that combines a few crumbs of justice with the seeds of even greater future perversions will certainly not do the trick. It just so happens that I have brought with me a paper I have recently written about 100% reserve banking. Some of the leading intellectuals in the financial community agree that such a system can prevent the kinds of problems we have faced every 15 to 20 years or so throughout our history, I'll give it to you to read. Unfortunately, I'm somewhat pessimistic about the prospects for its adoption because bankers will oppose it for no better reason than that it will reduce their ability to perpetuate their enormous power."

"Well I definitely want to read your paper, Grandpa. What you said about the Glass-Steagall bill's containing crumbs of justice and seeds of perversion, I'm not so sure I followed. As I understand it, the bill has three major provisions: it prohibits commercial banks from engaging in investment banking and vice versa; it provides for federally insured deposits of up to $2,500; and it forbids the payment of interest on checking accounts. The separation of banking from investment banking seems to make sense. The investment pools set up by the banks in the mid-to-late 20s seemed to have contributed to the excesses leading up to the crash. And if setting up federally insured deposits will help rebuild confidence in the system that doesn't seem like such a bad idea. So I guess the provision you object to is the elimination of interest payments on checking accounts. I must admit, I, too, wondered whether this was just the banks way of shifting the burden of having to pay insurance premiums from themselves to the depositors."

"Not really, Will. The separation of banking from investment banking is worthwhile as you suggest. The elimination of interest on demand deposits, even though it favors the banks, is also eminently reasonable. People should not be paid interest for the use of

money that they have not given up the right to use themselves. Interest only makes sense when the providers of funds transfer the right to use those funds to borrowers. If no such transfer is granted, no interest should be paid. In fact, before the 1920s, interest was not paid on checking account deposits. I opposed the introduction of the concept, at that time, because it was potentially dangerous in that the speculative bankers could bid funds away from the more conservative bankers. As you will see from my paper, I believe that bankers should not only not pay interest on these demand deposits, but I also believe they should not lend them out. They should merely keep them in their vault for safekeeping. It's as much a part of the money supply as the money in your pocket."

"No, by far the greatest problem with Glass-Steagall is the introduction of the concept of federal deposit guarantees. In effect, it induces people to put the first $2,500 of discretionary money they have into banks rather than into some other form of investment. Furthermore, it tells them, in effect, that all banks should be viewed as equally safe, because whatever risks do exist are borne by the government. This flies in the face of logic. The premium structure, also, is set up so that each bank pays premiums based on the amount of its deposits not based on some measure of the risk of the bank. In effect, this makes sounder banks pay more than they should, while unsound banks pay less than is justified by the market risk inherent in that bank."

"To tell you the truth, even if we have a choice between no reform and Glass-Steagall, I favor no reform. It's just that I can foresee a future scenario that can make deposit insurance a very dangerous concept. For example, suppose, over time, deposit insurance is raised to higher and higher levels and banks are given the right to pay interest on checking accounts again. That would be an outright invitation for speculative and fraudulent banking elements to pay

exorbitant interest rates to attract money into their banks. "

"In the absence of federal insurance, people would recognize that the banks paying the above-market rates can only do so if they are taking higher risks. And, without the insurance, the people would recognize that they would be taking a risk by putting their money into such banks. But with the federal guarantees, people won't have to worry about such things. This could produce a bank run of a totally different (and many times more dangerous) sort than any we have experienced over the last few years. Specifically, money would run from the relatively sound banks and into the unsound ones. Now I hope this never happens but the potential will be there. If you remember nothing else from this conversation, Will, remember this: if ever there comes a time when some banks start to grow at phenomenal rates because they are offering the highest interest rates at no risk to the depositor because of federal deposit guarantees, prepare yourself for the largest financial crisis the world has ever seen. Maybe I'm just getting a little paranoid in my old age. Maybe the President was right the other night just before he reopened the most stable banks when he said 'There is nothing to fear but fear itself.' But in my view the exact opposite is true: there is nothing to fear but the absence of justified fear." Just as Will was about to speak, a voice rang out, "Come in boys, breakfast is ready."

WHEN ALL THE BANKS CLOSED

On February 14, 1933, the Governor of Michigan declared an eight-day banking holiday to help alleviate a run on the Union Guardian Trust of Detroit that was owned by a holding company that included 19 other banks and assorted other financial institutions. From that day through early March, banking holidays were declared in state after state, and yet, to the casual observer nothing unusual was going on. *The New York Times*, for example, kept the news of this brewing disaster off the front pages. On March 2, *The New York Times* reported the overheating catastrophic buildup on page eight under the euphemistically mild heading, "Banks Protected in 5 More States."[1] From this headline, one could have very well concluded that some sort of positive development was underway.

As the bank runs spread throughout the country, banks began to call upon their deposit reserves held in the money-center banks. This, in turn, put extreme liquidity pressures on Chicago and New York. On March 3, Governors Horner of Illinois and Lehman of New York declared banking holidays in their respective states. President Hoover was prepared to call a national banking holiday but it was his last days in the White House and Roosevelt refused to take administrative responsibility until he officially took office. On March 6, Roosevelt took office and immediately took action. He announced that all the banks in the country would be closed. Then the Treasury Secretary classified every bank into one of three categories: 1.) to be reopened as soon as possible; 2.) to be put under government conservatorship; or 3.) to remain closed. About half of the banks were reopened within 10 to 30 days. Ultimately, however, 4,000 of the nation's 13,000 banks never reopened.

The Glass-Steagall Act became law on June 16, 1933. Its primary purpose was to require financial institutions involved in both commercial and investment banking to give up one or the other of these activities. Morgan, Chase National, and National City chose to give up investment banking; Kuhn Loeb and Dillon Reed chose, instead, to forsake commercial banking. Henceforth, these functions were to be strictly separate from each other. Each of the other two features of Glass-Steagall were viewed, at the time, as being of lesser importance. One prohibited the payment of interest on demand deposits; the other formed the Federal Deposit Insurance Corporation to guarantee bank accounts for small depositors.

UP, UP, AND AWAY

In 1969, FDIC coverage was increased to $20,000. Then, in 1974, as an appendage to legislation relating primarily to equal consumer credit rights for women, it was doubled from $20,000 to $40,000. In 1980, ironically as an appendage to broad based deregulation of financial institutions, it was raised, again, to $100,000 per account. Curiously, when the FDIC and FSLIC increased coverage levels, no one challenged or even questioned the wisdom of these moves. Clearly, artificial guarantees are incompatible with the very essence of the investment process---which requires joint consideration of risk and return. When risk considerations are removed from the equation, moral hazard totally perverts the process.

What justified increasing federally guaranteed deposit amounts on five separate occasions, without discussion, fanfare, or dissent? There was no particular public outcry demanding such increases. There had been no loss of confidence in the banking system preceding any of the increases that needed to be countered. There was no stated public policy goal that such increases were intended to help accomplish. In short, there wasn't one apparent justification and yet it was done over and over. One might try to argue that deposit insurance coverage was merely raised so as to keep pace with inflation. However, even that mindless goal would have only justified an increase to about $16,000 by 1980, rather than $100,000.

FDIC guarantees gave banks a promotional tool to coax money into their vaults. In 1984, for example, Citibank sent literature out to its depositors explaining how a family of four could legally insure $1.4 million at Citibank by using a series of individual, joint and trust accounts.[2] Banks prominently displayed their FDIC and FSLIC affiliation in printed advertisements and TV commercials. In connection with the Continental Illinois failure, the insurance concept reached its ultimate illogical stage. In that situation, FDIC publicly announced that even though it was legally required to only guarantee up to $100,000, it would, in Continental's case, guarantee all deposits. This was supposedly done because the risk of allowing a large money-center bank to fail to meet all its obligations is "unthinkable." No one, however, ever bothers to explain why this is the case.

Numerous commentators expressed the belief that Continental's failure would have widespread repercussions on the entire financial system. If Continental failed, these experts supposedly feared that other institutions would potentially follow, in domino-like fashion. George G. Kaufman---among others---explains why such fears were completely unfounded. Estimates at the time were that the loss would have been about 2 to 3 cents on the dollar for the uninsured depositors; later estimates were raised to 4 cents on the dollar. Even at 10 cents on the dollar not one of the 2,000 banks holding balances at Continental would have experienced losses in excess of its capital. Furthermore, only two of those institutions would have lost as much as 50% of their capital from Continental's failure.[3] Kaufman quotes Todd Conover, Controller of the Currency, (1984), Irving Sprague, a director of the FDIC (1986), and William Seidman, Chairman of FDIC (1988). Each of these administrators attempted to justify the "too big to fail" posture, but frankly admitted they did not know what might actually happen if Continental failed.[4] In 1990, Seidman, in an apparent major shift in thinking, suggested in an FNN broadcast that it may well be time for us to abandon the "too big to fail" concept; but in January, 1991, when the Bank of New England failed, Seidman quickly moved to protect all deposits---apparently reverting back to his former position as soon as a tough stand was required.

Until the S&L crisis hit, everyone seemed to be oblivious to the obvious dangers of FDIC deposit protection. Since the S&L crisis, informed opinion on the causes of the crisis generally acknowledges the role federal deposit insurance played in causing it. Most mainstream commentators have concluded that the protective cover of deposit insurance together with deregulation of interest-rate ceilings and the practice of brokered deposits created the conditions that allowed S&L criminals to loot the system of billions of dollars. Truly deregulated markets do not cause substantial amounts of money to "run" from relatively sound banks to speculative, fraudulent ones. In such markets, depositors who chase after supra-normal returns incur the losses, themselves, rather than pass them along to ordinary American taxpayers.

Why didn't many lawmakers call for the abolition of federally insured deposits once the perverse effects of these guarantees became clear? To be fair, a few did raise questions, but they backed away because of the perceived negative political ramifications. The most widely supported proposal merely called for restricting coverage to $100,000 per person rather than $100,000 per account. Unfortunately, the position that coverage should be completely eliminated has no natural constituency. Whenever a privilege is granted, the group that receives it tends to fight to preserve it regardless of how bad the privilege is as a general principle. Some people may fear that abolition would risk a loss of confidence in the banking system. But unless there is an unjustified, massive exodus of capital out of banks and into currency (a highly unlikely scenario), the system as a whole will be unaffected.

The Financial Institutions Reform and Recovery Enforcement Act of 1989 ("FIRREA") begged the issue on federally insured deposits; FIRREA recommended a study rather than a resolution. The study was to consider, among other things, whether premiums for deposit insurance should be based on risk; whether lower limits should be placed on the coverage; whether alternative private sources should be considered; and whether the FDIC should be prohibited from paying more than the legally covered amounts as it did with Continental.

According to Alan Greenspan, "If we were to start from scratch, the board believes it would be difficult to make the case that deposit insurance should be as high as its current $100,000 level." He went on to add, however, that the level of coverage has been "embedded" in the markets and in the financial decisions of households. Therefore, he concluded, any decision to reduce it would need a "substantial" transition period. Greenspan did give the nod to other suggestions such as risk-based premiums and/or coverage limits by person rather than by account.[5] Ultimately, risk-based premiums were put into place in 1993.

Robert Glauber, later an Undersecretary of the Treasury, was one of several authorities working on FIRREA for the administration. He suggested a tax on deposits to pay for the S&L bailout. If someone has to pay, this is certainly more logical than requiring all taxpayers to pay based on the current, obviously arbitrary tax structure. It's not as if our tax structure has somehow worked out the "correct" distribution for the tax burden. To the contrary, our tax system is a patchwork of regulations with no overarching rationale.

Glauber's approach at least makes some attempt to match costs with benefits. Yet, Martin Mayer, in a book replete with examples of various other peoples' illogical, irresponsible, criminal, and morally reprehensible behavior (*The Greatest Ever Bank Robbery*) reserves some of his most vituperative comments to attack Glauber and his proposals. Mayer characterizes Glauber's suggested tax as sheer idiocy, economically and politically.[6] Some mix of higher income taxes, excise taxes and government deficits arbitrarily impacting current and future citizens apparently wouldn't have suffered from the same idiocy according to Mayer.

As early as 1984, the much-maligned Federal Home Loan Bank Board ("FHLBB"), parent of Federal Savings & Loan Insurance Corporation ("FSLIC"), made some interesting suggestions for stopping the process that ultimately led to the organization's demise. Specifically, FHLBB recommended, first, that only $100,000 from any given money broker be insured at any given institution; second, FHLBB wanted to restrain the weaker institutions from obtaining any more than 5% of their total deposits from money brokers. The idea behind these proposals is eminently reasonable. As it turned out, had they been applied, billions of dollars of taxpayer's money would have been saved. Unfortunately, however, the courts overturned the proposal. Merrill Lynch issued its official comment that the FHLBB suggestion was an example of regulators out of control. That same year, the first of a long list of relatively large Texas thrifts failed. It was found that this failed thrift, Empire Savings and Loan of Mesquite, Texas, had received 80% of its deposits from money brokers. Some of these money brokers may not have been as "respectable" as Merrill Lynch, but they did have one thing in common with Merrill: they would send money wherever it earned the highest return regardless of how crooked the S&L bankers were and regardless of what their activities would ultimately do to the country---as long as bank deposits were federally guaranteed.

Large money brokers such as Merrill Lynch also began to make liquid markets in certificates of deposit. This allowed their customers to receive the benefits of higher interest rates without having to tie up the money. When these brokers realized that FSLIC was essentially bankrupt, however, they sought comfort letters from FHLBB assuring that taxpayer funds would bail them out if the issuing banks and the FSLIC both became insolvent. These brokers knew, in other words, that these high-yield investments they offered their clients only made sense for one (non-economic) reason: The U.S. taxpayer would pay principal and interest to them in the likely event of FSLIC insolvency.

By 1986, FSLIC required a taxpayer bailout that had to be voted by Congress. In 1987, it received $10 billion. By 1989, both FSLIC and its parent, FHLBB, had been disbanded. The ultimate taxpayer bailout, was a foregone conclusion---no other solution was seriously considered. After all, why should Merrill Lynch (for example) take losses if ordinary American taxpayers are available to bail them out?

Had the federal deposit insurance provision of Glass-Steagall either not been tampered with or had it been eliminated over time, it would not have, almost by itself, become the prime cause of a major financial catastrophe. Ironically, instead, the other two Glass-Steagall provisions were weakened and eliminated over time.

GLASS-STEAGALL LOSES ITS TEETH

Beginning in the 1970s and picking up momentum in the 1980s, the separation of banking and investment banking began to disappear. Investment bankers slowly began to acquire commercial banking and S&L operations; banks acquired discount brokers, insurance operations, instituted mutual funds and began limited underwriting activities. Through contorted logic, bankers argued that federal deposit insurance together with toughened securities disclosure provision in the Securities and Exchange Act of 1934 made the separation of commercial and investment banking less necessary.

Early on, commercial bankers encroached on investment bankers (and vice versa) through exceptions and loopholes. For example, brokerage houses would acquire banks and sell off the commercial loan portfolio thereby turning them into "non-bank banks." Citibank entered insurance by lobbying the South Dakota legislature to allow S&Ls to enter the insurance business---then it acquired a South Dakota S&L. By 1990, the Fed granted to Morgan the right to underwrite equity securities as long as it was done through a separate subsidiary with separate management and funding. Banker's Trust received similar permission. By 1997, Travelers, a large insurance company had acquired Solomon Smith Barney, a major investment banker and, then, in 1998, merged with Citibank, a major commercial bank, to form Citigroup. In other words, by the time the Gramm-Leach-Bliley Act formally overturned Glass-Steagall in November, 1999, it had already long since died.

The Glass-Steagall provision disallowing interest on demand deposits was also overturned. Brokerage house money market funds in the seventies and early eighties took deposits away from the commercial banks. NOW accounts were introduced in 1978 to help banks compete. In 1979, President Carter proposed legislation that allowed all federally insured institutions to offer interest bearing checking accounts. In the infamous Depository Institutions Deregulation and Monetary Control Act of 1980, interest on checking accounts was officially sanctioned, all interest-rate ceilings were scheduled for phase out over a six-year period, and---almost as an afterthought---federal deposit insurance was raised from $40,000 to $100,000 per account.

Ultimately, FDIC protection, which was initially viewed as a minor element of Glass-Steagall, remained in strengthened form while the two supposedly more important provisions disappeared. The exact opposite result would have served us much better.

"Ashes to ashes, and dust to dust..." the minister's voice droned on. Will stood passively and numbed as his grandfather's casket was slowly lowered into the ground. He thought back on those conversations from his childhood when he and his grandfather would discuss money and banking into the wee hours of the morning. By the time Will had reached his early twenties, his sister, Yolanda, who, for business reasons, now went simply by, 'Y.B.', would join in the conversations. Just one month ago, Grandpa, Y.B. and he had discussed the purchase of the bank that he, his sister, and a group of investors were negotiating to buy.

Even at 93, what Frank Speaker had lost in the sharpness of his analytical skills, he more than made up for in the succinct, philosophical wisdom of his years. His last comments to them, after agreeing that the bank deal made good sense, still rang in Will's ears: "Never, never follow the crowd---and if the crowd grows bigger chasing after easy money--- watch out; they will be endangering your money too."

The First National Bank of Fairfield Texas (FNBFT) was a mid-sized national bank with $50 million in deposits. The bank had relatively conservative management that had not taken full advantage of the growth that had taken place in that area of the country during the early sixties. From 1966-68, it had stable net earnings after taxes in the $1 million range. Will, Y.B. and the investors they represented paid $10 million for it. Will had done quite well as a senior loan officer at a Houston bank where he had started working over 20 years ago. Y.B. had achieved a high degree of success as the only female Sr. Vice President of a major New York money-center bank. Success of that magnitude for women, while not unheard of in 1968, was still relatively rare. Her success was primarily due to her high intelligence and her innate business instincts but was also not hurt by her classic good looks. She was certainly not adverse to capitalizing on her appearance in the predominantly male world in which she was forced to operate.

During the first three years under management and ownership by the Fehrs, FNBFT grew steadily through deposit growth, administrative efficiencies, and a more aggressive investment posture that seemed fully justified to both Will and Y.B. At the time the Fehrs took over, the deposits of the bank were split about 50-50 between time and demand deposits; it held a 20% reserve on demand deposits, had investments in government securities of $15 million and commercial loans of $25 million. By 1971, total assets had grown by 25%; Will and Y.B had emphasized short-term commercial loans at the ex-

pense of government securities and had been able to maintain their 50-50 mix of time and demand deposits even though a trend amongst depositors in the country, in general, toward time deposits was already underway. Will and Y.B. increased after tax profits to $2 million over the three-year period.

By 1973, however, things had taken a turn for the worse; money was flowing out of demand deposits and into the higher cost time deposits; the ravages of inflation had started to take a toll; administrative costs were increasing; and opportunities for profitable commercial investments had declined precipitously. In 1972, they had just managed to do a little better than break-even, and things were not improving in 1973.

Y.B. approached Will with two ideas she had been thinking about to help turn things around. "Will, as you know, my ex-colleagues in New York have recently gotten involved in some pretty profitable lending. Specifically, they have been making loans, as you know, to the lesser-developed countries, particularly in Latin America and some of the Communist bloc countries. Most of these loans have gone to Brazil, Argentina, and Mexico. I've been on the phone recently with New York and have found out that our client, Acme Engines, can be cut in on a massive sale of fighter planes to Argentina. The whole deal is $100 million at 20% for five years and we can get in for a cool mil. Besides, if we go with this, Acme will get a sorely needed contract and will deposit the funds in our bank. As you know, since the end of the Vietnam War Acme has been hurting. The deal seems to make sense all around."

"Well, Y.B., it does sound good---but somewhat risky. We are sitting here with relatively low yielding governments. So even though $1 million to a single borrower is almost in excess of our legal maximum, I think we can probably swing it. Why don't you speak to your people in New York and tell them we'll par-

*ticipate. I'd, personally, rather lend the money do-
mestically to tell you the truth, but if the money boys
are in for 100 we can get in also. What was your
other idea?"*

*"Well, Will, you know Nelson Bunker Quicksilver,
don't you? You may have heard that he and I have
been getting together socially, but that's neither here
nor there. He's actually got some interesting ideas
and has been shopping around for a banker. Basically, as you know, the price of gold was artificially
held at $35 per ounce for almost 40 years. Since
Nixon officially defaulted on the U.S. promise to redeem its dollars for gold in 1971, it has traded up to
$100 per ounce, but even this figure doesn't reflect
the amount of inflation we've had since it was artificially pegged at $35. So here's Nelson's plan. He
wants to sink a mil into 10,000 ounces of gold. He
will put up $200,000 and wants to finance the rest. As
gold goes up, he wants to refinance to 80% of market
value and to buy more gold with the proceeds of the
refinancing. From the figures he showed me, if gold
reaches $200 per ounce by next year, as some experts
predict, we stand to make $300,000 in interest on a
loan secured by a liquid asset and he will make about
$1.5 million on the deal. Furthermore, he'll cut us in
on the equity portion of the deal if we're interested in
the investment for our personal portfolios. If gold
doesn't perform the way we expect, we will be able to
call the loan whenever our investment is in jeopardy.
All in all, it's fast paced action, but I like the deal."*

*"Y.B., as bad as our circumstances have been and
as bullish as I am on gold, I don't think I want a
piece of this one. The problem with liquid markets is
that they are very volatile. So even though we'd have
a callable feature to the loan, an 80% loan to security value strikes me as a little too risky. I recommend
that we pass this one by."*

*Y.B. had to agree that Will's analysis was correct.
After all, they thought of themselves as relatively*

conservative bankers. But she didn't forget, in future years, that as it turned out, they had passed up a good deal.

THE GREAT DEPRESSION'S PERVERSE LEGACY

If we have been saddled with any perverse legacy from the depression, federal deposit insurance is it. FDIC protection grew, continually, through the intervening years; it flourished well beyond its initial modest intent. The S&L fraud should have made it clear that FDIC coverage served the interests of the worst elements of the banking community---the very elements from whom the insurance was supposed to protect us.

Federal deposit protection encourages money to flow into banks rather than into alternative uses. It encourages the riskier, speculative, and fraudulent elements within banking to gather a larger portion of available funds than these institutions would gather in the absence of such coverage. To that extent, therefore, it encourages higher interest rates, greater than prudent risk taking, and fraudulent enterprise. While these adverse effects are quite predictable in theory and quite demonstrable in practice, we have made no progress toward lessening the perverse effects of deposit protection.

Federal deposit protection does, admittedly, protect the depositor from bank failure. For that reason alone, some people will look no further: they will favor it. These people fail to consider that federal guarantees make bank failures more likely by artificially encouraging people to choose the highest interest rates available, which in turn causes bankers to seek riskier, higher-yielding loans and investments. The following exaggeration illustrates the perverse misallocation of funds engendered by deposit guarantees.

Let's assume there are only three banks in the country. The first bank lends to companies involved in legitimate productive enterprise; it can therefore, afford to pay no more than 5% interest on a 1- year CD. The second bank, openly admits that it will use half of the deposits to speculate in the foreign exchange markets using a sophisticated hedging system that has averaged a 30% annual return over the last five years; it can, therefore, afford to pay 10% on its 1-

year CD. The third bank does not reveal what it is doing but it offers 12% on its 1-year CD. With FDIC protection, virtually all of the money will flow into the third bank. In actuality, the bank is merely a front for a gigantic blackjack cheating scam; the deposits are used to bribe pit bosses and blackjack dealers and to bankroll the players. When the scam is uncovered, the bankers go to jail; the insurers make the depositors whole; the money now flows into the bank speculating in foreign exchange; and the country is well on its way down the tubes. In the absence of federally protected deposits, most of the money would have flowed into the legitimate bank; some of the money may have gone into the second bank; virtually none of the money would have gone into the third bank; and, of course, the country would have been much better off even though depositors would have only been receiving 5% on their money rather than 12%.

If the actual situation were only as clear as this hypothetical story, we would be much better off. Virtually everyone would favor---indeed, insist upon--- the abolition of federal deposit insurance.

Chapter VI

Dollars and Sense

"The abandonment of the gold standard made it possible for the welfare statists to use the banking system as a means to an unlimited expansion of credit...In the absence of the gold standard, there is no way to protect savings from confiscation through inflation."

-Alan Greenspan, 1967

Only two things in life are certain: death and taxes. Many people would be tempted to add inflation to that list. Every adult has experienced it first hand and could provide a reasonably appropriate definition. A typical definition is that inflation occurs because prices go up over time; or, inflation occurs because the value of money goes down over time. A better formulation is that inflation occurs when the stock of money grows at a faster rate than the stock of goods. Under this formulation, prices do ultimately go up and the value of money does ultimately go down---but as an effect rather than as a cause. Regardless of the formulation, however, the way this process works in our society is that fractional reserve banks piggyback newly created bank money on top of unredeemable paper money (fiat money) issued by the Federal Reserve.

FIAT IS NOT JUST A SMALL ITALIAN CAR

Three separate and distinct groups oppose the money creation process referred to above. They differ in that they each identify a different element of the process as the root cause of the problem.

Specifically, the point of view that *Special Privilege* has put forth is that fractional reserve banking is the root of the problem and the elimination of it is the solution. This would remove the money creation privilege from banks and give it to no one else. While maintaining this solution as the best solution, *Special Privilege*, nonetheless, sees merit to each of the other two positions. As different as these other two schools are from each other, either is preferable to the current system. One of these groups prefers to have government spend fiat money into existence rather than have private banks lend it into existence at interest. This policy is sometimes referred to as "social credit." This group, in essence, favors transferring the special money-creation privilege from private banks to the government, which theoretically, at least, operates in the public interest, and doesn't charge interest for money that it effortlessly creates. The third group favors commodity money. This group vigorously opposes the very concept of fiat money. To this group, money must be something valuable in itself not something that any privileged entity is allowed to create out of thin air as a liability against itself.

The Foundation for the Advancement of Monetary Education (FAME), a 501(c)3 organization, is among the most stalwart proponents of this third group. Dr. Lawrence Parks, Executive Director of FAME, has spoken and written convincingly that fiat money is dishonest and immoral. Dr. Parks points out that the fiat currency of the United States---the Federal Reserve Note---is not legally a "promissory note" at all. A promissory note requires four key elements: 1.) a maker; 2.) a payee; 3.) an amount; and 4.) a due date. Any instrument that does not contain all four of these elements is not a promissory note. Until 1963, Federal Reserve Notes, at least purported to meet all four criteria (although, it has not actually met all the criteria since 1933, when Roosevelt took us off the gold standard). Until 1963, the words "Will Pay To The Bearer on Demand" appeared directly over the face amount of the note. In 1963, these words were removed. Therefore, there is no longer a payee or a due date and two requirements of a promissory note have been eliminated. Dr. Parks, unswerving in his quest for honesty and morality in our money, suggests that "federal reserve notes" be renamed "federal reserve tokens" to honestly disclose their true essence.[1]

Surprisingly, the currencies of the world have only been totally unconnected to gold since 1971. From 1944 to 1971, the world operated under the Bretton Woods Agreement, hammered out by the leading countries of the world. Participating countries agreed to maintain the value of their currency within a narrow band of fluctuation relative to the dollar, and the dollar was convertible into gold at a fixed rate of $35 per ounce. While this didn't eliminate the opportunity to inflate the currency, it at least required each issuing authority to inflate at approximately the same rates---thereby keeping the inter-currency relationships relatively constant. In 1971, the United States defaulted on its promise to redeem dollars in gold at a fixed rate of $35 per ounce of gold. The currencies were, thereby, cut off from each other.

The world, today, consists of many different fiat currencies issued by different issuing authorities. Their respective values are allowed to vary---and they do. The Japanese Yen and the German Deutsche Mark changed substantially from the end of the Bretton Woods period in 1971 to later in that very same decade. Specifically, the Yen and the DM doubled in value--relative to the dollar--during just a part of the very first decade after the United States reneged on its pledge to honor dollar claims with specified amounts of gold. During that same period, the franc also improved relative to the dollar but not nearly in the same order of magnitude as the Yen and DM. The British pound, meanwhile, actually deteriorated against the dollar during this period. From 1979 to 1999, the Yen and DM continued to improve versus the dollar; the franc and the pound worsened.

The new European currency, the Euro, was instituted in 1999. It fell constantly relative to the dollar over the first two years of its existence. Specifically, during 1999, the value of the Euro fell about 15%; during 2000, it fell an additional 13%. Clearly, fluctuations of this magnitude are conducive to neither global trade nor multi-year planning.

The following (not so) hypothetical case drives home the impact of such intolerable fluctuations---even on a company that has no European operations of its own. U.S. Company A sells substantial amounts of product to U.S. companies B, C, and D. Companies B, C, and D, however, have substantial sales in Europe where they were very competitive in Jan, 1999 with European companies in the same industry. Because of the strengthening dollar against the Euro, Companies B, C, and D can no longer sell at a competitive price in

Europe and, therefore, cut their purchases from Company A substantially. Company A's stock price declines, executive stock options are under water, and Company A executives are, understandably, upset. Unfortunately, Company A was unable to establish an effective business plan because European bankers and central bankers, the Fed, and individual U.S. banks made decisions that company A could neither control nor foretell.

If Company A wants to lessen its exposure to currency fluctuations it can do so by purchasing individually designed derivative products that its banker is all too willing to offer. Currency derivative products are only necessary because the banking systems of the various countries cause their respective currencies to fluctuate in unpredictable patterns. In other words, companies buy expensive derivative products from their bankers because bankers create an environment that makes such protection necessary. This is somewhat akin to the "protection rackets" of the 1920s and 1930s: local shopkeepers bought "protection" from the mafia to assure that their businesses would not be harmed by acts of violence perpetrated by the very mafia from whom they bought the protection.

The banks make a very nice profit from such operations. They design high-priced tailor-made protection for clients, net their own exposure against other tailor-made derivative products they sold to other clients, and "lay off" the net risk in established currency, futures, commodities, and options markets. During much of the 1990s, many of the large money-center banks made much of their profits from currency trading! Their other major line of business was consumer loans at rates often exceeding 20%! To be sure, the picture this paints falls somewhat short of the ideal.

The currencies that we charted, above, are actually among the strongest and most stable. In addition to these relatively "hard" currencies are such soft currencies as Russian rubles, Mexican pesos, Thai bahts and---much to the delight of sun worshipping Americans---Jamaican dollars.

The seven miles of white sandy beach in Negril, Jamaica were largely unencumbered by resort complexes in 1978. A small, diverse, somewhat avante garde set of vacationers would periodically escape the rigors of their fast paced lives back home for the idyllic tranquillity they found here. Y.B. had gone for a walk on the beach several hours ago; Will sat under the protective shade of a palm tree on the beach with Delroy, a Rastafarian whom Will had befriended on an earlier trip. "So Wheel, when ya gunna check out a da money ge-eme, and join I and I in Jamee-i-ca?"

Before Will could answer Delroy, he heard Y.B.'s voice behind them. "Delroy, Will, I'd like you to meet Toby Free. We met down the beach." Will turned to see his sister hand in hand with a handsome, Aryan looking man about 10 years her junior. They had their free hands slung over their shoulders, loosely carrying their bathing suits. They were stark naked.

"Wha' hoppinin', Toby"

"Irie, mun." The nature of their interchange indicated that Delroy and Toby already knew each other. "I've got to run into town on some errands right now," said Toby slipping on his swim trunks, "but, why don't you all swing by my place for dinner around seven? Delroy knows the way. Catch you later."

The road to Toby's was scattered with people standing in the streets in front of their hut-like houses waving to the cars passing by. Neither Will nor Y.B. were quite prepared to see the palatial mansion looming ahead on the high cliffs overlooking the Ocean. "This is Toby's place" said Delroy, punctuating the obvious. A strikingly beautiful, very poised, exotic woman with jet-black hair in her mid twenties greeted them on the lawn and invited them in. It was Maya, Toby's wife. About 20 local Jamaicans, were apparently also there for dinner.

After dinner, Toby invited Y.B. and Will to join him in the library to discuss a mutual interest---the state of U.S and international finance. Toby was born, Ivan Tobifrieski, 35 years ago, in Poland. Abhorring the communist regime there, he had immigrated to the United States at the age of 18. He worked his way *through college and graduate school, worked for some time in international banking, and from 1972-1977 traded foreign exchange and precious metals using a sophisticated, mathematically complex arbitrage system he had developed. By 1977, he had built $500,000 of largely borrowed money into $15 million. He retired, spent some time living with an Incan Indian Shaman, in Peru, and then moved to Jamaica--taking Maya, who had been one of the Shaman's wives, with him.*

"The world's financial structure is clearly in a state of disarray, and I believe it has less to do with OPEC than with a declining morality. When someone can make the kind of money I made ---without producing a thing---something is seriously wrong. And I am sure I don't have to tell you two that the indiscriminately changing patterns of bank money creation and distribution is symptomatic and also causative of this moral decay. From what I can see, it is only the beginning, and I'm glad I have left that all behind. Don't get me wrong though. I am very thankful for my good fortune. I love the power and the control over my life that my money has afforded me. I only hope that I can effectively use that power to increase my ability to achieve what we are all seeking to achieve---whether we know it or not---to connect with everyone and everything, to love and to be loved. And I have found in both Peru and Jamaica, among the people and the spiritual leaders, a greater capacity to achieve that state than I have in the so-called more advanced cultures."

"Toby, I know what you mean about the spirituality here. It is infectious, and that's why Will and I come here several times each year. But, I am too attached to the "good life"--- from an advanced culture's perspective---to want to give that up. I also love being a banker. In addition to the obvious personal gains, we hope we help fuel the creative geniuses and entrepreneurial visionaries that create wealth. If so, we are

also doing our part to advance the general human condition. I must admit, however, that it seems less and less likely as time goes by that this traditional, laudatory view accurately describes the world as it is. And I am moving closer to the view that whatever must be done in order to survive, must be done with the new set of rules that we are forced to deal with."

"Toby, when you speak of indiscriminate lending you hit the nail right on the head," Will interceded. "I have seen it also. Too much money is flowing to gigantic consumers and not enough is flowing to genuine producers. The biggest of these consumers are governments---the U.S. government as well as others. The obvious effect of such lending is inflation---more and more money chasing too few goods. Now I've heard Walter Wriston justify the incredibly large amount of LDC lending on the basis that there is no risk lending to sovereigns. He has obviously been reading different history books than I have. Furthermore, the inflationary pressures this lending creates is a pernicious form of hidden, and unevenly distributed taxation, generally paid by ordinary citizens. We are also, in effect, 'thumbing our noses' at the governments in other countries that we have convinced to hold more dollars than is really needed to finance their international trade. In the absence of America's military protection of the rest of the capitalist world, it seems certain that nations would choose to hold much larger portions of their reserves in yen, marks or even gold. Other key currencies have experienced far less domestic depreciation, and continue to gain in foreign exchange trading relative to the dollar."

"Will and I have tended to differ, lately, on a proper course of action. We have been offered many more opportunities to participate in LDC loans than we've accepted. My feeling is that they are profitable on an accounting basis even if at some future time they will prove to be a colossal mistake. By participating in them, we would increase the book profits of

the bank and, if nothing else, we will be able to sell the bank for more money if we ever want to get out. Will, on the other hand, feels that if we have to distinguish between real profits and accounting profits, something is terribly wrong. He has more faith in what we actually both see as the ultimate reality."

"What is real and what is illusory is sometimes difficult to discern. In the world in which you and Will live maybe the course you want to follow, Y.B., is the real one. I'm sure we all shudder to think that this is so, but it may be. Everything ultimately rests on a perceived reality...we all require an order and permanence on which we can rely. When that order is shifting, we have to be visionary to see how things will ultimately unfold. From 1944 until 1971, a financial order was established that, at the outset, looked like it could last forever. I'm referring, of course, to the Bretton Woods period. In 1971, when Nixon defaulted on the promise to redeem dollars in gold at a fixed rate of $35 per ounce, he shook the very foundation that had allowed the world to function with a fixed, standard, immutable reality. For those 27 years, circumstances and U.S. economic and military power provided an effective world order and stability. The essence of its workability, on paper at least, was that finances were governed by the same fixed, immutable reality that had served for centuries---namely, that money, ultimately, is gold. On one hand, I agree with Keynes that gold is nothing more than a barbarous relic. On the other hand, it has been the one form of money that has kept governments and bankers most in check. It disciplines them and prevents them from abusing their power to control money. Any system that controls natural abuses in the creation and distribution of money can play the same role that gold historically has. My success in trading foreign currencies was primarily based on my recognition that without gold or an adequate replacement, the capitalist countries were entering a

state of flux. I merely capitalized on that very pre-dictable development. But now, I am less concerned with what will establish the new order than I am with the message that the Honorable Robert Nesta Marley is currently giving us from the stereo speakers."

One Love! One Heart! Let's get together and feel all right.
Hear the children cryin' (One Love!);
Hear the children cryin' (One Heart!),
Sayin': give t'anks and praise to the Lord and I will feel all right;
Sayin': let's get together and feel all right.

Let them all pass all their dirty remarks (One Love!);
There is one question I'd really love to ask (One Heart!):
Is there a place for the 'opeless sinner,
Who has hurt all mankind just to save his own be-li-efs?

One Love! What about the one heart? One Heart!
What about - ? Let's get together and feel all right
As it was in the beginning (One Love!);
So shall it be in the end (One Heart!), All right!
Give t'anks and praise to de Lord and I will feel all right;
Let's get together and feel all right.
One more thing!

Let's get togedder to fight this Holy Armagiddyon (One Love!),
So when the Man comes there will be no, no doom (One Song!)
Have pity on those whose chances grows t'inner;
There ain't no hiding place from the Father of Creation.

Sayin': One Love! What about the One Heart? (One Heart!)
What about the - ? Let's get together and feel all right.
I'm pleadin' to mankind! (One Love!);
Oh, Lord! (One Heart) Wo-ooh!

Give thanks and praise to the Lord and I will feel all right;
Let's get together and feel all right.
Give thanks and praise to the Lord and I will feel all right;
Let's get together and feel all right.

Maya, who had entered the room some time earlier, said, "Well that's about the first thing I'm sure I understood since this conversation began. I was fascinated, though, because money is so important. Too bad some people don't have more of it. Toby and I generally invite the people we interact with each day to have dinner with us. Our cooks arrange for fresh food to be sent, everyday, from the restaurants in Montego Bay. And yet, Toby tells me that our total yearly expenditures for all our needs is less than the money we make in a single month without doing a thing. I know it's impossible, but wouldn't it be great if everybody could be as free as we are in this regard."

BRETTON WOODS AND BEYOND

The world order that was established at Bretton Woods, New Hampshire in 1944 reflected the unchallenged U.S. economic and military superiority. The dollar's value was set to make American goods expensive relative to other goods available throughout the world; nonetheless, the U.S. maintained a comfortable trade surplus as other industrialized nations sought to "Americanize." We had to make loans, grants, and investments to provide others with the dollars to buy our goods. Therefore, even though we had a comfortable trade surplus, we had a payments deficit---more dollars went out than came in. By reducing the amount of domestically available money, this dollar outflow helped keep inflation in check. The receivers of these dollars used them to finance trade---not only with us, but with each other. The dollar was, thus, an international medium of exchange as well as a U.S. medium of exchange. This was ostensibly made possible because the U.S. stood ready to redeem dollars with gold (the traditional international currency) at a fixed price of $35 per ounce. But the realities were such that the world needed a new medium of exchange because 3/4 of the world gold supply was in Fort Knox.

Thus the U.S. became the world's banker. It held long-term assets in the form of loans and investments that it financed with short-term liabilities (dollars redeemable on demand in gold). The U.S., therefore, faced the same risk that every bank faces: a bank run. But having $25 billion in gold in 1950, for example, in a world that was eager to get all the dollars it could---not to redeem but to use---the prospects of a run seemed remote. By 1960, the gold supply was down to $20 billion, but still there was no cause for undue alarm. During the sixties, however, the gold supply dwindled further, and our payments deficits and consequent loss of gold did become a cause for concern. As has been the tendency of banks, in general, the U.S. had overextended itself. Clearly, however, any attempt to try to raise the dollar price of gold would have been counter-productive in that it might have caused the dreaded "run on the bank."

Instead of a run, of course, we eroded so that, by 1971, only $11 billion remained of our gold supply, and Nixon defaulted. This means we reneged on our promise to redeem dollars with gold at $35 per ounce. Looked at another way, the "bank" officially failed. Since that time, with the controls removed, the United States has compiled a poor inflation record---far worse, for example, than the records of either of its two primary foes in WWII. One might legitimately wonder why the U.S. dollar has fared as poorly as it has and why it continues to serve as the world's reserve currency under current circumstances. In a world of equals, actually, the dollar would have probably depreciated even more than it did and would have ceased to be the world's reserve currency. However, in a world where the U.S. is responsible for world order, the rest of the world continues to expose itself to the dollar---even as the dollar continues to decline. The reason for this bears repeating: the U.S. has responsibility for the world order by virtue, primarily, of its military might. Since the world is dependent on U.S. military might to keep the world order, it is also dependent on the U.S. dollar.

So even though the U.S. is now the world's largest debtor rather than its largest creditor, no one requires that we impose fiscal discipline to bring our deteriorated condition under control. To the contrary, even though the dollar remains overvalued from a trade perspective, our trading partners are happy that it remains so. For one thing, they hold so many dollar-denominated assets already that devaluation translates into a loss of their wealth. Japan and Europe now hold about 1/3 of the U.S. government's $3.4 trillion of publicly held debt. In addition, they hold vast amounts of dollars. When we defaulted in 1971, the size of the Eurodollar market was only about $100 billion. Now it is measured in the trillions. The overvalued dollar still allows Americans to buy the world's products at relatively attractive prices. A continuing devaluation of the dollar relative to other hard currencies would cost countries like Japan and China dearly in terms of lost markets for their products. The world appears happy to maintain a fictitious reality in order to avoid short-run economic repercussions. Throughout history, natural conservative tendencies lead to the preservation of the existing order long after a new reality is already evident. Generally, the longer new realities are ignored the more severe the ultimate readjustments. Any of a number of "triggers" could quickly cause such a new reality to require a new world order.

For example, what if the Eurodollar market suddenly shrunk precipitously for one reason or another. Reasons could range from a concerted flight to other currencies, on the one hand, to a massive investment of excess Eurodollars in America, on the other hand. As seemingly different as these two cases are, either could drive down the dollar to unhealthy exchange levels and/or create extreme inflationary pressures. These specific scenarios, of course, are only hypothetical examples, not predictions. As long as the United States remains the sole world's superpower and policeman it is unlikely that others would purposely engineer such developments. However, currency markets are highly liquid; liquid markets---by their very nature---are highly susceptible to unforeseen and/or unmanageable crashes and panics.

BANKS GO OFF THE DEEP END

For 70 years now, the U.S. monetary system has failed to maintain a stable dollar. For whatever reason, banks have consistently increased the money supply by lending both to gigantic consumers (U.S. and foreign governments) and to highly leveraged financial wheelers and dealers. During the 1970s, they somehow justified highly inflationary, shortsighted, and irresponsible loans to the

LDCs. These loans became the convenient source of book profits that ultimately turned out to require smoke and mirror accounting to keep afloat. When the money-center banks realized that the LDCs were in imminent danger, they generated still more book "profits" by rescheduling the loans for hefty fees. Reality was thus pushed off into the future. We should demand and expect more from the privileged class that gets to create and distribute money. To the extent that such a privileged class is allowed to exist at all, it should---at the very least---be required to channel the money into productive enterprises. At least when money is distributed to producers, the increased quality and/or quantity of goods ultimately offsets the inflationary impact of the money creation.

In the 1980s, the banks replaced the LDC consumer clients with clients largely engaged in purely financial, highly leveraged transactions. This activity, like the LDC loans, added nothing to the economic wealth of the nation but rather had the effect of redistributing it. Securities speculators, corporate takeover artists, dangerously leveraged buyout specialists and real estate developers were among the new clients. When money is channeled into real estate and financial assets instead of consumption, inflation (as measured by the CPI) abates. Instead, we have inflation in real estate and financial asset prices---but nobody complains when the price of real estate and financial assets go up. Nonetheless, too little money appears to go into the very activities that justify the bank's existence in the first place---*bona fide*, worthwhile commercial loans in support of productive economic activity.

In the 1990s there was an enormous growth in a financial vehicle called a hedge fund. A hedge fund, generally, is like a mutual fund in that the investments of many people are pooled together and managed by a group of investment professionals. Hedge funds, however, are structured, legally, as limited partnerships and that allows them to use a wider range of investment techniques. Typically, a hedge fund will use substantial financial leverage, play both long and short positions, and seek to identify arbitrage opportunities in order to outperform the markets within a tolerable (supposedly reduced) level of risk.

In 1998, when the huge hedge fund, LTCM, got into trouble, many banks were exposed as both counter-parties and direct lenders. LTCM's portfolio was highly leveraged ($4 billion in capital and

$100 billion in debt). This leverage ratio is similar to a money-center bank's leverage ratio. Because LTCM's portfolio was highly hedged as well as highly leveraged, however, it was not nearly as risky as a typical bank's portfolio. On the other hand, it didn't have all of the special privileges of a bank. On October 1, 1998, in describing what he called "a private bailout" of LTCM, Alan Greenspan stated: "quickly unwinding a complicated portfolio ...amounts to conducting a fire sale."[2] He then sanctioned a consortium that put up $3.6 billion to refinance/buyout LTCM. Since no one was suggesting that the predicated fire sale take place, Greenspan's justification appears fabricated. Were LTCM principals the victims of a power play on behalf of the banks or did they willingly participate in the ultimate resolution? More interestingly, why were banks making highly risky counter-party "bets" with a hedge fund? While LTCM held both sides of these huge relatively hedged positions, the banks involved were generally counter-parties on one risky side or the other. Can't they find more meaningful activities to do with their special privilege?

The problem may well be that banks do not have enough appropriate loan candidates. If this is so, they should go out of business. Instead, however, they fleece consumers with exorbitant interest rates, book bets for global gamblers, and rip-off corporate clients with sophisticated derivative products. These derivative products are only necessary because of the instability created through financial manipulation by a cast of financial wheelers and dealers. Throughout most of the 1990s, money-center banks made most of their profits from consumer loans and derivative products. That, in and of itself, should be cause for concern. Had these banks not been free to deny economic reality, they would have been forced to either lend to *bona fide* producers or downsize. Many budding productive enterprises may have been denied the opportunity to grow, prosper, and create jobs because banks misdirected activities into the alluring, quick buck, fast lane. One thing is for sure: continued abuse of special privilege is bound to cause the equivalent of a multi-car pileup sooner or later.

INFLATION AND THE MONEY SUPPLY

The following parable describes a simple concept regarding the relationship between the money supply and inflation. It is predicated on a simple society in which all money is in identical form (paper) and is issued by government. Since this conforms to what many people believe is actually the case (albeit, incorrectly), it should be particularly instructive.

One day, the government decreed that, for every green dollar a person had, two (additional) blue dollars would be issued. Henceforth, in all transactions, two blue dollars would accompany each green dollar. Furthermore, all contracts previously written would be automatically modified to conform to the spirit of the new system. If nothing else were changed, all prices, salaries, rents, etc. now would triple in that two blue dollars must now accompany each green dollar. Next, the government decreed that green dollars were, henceforth, worthless; they were collected and destroyed. Now instead of one green and two blue dollars in each one-dollar transaction in the original system, only the two blue dollars were needed. After a while, since people couldn't get used to blue dollars, the government finally replaced all blue dollars with green ones. At that point, relative to the original system, two new green dollars were needed for each one old green dollar in money transactions.

Of course, this somewhat laborious story could have been shortened if we just hypothesized what would happen if everyone's money supply were instantly doubled. But some people who view dollars as a fixed standard may not have immediately seen the natural consequence: that all prices would double and no one would either be better off or worse off than they were before. This is true, whether you double, halve, or change the money supply by any fixed percent--- as long as it is done equally, across the board. Under such circumstances, inflation wouldn't be a problem with which we would have to deal.

As we have already discussed, increases in the money supply don't even remotely approximate an equal distribution. The end result of uneven distribution is that wealth is redistributed to those who create the money and lend it out at interest, to those who receive it directly upon creation, or to those who receive it relatively early---at the expense of everyone else. The exact distribution reflects the decisions of bankers acting in their own narrow, short-term best interests. When they distribute it to consumers, the CPI goes up; when they distribute it to financial speculators, real estate and financial asset prices go up. Even the money used to acquire real and financial assets, however, represent an ultimate overhanging demand for consumption at some undefined future time. In *The Great Depression of 1990*, Dr. Ravi Batra graphs the relationship between the quantity of money and price level over a period of two centuries. The graphs demonstrate a high correlation. One of the primary reasons why the relationship isn't exact is that some dollars are stored in assets for future consumption rather than consumed immediately.

The process by which banks create and distribute money can and must be stopped, if our society is to endure. If ours is to be a fair, sound, moral, and vibrant society, we must remove control of the money supply from bankers. Unfortunately, to date, bankers have used inventive techniques to thwart the (so far, feeble) attempts to bring the money supply under control. The financial system has proliferated new financial products that obscure the money supply, itself, thereby, making the job of controlling it all that much harder. Alan Greenspan admitted the difficulties of controlling the money supply in Congressional testimony on February 17, 2000. Congressman Ron Paul complained that M-3 had grown over the last few years at far above the targeted growth rates; Greenspan responded that it has become increasingly difficult, in recent years to even define what money, in fact, is. Dr. Paul took this rare opportunity to ask the following pithy question: "So it's hard to manage something you can't define?" Greenspan was apparently taken off guard: rather than provide his normal, seemingly explicit, precisely worded, "Greenspeak" that people spend weeks trying to decipher, he answered directly: "It is not possible to manage something you cannot define."[3] In other words, the country is at the mercy of someone who---from his very own admission---is totally incapable of doing the very job he has been expected to do over the last 13-14 years! The stakes are high, the solutions are tough, but the time to start considering real reform is here. Not to do so soon risks an eventual mammoth collapse of the current world order.

THE SPIRITUAL BASIS FOR A SOLUTION

Y.B. had gone to check on some very disturbing reports they had received on some oil and gas loan participations with a bank in Oklahoma. She was due back on Sunday. Even so, on Saturday, Will felt an incredible need to get away from the relentless pressures that had been building over the last few months. He left word that he would see Y.B. on Wednesday, upon his return from Negril.

He walked down the beach, aimlessly, toward the town, deep in thought. He hardly noticed the ganja selling Jamaicans and the occasional frolicking nude sunbathers along the way. As he was about to turn back, a beautiful exotic woman emerged from the water and approached him.

"Will, long time no see," said Maya as she threw her arms around him and planted a big, warm, friendly kiss on his lips, "How long are you in for?" she asked as she led him, by the hand, to her large beach blanket.

"Just a few days. It's great to see you Maya," he replied as he plopped down on the blanket. An awkward moment passed.

"You look a little troubled, Will. I think, maybe, while your body is here in Negril, your mind is still back in the bank in Texas," Maya said teasingly, but aiming to put Will at ease.

"Well, Maya, Y.B. and I haven't been seeing eye-to-eye lately, and business hasn't really been too great at the bank...and, I guess I feel a little out of place sitting here on the beach with a beautiful nude woman."

"I think I can help you with all of those problems, Will, if you are willing to consider a spiritual point of view," she began, casually handing him suntan lotion and lying back on the blanket. "Your problem can be boiled down to a single word: 'separateness'. On the one hand, for example, you want to touch me now,

but on the other hand, you feel separated from me. Even as I have handed you the suntan lotion, you are confusing yourself by becoming entrapped by artificial boundaries you are erecting for yourself: What can I do? What should I do? What do I want to do? When you answer these questions, harmoniously, not as separate questions, but as one---guided by love--- you will be untroubled, unconfused, and not so isolated."

Maya's words had an almost mystical effect on Will. He began very gently rubbing every part of her body with the lotion. Instead of conflicting feelings of confusion, lust, timidity, and frustration, he experienced a natural, peaceful, harmonious and exhilarating oneness. "The spirituality which is you now, Will, is a microcosm of the spirituality which is you in every facet of your life. You may not see the connection, fully, now, but when you need to, just remember this moment; it will help. You will find, over time, that appropriate responses will become automatic."

"Will, great to see you!" It was Toby approaching from behind them.

"Toby, how the hell are you." Will arose from the blanket, hugged Toby, glowing from ear to ear with a warm broad smile. Afterwards, looking back on this moment, Will always marveled at how his responses in a world of oneness and love differed so completely from what his responses would have been in a similar situation in a world of separation and isolation.

THE GENESIS OF A SOLUTION

The following day, Toby had to drive into Montego Bay for some supplies and he asked Will to join him. "Toby, what do you make of the debt problem of your homeland? The reports are ominous. We have a million dollar participation with money-center banks who are putting pressure on us to reschedule, but my instincts tell me not to. Y.B., on the other hand, says if we don't go along, we can forget future good relations with the New York banks."

"I am pretty removed from these things, Will, but I sense that Poland is just the tip of the iceberg---especially for the U.S. Of the $25 billion Poland owes, most comes from other governments and the European banks---particularly Germany. I imagine that the U.S. banks have no more than $2-3 billion at risk. This is a reasonably large sum, but it is much smaller than your Latin American exposure, for example. I understand from some friends that sometime next year, around August I think, both Mexico and Brazil have big chunks of debt coming due. I would recommend that if others want to reschedule and you don't, they should get someone else to pick up your share."

"I tend to agree. That's what I should do. You know, this whole international debt situation has me scared, Toby. As Margaret Thatcher said last year: "never in the history of human credit has so much been owed." The scariest part is that the process seems to be gaining momentum rather than contracting, and the quality of the loans at double-digit interest rates is weakening rapidly. If just Mexico and Brazil can't meet their obligations, most of the money-center banks would be rendered insolvent. And if they can only meet their debts through rescheduling---with no hope of changing the underlying fundamentals---to my mind, the money-center banks would still be insolvent, they would just be refusing to recognize it."

"You are absolutely correct, Will. Reality doesn't change just because someone refuses to recognize it. Over the last seven years or so, banks have treated money as if it were some trivial commodity to be created and distributed with little regard for consequences. The dollar is a cruel joke on those who have

come to believe in it. In just the last decade alone, it lost more than half of its value. And virtue in the society has been debased right along with it."

"The problem is that with all one hears about the dangers of inflation, nobody cares to do anything positive about it. That is a clear sign of moral decay. The society has forgotten that money and wealth are not synonymous. Creating money does not create wealth; sometimes, in fact, wealth is destroyed in the money creating process. I believe a new world order will be required in the not too distant future. At this point, however, a popular base upon which such a world order could be built is nowhere to be found. It probably won't materialize until things get much worse. There is a natural tendency toward conservatism---to stay with the tried and true, the familiar and the comfortable. Not that I disagree with that. For example, any new economic order, in my opinion, must be firmly entrenched in the doctrine and spirit of the singularly most successful, moral, and rational order mankind has ever devised---capitalism. I left my native country because I believed so strongly in that. But concepts of fairness, oneness and love which are wholly consistent with capitalism must replace the special privilege, conflict, and greed which seems to pervade Western culture today."

"Toby, you would make a great leader and teacher. You have a way of putting things so clearly and have great vision on a wide variety of seemingly different, but really very similar, topics. My whole life has been devoted to banking. I imagine that on the level you look at things, this must seem very mundane. I would like to make a contribution to a new world order by concentrating just on how the banking system can harmoniously fit into that order. Over the years, from my own experiences and from insights passed along to me by my grandfather, I am confident that I can make a contribution in this area. But, like you, I also wonder whether people are ready right now for a

new order. I have put together my thoughts on paper and would like you to take a look at it for me. I would really appreciate any comments you could give me."

"At the heart of my ideas is a system of money and banking that effectively lubricates the process of wealth creation without enabling a privileged class of bankers to create money and distribute it to favored classes of borrowers. It involves a 100% reserve banking system with regard to demand deposits and a matching of maturities on time deposits. There would be minimal interference by the government. It is absolutely necessary, therefore, to eliminate federally protected deposits and to relegate the Federal Reserve System to clearing checks. We can even give them the responsibility of keeping the money supply constant as funds shift between various financial institutions and financial instruments. As long as they don't create and distribute money they can't do too much harm. The resultant system would perform all of the valid functions of banking, yet it would eliminate the aspects which have seemingly brought us to the brink of disaster."

"I can relate to your commitment to reforming an institution which has been in your blood since childhood. I, too, have made a similar pledge to myself, if the circumstances should ever arise. Specifically, if Poland should ever renounce Communism and hold free elections, I will return to my homeland and run for President in the hopes that I can share with my people the power of love. If you'd like to discuss your ideas now, by the way, I'd like to hear them."

Will was very happy to describe his ideas to Toby in more detail. While he had spent time writing up these ideas he hadn't really discussed them with anyone other than Y.B. Her attitude was that the ideas made sense in a fair and ideal world, but since the real world was far from ideal, it was better to go with the flow rather than try to become obsessed with reforms that would never be accepted. Y.B. always felt they should try to take as much personal advantage of the current ground rules, instead of trying to be white knights riding to the rescue of mankind. Will hoped that Toby would be more receptive to his ideas. Strangely, in a way he didn't fully understand, his experience with Maya on the beach gave him a greater belief in his own ideas.

"Several major changes have occurred since my grandfather first made similar recommendations 70 years ago. First, banks and non-bank financial institutions have proliferated new types of accounts which have blurred the distinction between money and short-term, liquid financial investments; second, banks and other financial institutions have engaged in practices that allow them to circumvent control of the money supply; third, commercial banks have made some very troublesome, very questionable, very large loans---to LDCs among others; finally, federally insured deposits have completely perverted the investment process. FDIC protection obviously has to go if we are to make any progress at all."

"Here is how I would deal with these issues in a proposed new order. They would all, admittedly, require substantial changes to current institutions, but they are necessary in order to get control over the money supply---which is of paramount importance. With regard to the proliferation of NOW accounts, 'checkable' money market funds, and such future possibilities (if things continue as they have) as inter-est-bearing checking accounts [1983], and insured money market deposit accounts [1983], etc., I would merely clarify the distinction between money and non-money and would implement rules which would maintain these distinctions. Specifically, any "money" account is not entitled to interest because the owners have not legally released the credits in such accounts and, therefore, potential borrowers may not borrow them. Any account that is not money, by definition, should not be accorded check-writing

144

privileges. Therefore, checking accounts would not earn interest and NOW accounts would cease to exist. Money market funds (which I would allow commercial banks to offer) would not be checkable. The value of such money market funds and money market accounts will depend on the return earned by the fund, and it will be illegal for either the bank or a federal program to guarantee such funds.

Traditional passbook savings accounts legally require 30 days notice on withdrawals. Such 30-day notices should be mandatory. Immediate withdrawals would be allowed but the amount withdrawn would typically be discounted 30 days at the prevailing interest rate and only if the depository institution agrees to make such early payment. The net effect of these changes is that all accounts would have clear and distinct characteristics of being either money or short-term assets---not both. Those that are money (i.e. bona fide checking accounts) would bear no interest and will require 100% reserves in support of that status. I would, however, allow the reserves to be in the form of short-term government obligations (marked to market on a daily basis). Those that are not money will bear interest, but will not be legally redeemable at par and not be allowed to include checking privileges.

As you know, the Fed currently reports several money supply figures: M1, M2, and M3. Under my proposed changes, the M1 items (currency, demand deposits, and traveler's checks) would be money while the M2 and M3 items (primarily, money market funds, savings accounts, and CDs) would not be money. Unfortunately, there are other huge elements in the money supply---by my definition---over which the Fed has no control and, for which, the Fed does not keep records. These items include lines of credit and Eurodollars (the Fed does account for the small portion of Eurodollars that have been temporarily repatriated). My solution to these items may seem even more radical than my insistence on 100% reserve banking, but the solution is absolutely necessary if we are to truly get control over the money supply. Specifically, I would require all extenders of credit lines to maintain 100% reserves on the amount of those credit lines. I would, again, allow these reserves to be held in the form of short-term government securities (marked to market, daily), and kept segregated for these purposes from other investments and activities. These credit lines must be reported in order to count them in the money supply statistics. After all, these credits can be spent as easily as cash, at par. The only difference is that they produce negative balances rather than reductions of positive balances in the owner's account. The same rules would apply to both bank and non-bank issuers.

Eurodollars are potentially the biggest problem of all. Current estimates suggest that the Eurodollar market is approaching $1 trillion. Twenty years from now, by the turn of the century, the figure could easily be four or five times that amount. Yet, we have absolutely no control over these funds that represent as much a potential claim on the goods, services and assets of our economy as any other portion of the money supply. I only see one way to deal with Eurodollars---outlaw them. Specifically, within some time frame, I would require every Eurodollar to come home and be reflected on the books of a domestic bank. Any dollars that are not repatriated within the agreed upon time frame would be repudiated. Let's face it. The only purposes for Eurodollars are: 1.) they allow those distrustful of the U.S. to use our currency while avoiding our control and 2.) they allow domestic banks and others to avoid regulation and control and to achieve secrecy. Neither of these is a legitimate purpose.

Domestic banks should not be allowed to circumvent regulations. Countries that are distrustful of what the U.S. might do to their dollars (e.g., freeze them in the event of an international incident with that country such as we did with Iran in 1979) should keep their reserves in yen, marks, gold, etc. Before moving on to the asset side of bank balance sheets, do you have any questions, Toby?"

"Well, Will, I see the rationale for all your proposals and recommendations and I see the benefits that would spring from them. My only problem is what I alluded to before. Namely, are people really ready for a change of this magnitude? When you tell people that they will not receive interest on NOW accounts and can't write checks on money market accounts, I'm afraid they are not going to see beyond that. They will, in all likelihood, not have the vision to recognize that the proposed system will leave them much better off. Banks that use the Eurodollar markets to dodge monetary control and offshore havens to dodge tax liabilities are going to be protective of these activities regardless of how indefensible they may be. Therefore, you are left with a constituency of enlightened people who regard fairness and soundness of the system more highly than the special privileges that they might greedily and short-sightedly want to maintain. I'm afraid that unless some calamitous collapse of the system makes people realize how fragile it is, you are going to fall far short of a majority in trying to sell your recommended modifications. An intellectually advanced and spiritually receptive society, however, would see the merit in your proposals. So, I would encourage you to speak out. I know you are sometimes reluctant to do so when you anticipate resistance to your ideas. But since you feel strongly on these issues, you should let people know what will happen if your proposals are not accepted. Then, when the inevitable does happen and because you correctly foresaw what would happen, your ideas will be accorded the attention they deserve. I also believe a major crisis will be necessary before the spiritual awakening I seek will come to pass. Tell me, what are

your ideas regarding the asset side of the balance sheet?"

To initiate the modifications I described, each bank will obviously have to convert enough of its assets to cash in order to provide the 100% backing on demand deposits. If banks had quality assets and loans as they should, the conversion process would not be difficult. Under current circumstances, however, the money-center banks, in particular, are holding highly questionable assets. I'm speaking, of course, about LDC loans. If the conversion to 100% reserves insisted (as it, ideally, should) on the best and most liquid assets to be sold to a Currency Commission, many of these banks would be left with garbage. One could argue that they would be getting what they deserve, but in order to get agreement on my plan, I would allow them to sell a portion of their questionable assets to the Currency Commission in meeting their 100% reserve obligation for their demand deposits.

I would also establish rules to prevent rescheduling of bad loans as a way to refuse to recognize bad debts, and I would establish rules that reduce exposure to a single borrower or class of borrowers. These rules would include such things as mandatory write-offs, would require participation by banks not involved in the initial loan before restructuring would be allowed without write-offs or penalties, and would include much more stringent rules regarding the percent of a bank's capital that can be lent to a given company, industry, or country. I would also provide for significant penalties for violations of these rules and for strict regulatory and enforcement mechanisms. That, in a nutshell, is what I would propose. My solution establishes a long-term solution to the root causes of our banking problems. If my ideas gain acceptance, we will have taken a giant step toward a sound, just system whereby everyone would benefit."

"I see the merit in your ideas, Will, but, again without first experiencing devastation, I see little chance for acceptance. The premise you are working on is that a sound, equitable, manageable system is what is needed. I'm afraid that the powers that be want a system that they can exploit to their own advantage. These powers favor a system that appears to be based on ethical principles—not one that actually is. As you've implied, the complexity and diversity of financial instruments is not so much a function of a complex society as it is a reflection of the deviousness of those elements of society that are looking to rip society off and/or circumvent appropriate rules."

"I'm sure you recognize that these people have successfully expended significant energies to convince the vast majority of people to see things as they want them to see things. I don't think you will get too far unless you highlight the moral basis of your approach rather than the logical and financial basis. You must get people to realize that the current structure is a con game in which they---the vast majority---are the suckers.

"You're probably right, Toby. Unfortunately, I tend to explain things in logical, analytical terms rather than in emotionally charged human terms. But, somehow, I think that this trip to Negril may begin to change all that. Both you and Maya have helped me in that regard."

The proposal in the above story is illustrative. Nothing in the story is inconsistent with an appropriate set of reforms, but neither is any particular detail necessary to an ultimate solution either. The first step, as always, is to get all of the issues and concerns on the public agenda---we are nowhere even close to that, yet. Alternative reform proposals may differ from each other in various regards and details, as long as they address, in some meaningful way, the root causes of the problem established throughout *Special Privilege*.

MONEY, DEBT AND INFLATION

Incredible as it is, the important concept of money is among the most misunderstood. A cynical mind might even suspect that those who do understand it have carefully rigged the game against those who don't. Why is it, for example, that the average person accepts the precept of "work hard and save" whereas the wheelers and dealers employ the principle of "work hard and borrow." Under the current system, convincing the majority to "work hard and save" provides the basis for bankers and borrowers to enrich themselves. Even those who are aware that the largest debtors are, paradoxically, the richest and most powerful, seem to accept the view that debt is necessary for the investors of capital to build productive capacity. In this way, so the theory goes, a better life will trickle down to all. Of course, debt, *per se*, is not bad. Sometimes debt lubricates the wealth creation process; more often, however, liberal bank lending enriches and empowers favored borrowers and specially privileged bankers. People's failure to understand money rests on their failure to recognize that in the current system money is debt. Paper money is the debt of the Federal Reserve System and checkbook money is the debt of the banking system. So when the Fed and the banks increase the money supply they are, by definition, increasing the debt supply. To the average person who feels that he has far too little money, the concept of increasing the money supply has some appeal. He hopes that some of it might even trickle down to him. Increasing the debt supply in the hope it is employed productively has far less appeal.

Since 1940 or so, growth in debt has outstripped growth in productivity. The predictable and inevitable result has been continuing inflation. Under inflationary conditions, a strategy of borrow as much as you can and use it to buy existing assets rather than employ it productively, works best if your goal is to enrich yourself. It is, essentially, a self-fulfilling prophecy that feeds upon itself. The Michael Douglas character, Gordon Geckko, in the movie *Wall Street*, says at one point, "I produce nothing. I own things." In so doing, he confirms the obvious strategy that current conditions dictate: borrow and buy.

By far, the single greatest macro-economic condition that has brought the American economy and financial system to the brink of disaster is inflation. Inflating a fiat currency thoroughly perverts the very foundation upon which society is based. It creates turmoil in institutions that operate on the premise of continued stability; it induces perverse behavior in saving, borrowing, and "investment"; and it causes destructive shifts in economic fortune. An example or two of each will help to clarify the devastating effects.

In the 1970s, inflation created such turmoil for the S&Ls that by the early 1980s the entire industry was insolvent based upon any realistic accounting methodology. The S&Ls were so susceptible because they operated on the highly unsound practice of financing long-term assets (mortgages) with short-term liabilities (deposits). Other institutions, however, were also damaged---although not so severely and dramatically. In the absence of inflation, the S&Ls could have rolled along, forever, paying 4% for deposits and lending them out at 7% to home buyers. Admittedly, the ill-advised governmental rescue plan of simultaneously deregulating investment restrictions while increasing federal deposit guarantees worsened the sorry outcome. However, none of this would have even happened had there not been a devastating inflation of our currency throughout the 1970s.

The inflationary 1970s brought about massive shifts of investible funds on every level. Among these were the substantial deposits of oil profits by the oil producers of the Middle East in the money-center banks. These banks were clearly not thrilled with the prospect of lending to General Motors at 10% or 12% under unpredictable inflationary conditions. Instead, they could lend to Brazil, Mexico and Argentina at double that rate (on paper, at least). When the folly of these loans became apparent, loans to the acquisitors of wealth rather than the producers of wealth became convenient. True investment is discouraged by inflation.

Inflation encourages leveraged buyouts and other highly leveraged transactions. Going into debt makes sense when you can pay back in inflated dollars and when the borrowed dollars are used to buy assets that will continue to go up in (nominal) value as long as the process continues. Junk bonds simply could not have become the rage had it not been for the preceding double-digit interest rates brought about by the double-digit inflation. Savers had become accustomed to such large returns---never bothering to question the underlying implications. The most fundamental implication, of course, is that high interest rates breed speculation. More precisely, perhaps, high interest rates are speculation. The extremely high real interest rates of the 80s were indicative of fraud as well as speculation. Paradoxically (or perhaps not so paradoxically), the really big winners in this speculative orgy were not the receivers of the lofty interest rates but the borrowers at these rates.

The destructive shifts in economic fortune are directly traceable to the inflation of the 70s and early 80s and the perverse investment flows which were its necessary consequence. In 1973, the richest 1% of the population owned 26% of the wealth; by the late 80s, the top 1% owned 38% of the wealth. Such rapid shifts of economic fortune have, historically, been associated with economic and financial upheaval or even revolution. The concentrations of wealth, today, have not been seen since the late 1920s.

THE CHALLENGE: A MORAL FINANCIAL SYSTEM

Debasement of the value of money through inflation is only perverse because it differentially affects the various members of a society. If everyone's individual money supply would magically double, all prices and asset values would also double and no wealth effect would occur. The same would be true if everyone's money supply were to be magically halved---all prices and asset values would be halved and no wealth effect would occur. Inflation is perverse solely because increases in the money supply are distributed unevenly and unfairly.

Those who receive newly created money first or early benefit at everyone else's expense. Over the last several decades, the Fed, together with the rest of the banking system, increased the money supply to finance government deficits and to make speculative, nonproductive loans. The government deficits benefited new or existing government employees and those who own or work in the industries in which the government spent its money. Over the last few years, the government has been less of a borrower. The new favored borrowers have included highly leveraged wheelers and dealers (e.g., LTCM) and those seeking to capitalize on the next geographic hot spot (e.g. South east Asia). No matter who they are, favored borrowers benefit at everybody else's expense. Since many of these loans have turned (or will turn) sour, they are only "profitable" on an (unrealistic) accounting basis, not on a real basis. Those bankers who do not participate in "go-go markets" survive without taxpayer bailouts. Those who do participate will probably be rescued. Perhaps some day soon, they will be forced to pay the price.

If meaningful reform is not forthcoming, a financial crisis dwarfing all previous crises is in the cards---we just don't know when. The reforms we need are straightforward and should appeal to virtually everyone. They would establish a basis from which we can prosper by building productive capacity, by gaining control of the money supply, and by eliminating the special privilege that is so pervasive in the system. We can gain control of the money supply simply by eliminating the ability of bankers---aided by an accommodating Fed---to create and distribute money. We must also eliminate or modify existing financial instruments and techniques whereby bankers---aided by accountants, lawyers, and consultants--- circumvent meaningful controls of money. These instruments and techniques exist---according to those who use them---because they are needed to deal with a complex society. This, however, is not true. They exist because clever people seek loopholes and escape hatches from the rules by which the rest of us play.

Chapter VII

Heads I Win, Tails You Lose

"Is there any reason why the American people should be taxed to guarantee the debts of banks, any more than they should be taxed to guarantee the debts of other institutions, including merchants, the industries, and the mills of the country?"

-Senator Carter Glass, 1933

The origin of the banking crisis of the 80s and early 90s is directly traceable to the massive buildup in international debt beginning in the early to mid 70s. Conventional wisdom holds that the 1973 and the 1979 oil shocks touched off the international debt explosion. Undeniably, the oil shocks and debt explosion are linked; but to say that the former caused the latter ignores too many other factors. These include, among other things, the floating exchange rates that were instituted in 1971. Floating exchange rates pervert the very essence of money. After all, money is supposed to be the fixed financial standard of reference by which all else is measured. In this context, the term "floating exchange rate" is counter-intuitive if not contradictory. More completely, however, the monetary system was put at risk by all of the special privileges discussed throughout this book. Special privileges pervert the underlying premise upon which free enterprise is based. This chapter discusses perhaps the single-most perverse of all of the special privileges: heads I win, tails you lose!

THE CAUSE OF THE INTERNATIONAL DEBT CRISIS

In *Paper Money* Adam Smith puts forth, better than most, the conventional point of view. This view is reasonably accurate---as far as it goes. It explains what happened but not why it happened. In a 1983 *Esquire* article ironically entitled, "Unconventional Wisdom: How Our Banks Got in Trouble," Mr. Smith states that "bankers used to be tightfisted, prune faced Scrooges in pinstripe suits who always said 'no'. In recent years, at least at the international level, they have become glad hand Charlies pressing money on anyone who would take it."[1] We now know that the "glad hand Charlie" syndrome was not exclusive to LDC lending. International lending was merely one of the earlier instances of it. In all fairness to Mr. Smith, however, back in the early 1980s, it may have legitimately seemed that LDC lending was an isolated, aberrant case.

OPEC's success in raising the price of oil from $2.50 per barrel to $11.00 per barrel in 1973 and then to $34.00 per barrel in 1979 is an example of one of those rare instances wherein substantial wealth is redistributed from more advanced industrialized countries to a small subset of lesser-developed ones---without bloodshed. What came to be called the "oil tax" produced a $100 billion annual surplus for the OPEC countries, a 2% to 3% reduction in the GDP of developed countries, and even greater reductions in the GDPs of non-oil producing LDCs. Except for a few highly populous OPEC members (Iran, Indonesia, Nigeria) the other beneficiaries of the "oil tax" could not find ways to spend their bounty fast enough. Instead, they deposited the money in banks in New York, London, Paris, Tokyo, Milan, Frankfurt, and Geneva. These large money-center banks then lent the funds to LDCs who paid their "oil tax." The OPEC countries then re-deposit the money in the money-center banks. This merry-go-round came to be called "recycling." Ultimately, worldwide recession created immense hardship on such countries as Poland, Mexico, and Brazil, for example, so that each had to reschedule its loans.

Loan rescheduling, of course, is a euphemism for default. The primary distinction---for the lenders---is that with default, they must acknowledge a loss on their books. With rescheduling, not only do they not book a loss, but they also book "profits" from fees they charge for the rescheduling. Unless money is ultimately paid back, of course, no real profit is ever made. From the borrower's perspective, rescheduling allows it to pay off old debts with new debts and it can maintain its official good standing (for still further future borrowing) in the international financial community. Large borrowers and large lenders, then, are highly dependent on each other to work out "solutions" to debt problems. When the amounts involved are measured in billions of dollars, even non-parties to the transactions are affected by the so-called solutions. *The Economist* put it succinctly, by expanding on the famous Keynes' statement: "When you owe your bank one hundred pounds, you have a problem; when you owe your bank one million pounds, it has a problem"---and *The Economist* added, "When you owe your bank one billion pounds, we all have a problem." Recycling oil money provided the first mechanism whereby a universal multi-billion dollar problem was created by the excesses of money-center banks.

Unfortunately, the so-called solutions to the LDC debt problem were really nothing more than denials of reality. In other words, while default and rescheduling are, ultimately, identical, the short-term effects of the two differ substantially. Human nature often favors short-term palliatives that avoid major changes in the faint hope that the problem will go away. In virtually every instance however the long-term effects of denial are many times worse than the effects of early acceptance of reality.

As far as it goes, recycling does explain how the international debt crisis mushroomed. Other broader based theories view the oil crisis and the international debt crisis as effects--both of which were caused by something closer to the root of the problem. To Davison and Rees-Moog in *Blood in the Streets,* the decline in the supremacy of the United States--particularly, in the military arena--was at the root of both problems. After WWII, for example, massive international credits were created through the Marshall Plan and other loan and aid programs. Yet, no international debt crisis ensued, even though the disparities in economic power were greater in the 1950s than they were in the 1980s. On the other hand, an international debt crisis did ensue in the aftermath of WWI. According to the theory, Great Britain was in a state of decline after WWI, and since Vietnam, the United States has been in a similar state of decline. In the 19th century, when Great Britain was militarily dominant, attempted defaults in Tunisia in 1857 and Egypt in 1879 were handled quite differently. In Tunisia the troops marched in; in Egypt, the country was, in effect, placed into receivership.[2]

It has now become apparent, that international debt is just part of a larger debt problem. Looked at in this still broader perspective, perhaps debt crises can be attributed to the institutional purveyors of that debt--the banks. Why did approximately 50% of all lendable funds of the money-center banks go to the LDCs from the mid 1970s through the early 1980s? Why did 10% of all lendable funds in late 1979 go to finance the Hunt brothers' attempt to corner the silver market? Why did a substantial portion of all lending go to highly leveraged speculators in real estate or corporate takeovers rather than productive alternatives during the 1980s and 1990s? The answer is that all these markets allowed banks to pretend they were profitable and to act as if they were profitable regardless of the underlying reality. The principle which led them down this destructive path was a pernicious variant of the "too big to fail" doctrine most aptly called, "heads I win, tails you lose!"

HEADS I WIN, TAILS YOU LOSE

Loans to the LDCs were clearly overdone and were irresponsibly inflationary. Yet bankers in the early 1980s didn't acknowledge that they had done anything wrong. Their attitude was not that they had over-lent; instead, they were merely caught up in economic circumstances beyond anyone's control or ability to foresee. The perversions that result from banker's natural tendency to concentrate loans in one or two countries (or investment areas) are counter to every concept of risk diversification. It occurs because bankers are primarily pyramiding newly created money on top of other people's money, because accounting rules encourage it, and, most importantly, because they get to play the game of "heads I win, tails you lose." Faced with the prospect of lending, say, $3 billion to Brazil or, instead, $1 million to each of 3,000 of the best opportunities among domestic entrepreneurs, bankers choose to lend to Brazil. If they were lending their own capital, of course, they would likely have decided otherwise. In a world of special privilege and bailouts, however, dangerously concentrating risk is rational strategy. Under the prevailing illogic, the riskier and more exposed the bankers are to huge losses, the better off they are! In the example above, if they follow the diversified approach and 5% of the loans go bad they will lose $150 million. On the other hand, if they put $3 billion into one project and things go well, they keep the profits; if the loan turns sour, special privilege bails them out, and they lose nothing.

A *Wall Street Journal* editorial concluded that banks often made LDC loans "with little or no analysis of whether the credit would create the production necessary to repay it." To bankers' complaints that writing down bad debt would cause them to be less able to pump fresh credit into the financial system, the Journal responded that, "crises are surely not caused by rewriting balance sheets to reflect fact rather than fiction...Capital is to be found in the marketplace, not in bookkeeping entries." In a *New Republic* article entitled, "The Great Bank Bailout," William Quirk reported a study by two MIT professors that estimated losses to the American economy due to the banks having made LDC loans rather than loans to productive domestic enterprises. They estimated that 30 to 50 million jobs or 70% of all jobs were lost during the 1970s.[3]

By August, 1982, overall LDC debt had grown to about $700 billion and U.S. commercial bank exposure was about $135 billion. Over 1/3 of the U.S. commercial bank exposure was concentrated in Mexico, Brazil, and Argentina. The largest 24 banks in the country had made 80% of all the U.S. loans.[4] Had these loans been more evenly spread throughout the system or more evenly spread among the borrowing countries, there may not have been an international debt crisis. Could it really be that the money-center banks were just naive about fundamental concept of loan diversification, or, alternatively, is it possible that they actually had a purpose in doing things as they did? Common sense dictates that they must have understood what they were doing and had their reasons for doing what they did.

If one can accept the notion that these institutions had no moral compunctions against endangering the world's financial system in pursuit of their own narrow, shortsighted self-interest, it becomes clear that they were actually better off doing what they did. Taking financial hostages, like taking political hostages allows small groups to gain leverage over much larger groups. Had they been financially prudent and exposed no more than, say, 10% or 15% of their capital to any single country and, say, no more than 50% of their capital to all such loans, they might have been forced to face the consequences of their losses. By exposing well over 100% of their capital (as virtually every money-center bank did) to Latin America alone, they actually increased their political clout. The same, of course, was true of the borrowers: the more they owed, the more political clout they had.

The $700 billion problem in 1983 had grown to a $1 trillion problem by 1986; and by 1990, it had grown to a $1.3 trillion problem. But a strange thing happened between 1983 and 1990. The money-center banks cleverly used the seven-year grace period to systematically reduce their exposure to LDC debt. Early on, they began to shift a greater portion of the debt to the International Monetary Fund and the World Bank. (Both, of course, are euphemisms for ordinary taxpayers---who are the ultimate financial supporters of these institutions.) Later, Japan agreed to pick up a larger share of the burden (under conditions favorable to them). By 1987, the banks had begun to build up reserves for the potential bad debt. Europeans had done so at the inception of the crisis. Miraculously, by 1990, even default by a major debtor would no longer have necessarily rendered the money-center banks insolvent. Unfortunately, the debtor countries did not fare so well. They still owed more than they could ever expect to pay, but it was now spread out and had been partially provided for. To that extent, the LDCs had lost some of their political clout.

In a fair, equitable, and just society, such things could not have happened. In a system based upon free enterprise, the banks would not have attempted the irresponsible LDC debt expansion in the first place. If some random bank had attempted it, it would have long since failed---and everyone would be the better for it. Instead, in a system of special privilege for a privileged class, U.S. taxpayers rescued the banks from their folly.

THE BIG BANK BAILOUT: PHASE I

From the beginning, "solution to the international debt crisis" was a euphemism for "bailing out the big banks." Had there been an international bankruptcy court in 1982-83, every money-center bank would have been deemed insolvent. However, since everyone accepts the "too big to fail" concept, solutions that render even a single large bank insolvent are rejected out of hand.

The solution to the LDC debt crisis involved clandestine swaps of dollars for pesos between the Fed and the Mexican Treasury; clandestine purchases by the Fed of Brazilian bonds with dollars; an increase in IMF contributions; persuasion and strong arm tactics to get smaller banks to put up new money against their will and against their best interests; and loose regulatory practices that allowed flagrant violations of supposedly prudent regulations. These were the primary steps taken in the 1982-84 period. The purpose and effect of all of these steps was to buy time for the money-center banks to reduce their exposure---at everyone else's expense.

Money-center banks had made relatively long-term loans to foreign governments and had risked a larger portion of their capital; regional banks had made mostly short-term, self-liquidating trade loans and had not risked a large portion of their capital. The regionals, therefore, had a vested interest in taking their lumps, if necessary, from defaulted loans. However, the money-center banks and their agent, the Fed, "persuaded" the regionals to participate in rescheduling. Recalcitrant regionals did spring up on occasion. The President of the Bank of Detroit spoke out publicly: "the role of the Fed and the Comptroller of the Currency is to protect the soundness of U.S. banking. I'm not sure that requires leaning on me to roll over my Mexican exposure and extend my maturities." The Michigan National Bank, which had extended and rolled over debt three times to Pemex (the state controlled Mexican oil company) sued Citibank for renewing loans without its permission. The President of this bank was subsequently required to step down and faced penalties for irregularities on other matters. This may or may not have related to the decision to take on Citibank.

During the first phase of the big bank bailout, irregularities by the regulators were the rule not the exception. Bank supervisors accorded new loans privileged status. Pesos, for example, were used as temporary security for dollar payments and banks were allowed to count the pesos as income. Loans that were in arrears on interest for more than 90 days, were not required to be classified as non-performing. Loans in excess of 15% of capital to a single borrower were not only tolerated but also openly encouraged. Prudent reserving for bad debt---instead of being required---was discouraged. Implied government guarantees were given on new loans despite denials and the lack of documentary support. Of course, governmental guarantees bail out the banks even before they need to be! Volcker publicly admitted that "we are all being induced to close our eyes to loose banking practices."[5] Irregularities, in other words, became the rule not the exception. Apparently, irregularities of "outsiders" are punished; irregularities of "club members" are overlooked; and irregularities of the regulatory body are creative policy initiatives.

THE BIG BANK BAILOUT: PHASE II

Phase II of the bailout (the so-called "Baker Plan") lasted from 1985 through 1989. This "plan" was more of a loose collection of concepts than a coherent plan, and it was regarded as a failure when the Brady Plan replaced it in March, 1989. If the Baker Plan was ever intended to "solve" the international debt crisis, then, indeed, it was a failure. The debtor nations were in worse shape in 1989 than they were in 1985. But the Baker Plan was a bailout plan, and, as such, it did succeed in buying more time for the big banks. From that perspective, it was a success. The guiding principle of the plan encouraged banks to a.) continue to make loans to the LDCs; b.) to neither write-off bad loans nor reserve for them; c.) swap loans for equity; d.) swap loans for bonds; e.) oppose both debt relief and debt forgiveness.

Continued lending was dictated by the reality that without it defaults would render most major banks insolvent. Even with continued lending, more money flowed from debtor to creditor than vice versa. Then, in early 1987, Brazil suspended interest payments. It owed over $100 billion to all creditors---$28 billion to U.S. banks. These loans should have been written off or offset by reserves for bad debt. But since the U.S. banks had only reserved about $20 billion against all foreign debt, normal procedures were ignored. In January 1988, nine months after Brazil suspended interest payments, the Fed specifically cautioned money-center banks not to write down the debt even though the regional banks had already done so. In trying to explain that things weren't as bad as they might seem,

The New York Times went so far as to suggest (seemingly, in all earnest) that if, for example, Manufacturers Hanover were really strapped, it could always raise at least $600 million by selling its Park Avenue Headquarters![6]

In 1985, debt to equity swaps reduced Latin American debt. In this process, prospective equity investors in Latin America bought debt (generally, at a discount), and, redeemed it in local currency (possibly, again, at a discount). The investor would, then, either buy existing assets or build new production facilities. In the latter case, there may have been some merit to the process from the debtor country's perspective. Since the government had to either borrow or print the money needed to redeem the debt, an initial inflationary effect was guaranteed; but if the money was used for productive purposes, the process might ultimately justify the increased money supply. Throughout Phase II of the big bank bailout, only about $20 billion of debt was retired through debt for equity swaps.

Banks also sold debt back to the debtor countries at a discount on a voluntary basis. The banks defended this approach as the free enterprise approach: those who wished to cash in did so; those that wanted to hang on, were allowed to do that as well. The problem with this approach is that none of the money-center banks chose to cash in at a discount even though they were precisely the banks that had the greatest exposure. From their perspective, why should they take less than par when they could, instead, play the more profitable game of "heads I win, tails you lose."

The Baker Plan specifically rejected debt forgiveness as a means for dealing with the crisis. Over $1 trillion in debt would never be repaid, and someone had to take the loss. Most of the plans---stripped to their essence--- "billed" U.S. taxpayers. The debt for equity swaps "billed" citizens of the debtor country. Those responsible for the international debt crisis---the money-center banks---did not shoulder much of the loss at all. The banks were shielded from reality even when nobody was immediately available to pick up the tab. The loss was merely ignored as if it didn't exist. Nevertheless, the money-center banks ultimately began to provide reserves for potential losses. Within a year, Brazil realized it did not achieve any clout from its discontinuance of interest. It agreed, again, to work with its creditors. As it turned out the biggest gainer from this decision was Citibank. In September 1988, Citibank came up with a plan that it proclaimed was "the most extensive and innovative menu of options of any package to date."[7] By March of 1989, the Brazilians had already suspended this agreement---but not before Citibank's rescheduling fee, of course. Jeffrey Sachs (who was dubbed the "Debt Doctor" in a *Time* article for his work on behalf of several Latin American countries) suggested that Citibank was well aware that its "innovative" solution would probably not work. The new financing, however, allowed Citibank and other big banks to "book" record earnings in the fourth quarter of 1988.

THE BIG BANK BAILOUT- PHASE III

In March 1989, the Brady Plan was hailed as a major shift in policy. Six months later, there was still significant confusion about what the plan really entailed. The primary impediment to understanding was fundamental: lack of definition. Much was said about how new and innovative it was, but, upon questioning, little was said about what aspects of the prior policy were being rejected and what new initiatives were being undertaken. Part of the problem was political. James Baker, the prior Secretary of the Treasury, was now Secretary of State. The prior plan could not be rejected as a failure without embarrassing Baker. So, instead, vagueness prevailed. For a period of six years, various prior plans purported to address the international debt crisis. But the real goal of all these plans was to bail out the money-center banks from their incredible self-inflicted wounds. In truth, any plan had to incorporate one or more of a finite set of options:

1. Provide new loans
2. Offer debt relief
3. Offer debt forgiveness
4. Accept payment in equity rather than debt
5. Write off bad debt
6. Obtain international and other support.

The first bailout highlighted 1 and 6; the second highlighted 1 and 4; the third highlighted 4, 5, and 6.

Leading up to the announcement of the Brady Plan, there appeared to be a split between the Treasury and the Fed. The Treasury sought to get the banks to reserve more for the bad debt while the Fed maintained that such action would "pose hazards for the integrity of the banking system."[8] The day after this statement, the Brady Plan was announced acknowledging "realities we cannot deny."[9] Because the Brady Plan urged the banks to reserve more against their bad debts, the banks generally viewed it unfavorably.

Japan had urged something akin to the Brady Plan for years (i.e., debt reduction emphasized over new credits). It agreed to put up $4.5 billion but sought guarantees. After all, their goal was to ease the LDC debt crisis, not bail out overextended U.S. banks. The IMF and the World Bank agreed to put up $25 billion. The big U.S. banks, meanwhile, remained cool toward the Brady Plan. Any plan that paid lip service to facing reality was seen as insensitive to their needs.

In September 1989, however, Morgan Guaranty took steps that did more than all the government programs and policies. In a single move, Morgan increased its reserve for bad debt from about 25% of the total to over 80%. In so doing, it was not only complying with the spirit of the Brady Plan, it was also freeing itself from future government policy. Since its past loans, for all practical purposes had been written off, Morgan could now refuse to participate in any future credits. Morgan's move indirectly put pressure on the other money-center banks to make similar write-offs. Not one of the other money-center banks was in a position to do so, however, without significantly impairing its reported performance. According to a Solomon Brothers chart appearing with the Morgan story, Citibank's loans exceeded its reserves by $6.5 billion; Bank America, by $5.5 billion; Chase, Chemical and Manufacturers, by $3.5 billion; and Banker's Trust, by $2.5 billion.[10] If any of these banks attempted to match the Morgan move, they would, in effect, be admitting they were significantly undercapitalized---even before considering the problems of real estate and other highly leveraged transactions on their books.

Morgan's action, in combination with the new money coming from other sources, tended to move the international debt crisis to the back burner. In 1989, *The New York Times* averaged three major stories per month on the crisis; by 1990, there were only three major stories during the entire year. This does not mean the crisis had disappeared. For example, Mexico announced in late 1989 that it would require $6-7 billion per year in net inflows over the next 6 years just to stay afloat.

The problem was downgraded in the early 1990s because crises measured in mere billions were no longer big news. We now had newer and bigger problems. While we had spent seven years bailing the banks out, they were busy creating still greater problems for themselves and the country. For explanatory purposes, let's call the new problems that were emerging "The Trump Syndrome" and "The Milken Syndrome."

THE TRUMP SYNDROME

By 1990, the combined commercial bank portfolio in commercial real estate loans was over $700 billion. Most of these loans were highly leveraged and were, therefore, highly risky by any prudent standard. From 1980 to 1988, commercial and industrial loans grew by about 50%. Real estate loans grew by 150%--three times as fast. In 1980, $1 of every $4 in loans by commercial banks was classified as a real estate loan; by 1988, more than $1 out of every $3 was so classified. Even these numbers, however, obscure the true degree of exposure because of accounting leeway that allowed banks to reclassify certain real estate loans as commercial loans after development was completed.

Perhaps, real estate loans grew at such a torrid pace, partially because bankers had noticed that real estate values seemed to go in only one direction: up. They, therefore, concluded that any loan secured by real estate can't lose. Furthermore, real estate loans benefited from some rather faulty accounting procedures that allowed them to be treated as profitable on the books even if more sensible accounting indicated otherwise. We will address this aspect of real estate loans in the next chapter. Finally, by concentrating loans in a single area (and real estate was as attractive a candidate as any), the money-center banks got to continue playing " heads I win, tails you lose."

The conclusion that real estate values only go up truly requires a myopic view. One must ignore all history that began before his birth. For example, he must ignore the experiences of the various 19th century panics, the crash of the Florida land boom in the 1920s, the 70 year bear market in England real estate from 1870 to 1940, and so on. Crashes in real estate regularly occur after aggressive expansion of bank credit to finance real estate acquisition and development---the collapse in the late 1980s was just the most recent example. Such occurrences are virtually always punctuated with a universal belief that real estate can only go up. Historical examples demonstrate, however, that even raw land can go down in value. In addition, one has to ignore basic economics not to realize that the values of golf courses, hotels, shopping centers, condos, and office complexes are a function of supply and demand. Most speculative of all are properties whose value depends on people's willingness to seek out the most extravagant of a given genre (e.g., Trump Tower, Taj Mahal, etc.).

Donald Trump is merely one ostentatious example of thousands of smaller developers and wheeler-dealers who were the favored borrowers of the go-go 80s. He is highlighted here because of his high visibility. In 1990, Trump owed approximately $3.3 billion. Against this, he owned assets that very roughly were valued somewhere between $3 billion and $4 billion. The wide range of possible values indicates the folly of making loans secured by such illiquid assets.

Assuming that none of the borrowed money had been siphoned off to numbered Swiss bank accounts and the like, Donald Trump was worth somewhere between minus $300 million and plus $700 million in the early 1990s. In other words, based on net worth, he was either one of the richest or one of the poorest men in the country. The illiquidity of his assets left no way of knowing. At the time, though many people seemed to suggest that he was probably one of the poorest---using reality-based accounting. Since then he is generally recognized to have made a miraculous comeback. One can only wonder how much creative accounting was required to create that fiction. When everyone has a vested interest in it, any fiction can be fashioned into reality.

If some random other person had borrowed $3 billion over the same time period, it's a tossup whether that person would have been richer or poorer than Trump. In either event, however, that person would live a rich lifestyle---even if his net worth were negative. Furthermore, that person would be "propped up" by the banks since they would have a vested interest in creating the perception that everything was all right. Trump's primary skill, therefore, boiled down to this: he was able to convince bankers to make loans to him. What he did with the money is relatively immaterial. Had 3,000 smaller entrepreneurs borrowed $1 million each instead of Trump borrowing $3 billion, our economy would probably have been far better off. If banks lent their own capital, they would have likely taken the diversified approach. Even if they operated as they do but were accountable, they would have diversified. But on a "heads I win, tails you lose" basis, they were virtually guaranteed to look for and find some suitable favored borrower into whose hands they could funnel obscene quantities of money.

Of the $3.3 billion that Trump owed in the early 1990s, $2 billion was in the form of bank loans. Some of those loans were, theoretically well secured by real estate properties. Foreclosure on such ostentatious, one-of-a-kind properties would have been a headache, but based on the prevailing accounting rules, it would have been easy to maintain the fiction that the bank was well protected. Other loans to Trump were not collateralized. In May, 1990, while everyone in the country was learning of Trump's financial problems, he borrowed $35 million on his signature. He certainly could not have borrowed $35 million from a bank that he didn't already owe. Even with other people's deposits, such a loan makes no sense. Banks to which he was already in hock, however, apparently felt it was worthwhile to lend still more money to Trump.

In 1988, Trump sold $1.3 billion in Taj Mahal junk bonds to a public that believed he had the Midas touch. Within three years, these bonds were only worth 30 cents on the dollar. Had junk bonds been sold directly to the public, they would have been worthwhile financial innovations. In theory, they funnel money directly from investors to borrowers. Unfortunately, all too many were pedaled to insurance companies, pension funds, and S&Ls investing other people's money---and each of these types of institutions got into trouble because of them. Even the commercial banks that invested in the senior debt issues associated with the junk financing felt the negative effects.

As late as 1993, the banks were still looking for suitable suckers to dump their losses on. The vehicle was a new junk bond for which Merrill Lynch was the lead underwriter. Could Merrill possibly solicit clients to invest in this issue it was "cooking up" (Forbes' language)?[11] Even institutional investors investing other people's money were unlikely to want this one. $60 million of the financing was in PIK (payment in kind) bonds. This portion offered no cash interest---just more bonds! The proceeds of this portion were to be used to pay off Trump's personal bank debt. Therefore, even if the banks bought the issue, themselves, they could replace $60 million of non-performing debt with $60 million in bonds that "pay" interest. The banks could pretend this worthless paper had value for another 10 years.

Stuart Hoffman, Chief Economist of PNC Financial Corporation said of the financing, "It's like Brazil coming back to the market...from an outsider's point of view, I am always amazed how quickly people forget. But when you're managing other people's money you do that."[12] Even though the *New York Times* reported that Trump had announced that the financing was a "tremendous success," Merrill told callers, weeks later: "I think some may still be available. How much were you thinking of taking down?" Apparently, some of the initial public offering was still available even though The Donald, himself, had announced that the issue was fully subscribed. He had even bragged that it was priced to yield less than 11% interest. Ultimately, further calls to Merrill Lynch revealed that the deal had "fallen through." Merrill directed callers expressing interest to contact the Trump Organization, directly. The mere fact that Merrill Lynch was ever associated with this thinly disguised rescue mission speaks volumes about where we are heading.

THE MILKEN SYNDROME

Junk bonds did not begin with Michael Milken, but he, more than all others combined, formalized this market. Lower quality, higher yield bonds have existed for decades as a relatively small component of total bond financing. The go-go 1980s and a super salesman interested in specializing in this area provided the environment whereby junk financing achieved the status of "market" rather than fringe element of traditional bonds.

In the past, high-yield bonds were traditional bonds that had deteriorated due to financial reversals. The market for such bonds was thin and illiquid because the issuing companies were known to be in trouble. When junk bonds began to be issued, as original issue high-yield instruments, the high yield was a function of the riskiness of the financial structure, itself, rather than any weakness in the underlying economics of the issuing company's operations.

During the 1980s, performance oriented financial institutions were willing to take on additional risks to earn a 5% to 10% higher interest return. This set the stage for an explosive growth in junk bonds from $10 billion in 1980 to over $200 billion at the height of the market in late 1989 and early 1990. Insurance companies, pension funds, and junk bond mutual funds held about 85% of this paper in approximately equal proportions. S&Ls held two-thirds of the remaining 15%, although the Resolution Trust Corporation ultimately held over half of these holdings since most S&Ls dealing in junk bonds became insolvent.

Junk bonds are merely the most visible component of a concept in financing that has developed over the last 20 years or so. Commercial banks refer to them as highly leveraged transactions (HLTs). While such transactions can take a number of forms, a typical one involves a small amount of equity capital, a relatively large amount of junk bonds, and a relatively large amount of senior debt. HLTs are used to finance hostile takeovers, leveraged buy-outs, and capitalization of new companies. While the commercial banks generally hold the senior debt in such transactions, even this portion of the HLT is speculative because of the risky financial structure. When equity capital is replaced by junk bonds, an expectation of dividends is replaced by a legal obligation to pay (relatively high) interest. Therefore, in a non-leveraged company adverse results may lead to dividend cuts without too much fanfare. In an HLT, however, even short-term reversals can cause a legal default. In other words, bankruptcies can result merely because of the riskiness introduced by the leveraged financial structure. HLTs that pay buyout premiums in hostile takeovers or leveraged buyouts are particularly vulnerable to the prospects of bankruptcy.

So what justifies the phenomenal growth in HLTs over the last decade? Who benefits from them? For one thing, buyers get to purchase companies using largely borrowed money thereby gaining substantial financial leverage. If things work out, the buyer makes out far better than with traditional financing; if things don't work out, relatively little equity capital is lost---the brunt of the adverse effects is borne by the junk bond holders.

Investment bankers make out by collecting fees for putting these deals together. Some individual investment bankers, in fact, do even better than their firms do. The firms must maintain the market in the junk bonds they underwrite, and are therefore exposed to portfolio risk. The individuals, however, make huge sums of money. That Michael Milken went to jail for illegal activities tends to obscure this point. Whatever Milken may have made from illegal activities pales in insignificance to his salary and bonus of several hundred million dollars per year. An argument could be made that Milken went to jail and his firm---Drexel, Burnham, Lambert--went bankrupt because they were very powerful, successful outsiders who "stole" billions of dollars of business from the money-center banks and who were not willing to share business with the white shoe investment bankers through syndications. But that's another story.

The insurance companies, pension funds, junk bond mutual funds, and S&Ls presumably bought junk bonds in order to earn a higher return than they otherwise could. In order to do so, they had to take on additional risk. As it turned out, the additional risk was not worth taking. Said less charitably: every game needs a sucker. Institutions playing fast and loose with other people's money were the designated losers in this game.

Most of the money-center banks had exposed over 100% of their capital to these highly leveraged transactions by the late 80s and early 90s. Of course, they earned substantial fees for putting these deals together, and, of course, they knew taxpayers would rescue them if the loans went sour. The fees earned in 1989 from HLTs often represented 1/3 (Banker's Trust, Manufacturers Hanover) to 1/2 (Bank of Boston) of total annual income.

Hostile takeovers and leveraged buyouts add nothing to the wealth or economic well being of the country. They only merely repackage and redistribute what already exists---with substantial rake-offs for the bankers and investment bankers who put the deals together. Perhaps these institutions are unable to find *bona fide* opportunities, or maybe they merely find it more convenient to rip-off the system through creative financing that does nothing for the productive capacity of the society. Either way, for the better part of three decades, commercial bank loans have focused on redistribution of wealth. It is hard to justify giving commercial banks special privileges if their primary activity boils down to lending activity that merely redistributes existing wealth. The special privilege commercial banks enjoy must minimally require them to redirect their efforts back to productive enterprise and away from shuffling paper ownership of existing productive capacity.

Finally, another financing technique that allows banks to make big profits is the standby letter of credit. In these transactions, the banks earn fees ranging from 1/2% to 2% for guaranteeing the bonds of an issuer whose financial rating is below investment grade. Everyone benefits---except the taxpayer, of course. The issuer gets to raise money at lower interest because of the guarantee by a money-center bank; the investor receives the comfort that a money-center bank stands behind the transaction; and the bank, itself, earns easy fees without "expending" reserves. This is all made possible because of the money-center bank's guarantee. The ultimate guarantee actually comes from the government and, therefore, the taxpayer. In the early 90s, Citibank had over $25 billion in SLCs-- more than in HLTs and real estate loans combined! Most of the other money-center banks had upwards of 200% of their capital pledged to these transactions.

A PERVERSE SET OF RULES

LDC lending was, in retrospect, particularly suited to the money-center banks. They could make huge loans at high rates without having to worry about risk. The international political overtones provided a convenient justification for the bailout, when that became necessary. For the most part, however, LDC lending just happened to be the first bank excess that resulted in the introduction of the perverse new rule of "heads I win, tails you lose." Variants of it have been applied with equal fervor to other areas of lending.

The "too big to fail" doctrine is, also, unfounded, unfair and counter to the very essence of capitalism. The manufactured justification has always been that it's in everybody's best interest to save failing large financial institutions. Rarely is the position defended by logic. We are asked to accept it on faith, or as being too obvious to require an explanation. "Heads I win, tails you lose" is even worse than "too big to fail": the latter implies that if unfortunate circumstances should befall a large institution, it should be accorded relief; the former implies that these institutions should conduct normal operations outside the laws of reality. This goes well beyond special treatment in special circumstances. It entails ongoing special status that is inconsistent with democratic societies. It simply should not be tolerated. Nonetheless, it is the way money-center banks operate.

In 1982, our money-center banks were virtually all insolvent, or nearly so, based on anything approximating a reality-based accounting. They had staked more than they had on Mexico, Brazil and Argentina. They didn't seek to insure repayment by employing normal prudence. They were blinded by the high "book" profits they could show from this activity. Such shortsightedness could only have been justified if they believed they would be rescued if things went wrong. We didn't disappoint them. This freed them to move on to other reckless lending on the assumption that they would again be rescued when things went wrong---the guaranteed result of special privilege. Somewhere down the line, the country will be destroyed if we don't act, purposefully, to put an end, once and for all, to this insanity.

Our financial system is on a collision course with reality. We can still choose, however, to reform it before a sudden crash takes us by "surprise." The flaws in the system---some of which can be traced back for centuries--only first reached cataclysmic proportions with the final removal of any last vestige of monetary discipline. The entire world is now on a full-fledged fiat system on top of which bankers create electronic money. In the 1930s massive breakdowns caused all but the strongest to fail. The system was resurrected on the shoulders of the strongest and most powerful elements with relatively little structural change. Today, the strongest and most powerful may, paradoxically, be the weakest. The strength of the institutions at the cornerstone of the system rests entirely on special privileges that allow them to deny---even defy---reality. Any long-term solution requires a major overhaul. We must remove special privileges that allow powerful institutions to pervert the very basis of free enterprise.

Within our society equality of opportunity and the absence of special privilege are widely accepted general principles. Bankers not only have such special privileges, but they have also consistently abused them to gain advantage for themselves and their favored borrowers. In conjunction with "too big to fail," FDIC deposit guarantees, creative accounting, and money-creation privileges, "heads I win, tails you lose" virtually guarantees "tails" will be the ultimate result.

BAILOUTS OF THE 1990s

The LDC crisis of the 70s and 80s required years and years to resolve primarily because bailouts were not yet common occurrences. In fact, the 1980 edition of *The Random House College Dictionary*, defines "bailout" only as "the act of parachuting from an aircraft especially to escape a crash." No reference is made to any financial definition. The 1995 *Webster's II New College Dictionary* defines "bailout" as "a rescue from financial difficulties." In the 1995 dictionary, no definition other than the financial one is given. At the time of the LDC crisis, skeptics may have felt the handling of the crisis boldly defied and ignored reality. Compared to the bailouts of the 1990s, however, it appears we dealt with the LDC problem with relative candor. Maybe those with special privilege are only first realizing, themselves, the degree to which they can defy reality under the current system. Perhaps they always realized, but felt they could keep the rest of us in the dark by pretending that they were struggling to obey the same universal laws the rest of us do. For whatever reason, however, people are desensitized to, and mystified by, one bailout after another.

In the early 1990s we started with the S&L bailout with a price tag somewhere between $150 billion and $1 trillion. When even $1 trillion is socialized, that only amounts to about $4,000 each and when the whole amount is borrowed it only amounts to $200 each, per year---forever. Two hundred dollars is hardly worth breaking a sweat over. When people think to themselves that the S&L bailout cost several hundred billion and yet they didn't even seem to notice the "pinch," that helps them to not even think about it the next time they hear the word "bailout"---particularly, when a mere $20-$50 billion is involved as it was in the Mexican bailout of 1995.

From 1982 to 1990, Mexico maintained its current accounts deficit at under $8 billion annually. Then, in 1991 it approximately doubled to $15 billion and, again, by 1994, it almost doubled again to $28 billion. On December 20, 1994, the peso was officially devalued by 13% (it, then proceeded to dwindle to half its pre-crisis value over the next 75 days). On January 3, 1995, President Clinton announced an $18 billion bailout; by January 12th, the estimate had increased to $40 billion, primarily in U.S. loan guarantees; ultimately the price tag was placed closer to $50 billion. Meanwhile, numerous economist commentators (Milton Friedman, Lawrence Kudlow, and Pat Choate, among others) publicly called attention to the fact that the bailout was actually a bailout of U.S. commercial bankers and Wall Street investment bankers who were over-exposed to short-term Mexican debt. Treasury Secretary, Robert Rubin, formerly of Goldman Sachs, tried to sell the unpopular bailout using familiar scare tactics: we would lose 700,000 jobs that depend on the health of the Mexican economy, and we would open the floodgates to illegal Mexican immigration if we don't proceed with the bailout. Ultimately, the so-called Mexican bailout got done despite its supposed lack of popularity. To not do so, would have been unthinkable, right?

In a *Wall Street Journal* article on October 13, 1998, Milton Friedman wrote: "The Mexican bailout helped fuel the East Asian crisis that erupted two years later. It encouraged individuals and financial institutions to lend to and invest in the East Asian countries, drawn by high domestic interest rates and returns on investment, and reassured about currency risk by the belief that the IMF would bail them out if the unexpected happened and the exchange pegs broke."

Liberal extension of credit fueled fast paced investment in Thailand, Malaysia, the Philippines, and South Korea among other places---and, again, weaknesses in the local currency precipitated the crisis and led to other bailouts---this time with the IMF taking the lead role. These crises spread not only throughout Southeast Asia but also to Russia and Latin America. The IMF, as Milton

Friedman has pointed out, came into being for the single explicit purpose, in 1944, of supervising the fixed exchange rate system. When the U.S. defaulted in 1971, the IMF was an organization in search of a purpose. Its new purpose is, presumably, to assist emerging nations when their economies get over-extended. In actuality, it serves the creditors of the troubled nations by socializing losses. Ordinary citizens of the emerging nations and/or ordinary citizens of the creditors' nations ultimately pick up the tab.

In an article entitled, "Mother of All Stings" in *Truth in Media*, October 21, 1998, Australian writer, Graham Strachan, explained the bailout process quite well using the movie, "The Sting," with Paul Newman and Robert Redford to make his point. Specifically, a successful "sting" requires that the victim not be aware that he has been defrauded. In Strachan's words, the banking "sting" goes like this:

> *"Over a trillion dollars zooms around the world each day in the global markets, buying and selling currencies, corporate shares and government bonds...and derivatives....Some of the money (not much) actually gets to be invested in productive enterprise, but most of it is used by speculators playing a huge global gambling game....*
>
> *The sting is made possible because most of the 'money' the 'players' gamble with doesn't actually exist. It's pretend money, credit money extended to them by various banks, and ultimately the international bankers. The banks are able to do this...invent imaginary money out of thin air and charge interest on it....because of the 'fractional reserve banking system'....*
>
> *....An area is targeted, like Asia. The world media then talk the area up. They run stories about 'Asian Tiger Economies', and how the 'future lies in Asia', fortunes are there for the asking. ...At the same time the local banks in the target country are encouraged to borrow from the international bankers and make reckless loans, hardly bothering to assess the viability of ventures or requiring adequate collateral. The*

myth is promoted that it's almost impossible to fail in the 'emerging economies'.

Then a crisis is precipitated. ...What happens then is a massive flight of capital from the target country. ...What is euphemistically called in banking circles the 'non-performing loan' becomes a local plague....

At this point the debt collector for the international moneylenders, the International Monetary Fund (IMF), is sent in to 'review' the situation, and to recommend a 'bailout package'. The pretext is 'to prop up the country's economy', but what that really means is bail out the country's private banks. And where does the money for the 'bailout' come from? .... In munificent mode [governments] 'pledge' billions of dollars of their taxpayers' hard-earned money....real money, backed up by sweat....to the IMF to bail out the profligate bankers in the target country. Losses by private bankers, who deserve to be driven out of business by the 'free market' they claim to espouse, are made good by hard-working taxpayers in the developed (G-7) countries....

The governments who pledge their taxpayers' money don't actually deliver it in cash. They borrow it from the international bankers at interest, thereby increasing the national debt, ultimately repayable by taxpayers ....It is fraud and slavery on a massive scale, a scale so massive nobody would ever believe it was deliberate.

It began when the value of money was severed from the gold standard by America. This enabled almost unlimited credit 'money' to be created...To make sure the victims don't wake up that they are being defrauded, the sole purpose now of the Western media is to keep the people ignorant, to prevent them from understanding anything of any consequence, to keep them in the dark or distracted with sex, sport, and the private lives of people like Princess Diana. Economics is portrayed as being beyond human comprehen-

sion, even of the best brains in the world. It's 'just happening'. Like the weather.

No it's not. This is fraud on a global scale: the milking of captive taxpayers by scoundrels with the help of paid liars in government and the media....

As Doctor Goebbels said, if you're going to tell a lie, tell a big one, then nobody will believe it's a lie. The same goes for fraud. Do it on a global scale, and who would ever believe it was a sting?[13]

While it is hard to predict exactly where the next crisis will hit, one can be reasonably sure it will occur where liberal extensions of credit taking advantage of "can't miss" opportunities have preceded it. Once the inevitable crash occurs, the specially privileged players of "heads I win, tails you lose" will be made whole. Ordinary taxpaying citizens will be left holding the bag. Unfortunately, it happens every time.

Chapter VIII

Who's Watching the Watchdogs?

"When plunder becomes a way of life for a group of men living together in society, they create for themselves in the course of time a legal system that authorizes it and a moral code that glorifies it."

-Frederick Bastiat, (economist, statesman, author of *The Law*)

Theoretically, the combined efforts of bank regulators, bank examiners, and independent bank auditors should provide some measure of assurance to the general public that the nation's banks operate according to some specified standard of appropriate behavior. Bank regulators do, indeed, establish supposedly appropriate standards; bank examiners do, indeed, periodically evaluate compliance with these standards; and independent CPAs do, indeed, perform annual audits in which they attest that financial statements fairly reflect the financial condition of the institutions. But usually these activities do not prevent---or even warn of---impending insolvencies, abuses, and/or frauds. The trillion-dollar question is "how can this be?" How can several layers of regulators, examiners and auditors be so ineffectual?

In 1983, a blue ribbon panel chaired by then Vice President George Bush, and consisting of such other heavyweights as Donald Regan, Paul Volcker, and Martin Feldstein, concluded that there had to be more co-ordination among the various overlapping regulatory bodies. Interestingly, several prior study groups had observed the same wasteful duplication and made similar recommendations. In 1975, the FINE Committee (Financial Institutions in the National Economy) also studied the situation. Its conclusions were embraced by Senator William Proxmire, then head of the Senate Banking Committee, who proposed that all banking regulation and examination should be performed by a single authority to prevent banks from switching from one to the other every few years as a way of keeping the regulators in the dark. Several other groups--going back to the Hunt Committee in 1941--had made similar recommendations. In other words, over and over throughout a 40-year period, relatively minor, eminently reasonable reform was recommended but never implemented. The Bush study group specifically recommended that FDIC and FSLIC be combined. FIRREA finally took that step in 1989---but only after FSLIC was already insolvent and the S&L disaster had already surfaced. It is discouraging that even such relatively minor non-radical reform is difficult to achieve.

The current regulatory environment is a crazy patchwork quilt. The Fed regulates all member banks; the Office of Comptroller of the Currency regulates all nationally chartered banks; the FDIC regulates all federally insured banks; state banking departments regulate state chartered banks; and, finally, both the Fed and the SEC, regulate bank holding companies. Three separate regulatory authorities have regulatory responsibility for example, over a state chartered, federally insured, Federal Reserve member bank. Regarding examinations, some of the overlap has been eliminated: the OCC examines all national banks; the Fed examines state-chartered member banks; and the FDIC examines federally insured non-member banks.

Since banks can, if they wish, switch back and forth from state to national charters and may join or leave the Federal Reserve System at will, they can easily switch from one examiner to another. Proxmire's proposal in 1975 obviously made some sense. With a single examining authority, banks would not be able to play off one bureaucracy against another. Since none of these bureaucracies want to give up authority, inefficiency persists. The industry, meanwhile, resists effective regulation like the plague. In 1976, for example, Walter Wriston, then CEO of Citibank, stated, "one of the worst things that could happen to the banking industry would be to have a single regulator."[1]

Another troublesome aspect of banking laws and regulation is bank secrecy. A fundamental tenet of our society is that nobody should impede free exchange of information without good reason. Yet, bank secrecy is the rule rather than the exception. Examiners are sworn to secrecy in virtually every aspect of their duties. Although the FDIC rates institutions on the basis of their soundness, these ratings are withheld from the general public. The rationale is to avoid creating an atmosphere wherein confidence in the system is shaken. On the surface, it seems that public ratings would increase confidence in the system by reducing confidence in weak institutions. After all, knowing, for example, the composition of a bank's portfolio is critically important to evaluating its health. Yet, bank secrecy rules permit this information to be withheld from stockholders, depositors, and the general public.

Some special privileges relating to secrecy were built right into the original Federal Reserve Act of 1913. For example, the act provided for a body called the Federal Advisory Council (FAC). Directors of the Boards of the Federal Reserve Banks select the members of FAC. Today, FAC members consist of the top management of banks whose combined assets exceed $1 trillion. These members meet regularly with the Board of Governors, in secret and without oversight, to air their concerns and provide advice. No other regulatory agency meets in secret like this with the entities it regulates.[2]

Other special treatment relating to secrecy was built into subsequent legislation. For example, most federal employees are provided whistleblower protection for revealing criminal or fraudulent activities that they come across in the conduct of their jobs. Bank examiners, however, were specifically denied such protection within the provisions of FIRREA--an act supposedly dedicated to bank reform.

Bank secrecy has also played a role in interfering with the prosecution of criminal cases. For example, even after Jake and Cecil Butcher's banking empire had collapsed because of criminally prosecutable behavior, the FBI had trouble obtaining files from the FDIC. Only after the FBI complained to a Congressional subcommittee about the FDIC's lack of co-operation, did it get some of the documents it needed to prosecute the case. The FDIC's reluctance to co-operate with the Justice Department prompted a *Wall Street Journal* editorial to wonder whether part of the problem was that the documents revealed the FDIC's own ineptitude.[3]

Sometimes, even after lower level bank examiners discover and report abuse or fraud, politicians apply pressure on behalf of the institution. The regulatory bodies are often inclined to protect rather than regulate the banks. Advising bank management is generally preferred to even marginally more severe action---let alone something like criminal referrals.

Bank regulators can attempt to regulate the excesses of banks and bankers only if they are relatively independent of the industry. However, chief regulators are often drawn from the industry and, therefore, tend to see things from a banker's perspective. There is a cozy relationship between the regulators and the regulated. When senior bank regulators spend a good deal of time, for example, attending banking seminars at luxury hotels, there will be a natural tendency to begin seeing things as the industry sees them. Dr. Carol Greenwald, a past Commissioner of Banking in Massachusetts, reports that Comptroller of the Currency, James Smith, in 1975, spent 154 days at banking seminars.[4] That represents approximately 60% of his total work year. Presumably, some of the remaining 40% of his time would have been spent with bank lobbyists elsewhere, as well. Another factor is that bank examiners are not as highly paid as those whom they regulate. Therefore, they are often motivated by a desire to obtain a job in the industry more than anything else. A friendly non-confrontational attitude toward the regulated bank clearly furthers such ambition.

There has also been substantial evidence of political interference by political leaders at the highest levels of government. Jake and Cecil Butcher's operation was like a "chain" of banks in Kentucky and Tennessee. As early as 1976, a local examiner alleged that these banks were involved in a pattern of insider lending, family deals, and loan shuffles. The politically well-connected brothers, however, persuaded "higher ups" to transfer the examiner in question to another district. In 1978, the FDIC supervisors issued cease and desist orders indicating "serious banking abuses and possible criminal misconduct."[5] The Butchers, however, were not apprehended until 1983. As Senator William Proxmire said, in another context, in 1990, political influence pedaling is a real problem:

> *"I recently suggested to a group of Members of Congress that they refuse campaign contributions that come from special interests...These legislators are not crooks...[but] I am also convinced they are sincerely honestly hypnotized by a system of thinly*

concealed bribery that not only buys their attention but frequently buys their vote." [6]

Subtle, or even overt, political interference was a factor in many of the major bank failures throughout the 1980s. In addition to the Butcher case, both the Ohio and Maryland banking crises were tainted by overtones of political interference. In 1989, Jim Wright, Speaker of the House, was forced to resign because he interfered with FHLBB and FSLIC in their regulation and examination of Texas S&Ls. The FSLIC recap bill was not passed in 1985 because politicians in high places went to bat for the S&L industry. As a result, FSLIC was inadequately funded and institutions that should have been closed down were left open.

The most highly publicized case of Congressional interference involved the so-called "Keating 5." Each of the five senators involved (John McCain, John Glenn, Dennis DeConcini, Don Riegle, and Alan Cranston) received political contributions from Keating, Lincoln Savings, and/or Lincoln's parent, the American Continental Corporation. These senators' met with representatives of the national board and members of the San Francisco Home loan bank to elicit special treatment for Lincoln even though they had been informed that criminal referrals were being recommended against the bank's management. Ultimately, only Cranston's case was referred for further congressional investigation. The others received various lesser degrees of rebuke.

In 1985, then private consultant, Alan Greenspan, interceded on Keating's behalf with the San Francisco Home Loan Bank. Others, such as Donald Regan, were reported to be furious with Edwin Grey, Director of FSLIC, for his opposition to brokered deposits and the direct investment rules that significantly expanded S&Ls ability to risk federally insured deposits. In short, high-level political figures were not in short supply when it came to interfering with regulators' efforts to contain a major crisis in the S&L industry.

Unfortunately, banks have almost unlimited leeway to create their own reality. As long as this situation continues, no reform is possible. As Robert Willens, a Shearson banking analyst, put it "bank accounting is so subjective and susceptible to manipulation, that it gets to a point where all the items in the balance sheet and in the financial statements have no meaning at all." In other words, even having a single regulatory authority that fully divulges financial information without political interference is still useless if the information revealed is meaningless.

BANK ACCOUNTING- GENERAL

Financial accounting, in general, is a discipline whose goal is to provide meaningful financial information to stockholders, creditors, potential lenders, potential investors, etc. The discipline suffers because of its orientation toward historical costs. The true health of a company is more dependent on future prospects than on even a perfect accounting of its past performance. Furthermore, during periods of unstable prices (either inflation or deflation) historical costs mix apples and oranges and do not, therefore, reflect historical results accurately. Moreover, accounting techniques designed to deal with these problems merely create further confusion. For example, during a period of inflation, two absolutely identical companies--- one using LIFO (last in, first out) inventory accounting and the other using FIFO (first in, first out) inventory accounting ---would have entirely different balance sheets and income statements while each still uses generally accepted accounting principles.

These general limitations and inaccuracies of financial accounting are minor compared to those of bank accounting, specifically. The primary inaccuracy of bank accounting results from the valuation of investment assets at cost, rather than at market. This, alone, is sufficient to render all reported figures meaningless. In addition, however, various, totally illogical accounting treatments of specific bank accounting areas give banks an almost unlimited latitude to create whatever reported results they wish to report.

Historical costs are used in accounting for industrial enterprises because there is no reasonable alternative and because the distortions do not totally blur the true picture of the company's performance. Even, then, however, the general rule is to use "lower of cost or market." If an industrial company bought land in 1980, built a plant in 1990, and holds inventory produced in 2000, clearly, the 1980, 1990, and 2000 dollars lack comparability. The land and plant, however, are incidental, in a sense, to the business of the company. These assets were not bought for resale nor were they bought to be earning assets, *per se.* Therefore, if the land is underreported in terms of its 2000 value on the balance sheet, it does not materially misrepresent the financial viability of the company. Under inflationary conditions, the balance sheet will merely understate assets in current dollars.

Bank assets, on the other hand, are primarily earning assets-- they are financial assets acquired for the specific purpose of generating a return. It is perfectly reasonable, therefore, to reflect the value of these assets at their current market value rather than at their acquisition cost. A loan to Brazil of $3 billion can be reported on the books at $3 billion whether or not the loan is expected to be repaid. If a loan is never going to be repaid, its true value is zero. If there is a 50% chance of repayment, proper financial accounting should reflect that too. Virtually every independent economist takes this position. Accountants acknowledge the merits of this argument and pay lip service to moving in the direction of market value accounting for banks, but precious little progress has been made.

In November 1987, the Financial Accounting Standards Board ("FASB") attempted to introduce a limited set of market value accounting rules. Specifically, they suggested that market value of investments be disclosed in a footnote to audited financial statements. Predictably, banks strongly protested the idea. Years later, the issue was still being debated and no definitive progress was made regarding a reasonable set of rules. For a time, the accounting profession (half-heartedly) promoted the concept that market values should be reported for assets that would not be held to maturity. How one could determine whether or not a given asset would be held to maturity was left undefined. Bankers objected on the grounds that any such rule would create too much instability in reported earnings. This may be so; it would also inject a degree of truth to reported earnings. Banks also argued that such a rule would discourage investment in the more price sensitive longer-term government debt (the scare tactic argument), and that it would necessitate sophisticated interest rate hedging techniques to the disadvantage of the smaller, less sophisticated institutions (the poor little underdog argument).

In October 1990, under pressure from the SEC to come up with some kind of appropriate market value rules, the AICPA promised to recommend something in time for 1991 year-end financial statements. The pressure from the SEC came only after the AICPA announced in September that they were ready to back away from trying to establish any sort of market value rules. Prior to that time they had solicited reactions to a proposed rule and reportedly received 374 letters---all of which were unfavorable to the rule under consideration.[7] One might legitimately wonder who was solicited for comments. Based on the one-sided reaction, it is probably fair to guess that comments were solicited only from bankers. They have, of course, opposed any form of rules moving in this direction since they were first suggested. While FASB, the AICPA, and the accounting professional, in general, accommodate the bankers, they did come out in January of 1993, with a rule mandating limited footnote disclosure. Will these rules actually be employed in instances where doing so paints a bleak (but accurate) picture of the bank's condition? If history is any guide, the answer, sadly, is "no."

THE CRAZY WORLD OF BANK ACCOUNTING

In 1985, Y.B. Fehr had decided to learn a little more about the tricks one could perform using creative accounting. She had asked Smallville's Financial V.P., Jimmy Booker, to arrange a meeting with the financial services consultant from their outside audit firm, Dewey, Fulem, & Howe. Smallville had recently switched to the Dewey firm based upon their apparent willingness to bend over backwards in accommodating accounting treatments that Smallville wished to use. After they were engaged, Y.B. continually sought assurances that they would be as compliant as they had initially implied.

"Y.B., I'd like you to meet Howie Markham. He's the partner in charge of bank consulting at the Dewey firm. I have already given him a broad overview of our basic goals."

"Hi, Howie. Jimmy tells me that you have done some pretty interesting consulting work for some of

*the other S&Ls in the area that they were very
pleased with. We are interested in any ideas or programs you could recommend to us. Our goal is to examine alternative loan and investment programs that
we can use to optimize our reported results. I want to
be as aggressive as possible in this regard. Can I assume that anything you suggest or agree is appropriate will also be accepted by the audit department of
your firm?"*

*Y.B.'s final question was, of course, the real reason
for the meeting. She was less interested in Howie's
ideas than in his assurances. She wanted to know
whether Howie's involvement in a course of action
would make the auditors more accepting of it.*

*"I can't give you any official confirmation on that,
Y.B. You have to understand that the mission of our
consulting group is to be as helpful as possible to our
clients. The audit department's role requires it to be
questioning and challenging on techniques or procedures that deviate from what they are used to. Having
said that, I can tell you this---none of the recommendations I have ever made to a client has ever been
disallowed by the auditors." Reading between the
lines, this meant that the Dewey firm knew the score
and was more than willing to play ball. Howie's inability to officially confirm this was just part of the
way the game is played.*

*"That's good enough for me, Howie. Let me start
with our real estate portfolio. My first question re-
lates to acquisition, development, and construction
loans, in general. It is my understanding that if we
make, say a $1 million ADC loan and charge up front
fees for initiating the loan there is no problem taking
in those fees as income at the time the loan is made.
Also, I understand that we are allowed to add multi-
year interest charges to the amount of the loan to insure that the loan performs during the development
period. Now let's assume that the project is com-
pleted but the space cannot be leased out by the de-*

veloper and the borrower can't meet the interest payments. What are our options under these conditions?"

"For one thing, if you think the problem is temporary, you can reclassify the loan as a commercial loan and continue making loans on that basis. In this way you will continue to receive interest on the original loans. Alternatively, you can obviously foreclose. In this case, however, you would be replacing an interest bearing $1 million loan with a non-interest bearing asset. Certainly, if the situation can in any way be viewed as a temporary problem, you would want to seriously consider the reclassification option seriously."

"Okay. I see your point. What can we do, however, if the loan runs into trouble before the land is fully developed? If we foreclose, we will obviously have expenses such as taxes, salaries, interest, etc. Can we carry the property, at cost, on the books? Can we increase the original valuation by the expenses we incur to carry the property on our books?"

"Yes. You can document the initial valuation by the acquisition, development and construction (ADC) costs before foreclosure. Also, if this property is held rather than sold and if you put more money into developing or carrying the property, this will increase the property's value and can, therefore, be capitalized in its asset value. The reasonable assumption, here, is that you certainly wouldn't incur such expenses unless you saw economic merit in doing so."

"It's good to hear you say that, Howie, because that's exactly how we feel about it."

"Another question, Howie," Jimmy chimed in. "Several years ago, due to a foreclosure on some beach-front property up along the New Hampshire coast, we came into some property that we have subsequently sold and re-bought on several occasions. This has come about because, after the profitable summer months, the buyers have encountered diffi-

187

culty meeting their payments. Our previous auditors have questioned these transactions in past years, especially last year, even though they did, ultimately, see things our way. Can you comment?"

"Yes. The reason your previous auditor's questioned these transactions is because some banks have entered into sweetheart deals with related buyers for the purpose of siphoning off the profits from these properties during the high rent summer months. As long as the transactions are arms-length deals, without recourse, you don't have anything to worry about. Our auditors sometimes like to question these transactions, too, but we are all well aware that they can arise within the normal conduct of business. My audit partners have, ultimately, always accepted our client's treatment of these transactions. That should, hopefully, give you comfort that we do understand the legitimacy of these transactions."

"Well, Howie, I think we now have a good feel for your attitudes regarding our commercial real estate portfolio. I'd also like to get your ideas on our financial assets, as well as our home mortgage portfolio. We have, perhaps, been much less aggressive in these areas than we should be."

"Okay. Let's start with your home mortgages. Jimmy tells me that Smallville's mortgage portfolio consists of about $30 million. Of this amount, about $10 million is still outstanding from loans made before 1980 at an average interest rate of 7% and an estimated weighted average remaining maturity of about 15 years. It is now possible to sell these mortgages to Freddie Mac or Fannie Mae or through the collateralized mortgage obligations put together by various Wall Street firms for about $7 million. Now here's the good part. The $3 million dollar loss can be immediately taken for tax purposes but the paper you will receive in return can be recorded on your books at $10 million. Even better, the losses can be carried back ten years to offset against those prior

year's tax payments. Since the face value of the new mortgages is only $7 million, the $3 million difference can be written off over the life of the assets for book purposes. Therefore, you will get an immediate tax benefit in exchange for a reduced amount of principal repayment at some indefinite time in the future. Now the IRS is likely to challenge this treatment, but a good portion of the accounting profession and the bank regulators accept it and will combine to challenge any such IRS effort. Most of the S&Ls in the country are currently taking advantage of this benefit."

"Well, this certainly looks like something we should do. I noticed that Jimmy was nodding in agreement and understanding as you spoke, so I'll leave it to the two of you to work out the details for moving forward on this immediately. Tell me more."

"Continuing with a similar principle, assume that there are two banks with identical government bond portfolios and carried on their books at cost. Now, at the end of each year, one bank sells that portion of its portfolio that is selling above its acquisitions cost and buys it back on the first day of the following year. The two banks will continue to have identical operations but will report entirely different annual profits. Depending on your need to reflect profits in any given year, you can determine to what extent you want to engage in such transactions. These effects can also be achieved without going through with the sales and repurchases. For example, by a well-managed control over your portfolio and trading accounts ---the former of which is recorded at cost and the latter of which is booked at market value---you can achieve the same results. As crazy as it seems, in other words, results can differ just on the basis of internal classifications."

"Howie, this sounds like some pretty good stuff. As I understand it, perfectly legal techniques exist whereby we can recognize gains while we defer

losses. That's great. I must say I find you very re-
freshing for an accountant. You guys, are usually
pretty easy to get along with---but only after you have
given us some grief, first," Y.B. said with a smile on
her face.

"Well, as you know, I'm in the consulting depart-
ment, and our outlook is somewhat different than our
auditors. But as you suggest, we all come out in the
same place, ultimately. By the way, everything I've
suggested to you, so far, has been with regard to your
existing portfolio. One of my favorite ideas -- if you
want to be proactive --- involves some pretty interest-
ing trading concepts with call options on T-Bond fu-
tures.

Specifically, suppose you buy deep in the money
calls on T-Bond futures. Deep in the money calls can
be purchased for very little time premiums. If, now,
interest rates go down, the T-Bond futures will go up
and you will have a gain on your calls and can sell
them at a profit. If, on the other hand, interest rates
go up, the futures will go down and you will have a
loss in the calls. But since these calls still have intrin-
sic value, they can be exercised at expiration. Even
though these instruments are settled in cash, if the
equivalent securities are now bought with the pro-
ceeds, a case can be made that the securities were
acquired at a cost that includes the cash purchase
price plus the cost of the calls as well as any transac-
tion costs. In other words, you bury the losses in your
balance sheet, at cost. They do not have to be recog-
nized, therefore, until you ultimately dispose of them;
profits, on the other hand, are taken through the sale
of the calls. There will, of course, be a growing dif-
ference between your balance sheet at cost versus
what it would have been if it were reported on a mar-
ket value basis, but your profit and loss statement
will always look good."

"Well, that sounds good, Howie, but I must ask
you, again, if your Audit Department has audited any

such programs and, if so, what has been its attitude toward them?"

"This is a new program I am recommending. Several other clients are taking advantage of it for the first time this year. Informally, however, I have discussed it with some auditors who answered, in typical cautious fashion, that they would have to evaluate the specific circumstances and the rationale behind the program. In the past, I have always taken anything other than an outright 'no' to mean that a concept was acceptable, and I have no reason to believe this program will be any different."

"In that case, meet with Jimmy to discuss the details. If there is nothing else that needs my attention, I should get going. I'm late for another meeting. It was a real pleasure meeting you, Howie."

CRAZY ACCOUNTING--CONCEPTUAL SUMMARY

Although accounting gimmicks come in a variety of forms, there are three main categories: legislative and regulatory initiatives, accounting initiatives, and sham transactions. Congress or the government regulators create the first of these. However ludicrous these gimmicks may be, accountants cannot be faulted for taking advantage of them on behalf of their clients; the second category involves accountants working with their clients to reflect certain transactions in a manner which benefits the client but misrepresents the true financial condition of the institution; the third category involves outright fraudulent transactions with thinly veiled (or non-existent) justifications. All three categories have the effect of presenting a picture of financial health when, in fact, no such health exists. Independent accountants often accept items in each of these three categories.

The treatment of the sale of mortgage portfolios that allowed S&Ls to obtain tax write offs (by merely swapping their existing mortgage portfolios for an identical portfolio obtained in the secondary market) resulted from a law passed by Congress in September

1981. It is difficult to justify this act of Congress as anything more than an outright gift from ordinary citizens and taxpayers to the S&Ls. Although the IRS subsequently challenged it, the courts ruled against the Service and in favor of the S&L industry. In addition to being a boon to the industry, it was also a major plum for Wall Street. The investment bankers provided the relatively mundane service that enabled an S&L to swap paper with other S&Ls in order to generate tax gifts. Of course, Wall Street was not adverse to earning several hundred million dollars per year in fees and other transaction costs in the process.[8]

Another regulatory gem allowed two insolvent institutions to merge in a manner that produces a "viable" joint entity solely because of accounting gimmicks in the form of goodwill accounting. Under these rules, the difference between the market value of an institution's portfolio and the value at which it was carried on the books can be written off over a 40-year period. In the meantime, the capital of the bank is overstated by the amount of the un-amortized goodwill, providing a capital base from which to grow. In effect, the more overstated an institution's books are, the more attractive it is as a merger candidate! The rules are so insane that it led *Fortune* magazine to propose the following (tongue in cheek) solution to the international debt crisis: create one monster institution that acquires all the banks with LDC exposure. The goodwill rules would then allow the newly created superbank to write off the bad debt (which was already a reality) over a 40-year period.

The second category of accounting gimmicks includes those gimmicks that are created by accountants and their clients. These generally fall into one of three areas: capitalizing expenses as assets on the balance sheet; allowing the selective recording of profits and losses on the P&L statement; and, permitting the valuation of assets at cost rather than current market. The former essentially allows a bank to never recognize a loss on overvalued real estate in its inventory. The bank increases the book value of the property to reflect carrying costs. The resulting distortions can best be clarified by a familiar example. Assume that you buy a house for $200,000 with a $75,000 down payment and $125,000 mortgage; assume, further, that the market value of the house falls to $150,000. Your real equity in the house is 25,000 ($150,000 market less the $125,000 mortgage). If, however, you could use bank accounting and you spent $50,000 on the upkeep of the house over the three-year period, you would be allowed to carry the house at a value of $250,000 (cost plus additional expenses). Your equity in the house, therefore, would be recorded as $125,000 ($250,000-$125,000) rather than the actual equity of $25,000 ($150,000-$125,000). Your real equity would be overstated by a factor of five. This seems ludicrous for a very good reason: it is! Nonetheless, that is roughly the way a bank is allowed to, and often does, account for foreclosed property---with the full acquiescence of the auditors.

Selectively taking profits and losses distorts results. For example, assume you bought $100,000 of each of two stocks. One goes up by $25,000; the other goes down by $50,000. You, therefore, have a real net loss of $25,000. If you were a bank, however, standard techniques of accounting would allow you to report the $25,000 profit while carrying the security in which you have a loss at your original cost rather than at market value. In other words, you can report a gain of $25,000 rather than a loss of $25,000.

Finally, there are the outright sham transactions similar to the New Hampshire beachfront property transactions in our fictionalized account. If you can find an accountant to go along with it---and you can rest assured that you can---you can basically create artificial profits out of thin air. For example, you own a property on your books for $1 million. You, then, lend someone $2 million to buy the property from you for that amount in December of 2000 (agreeing to buy it back at the same or higher price in January). You made a $1 million profit in 2000 and you now have a $2 million property on your books in 2001. A similar deal at the end of 2001 with still larger amounts will allow you to make another "profit." Simply amazing.

Why do accounting firms regularly attest to the books of banking institutions that are on the brink of insolvency? Three possible reasons come to mind. First, accounting deficiencies thwart accurate assessments. Second, accountants are inclined to maintain confidence in the system. Third, accountants have a vested interest in not seeing their client base become extinct. All three of these factors probably play some role. Deficiencies of accounting do indeed make it difficult, for example, to determine the credit-worthiness of a borrower. Since this issue is of crucial importance, however, even imperfect rules are useful. For example, if borrowers can only pay interest by taking new loans or rescheduling their debt, the credit-worthiness of these borrowers is obviously suspect. Without rules that require write-offs under such circumstances, accountants are essentially allowed to attest to books carrying bad loans that would be obviously suspect even to lay persons.

Accountants, as well as others, will generally justify suspicious accounting if it helps to maintain confidence. Even government regulators look the other way in pursuit of the mindless goal of maintaining confidence in the system. Ironically, justifying treatment favorable to the bank's best interests ultimately produces the opposite effect. The evidence suggests that the third potential motive---the self interest of the accountants---is most responsible for the failure of these firms to call attention to trouble spots before they culminate in unrecoverable insolvency.

FIGURES DON'T LIE, BUT LIARS FIGURE

One might wonder whether there are, perhaps, a few bad apples in the accounting profession ruining it all for the vast majority of honest accountants. Unfortunately, each of the "Big Five" accounting firms (as well as virtually every smaller firm) indulges in questionable accounting gimmicks. Ultimately, as it becomes widely known that accounting firms operate along these lines, the reputation that they have painstakingly developed over many years will be besmirched beyond repair. Several of them have settled multi-million dollar lawsuits relating to their participation in the S&L fiasco. A short list of sample transgressions follows (alphabetically) to show how widespread these indiscretions within the profession are.

Arthur Anderson--- AA audited two of the largest failed S&Ls: FCA and Lincoln Savings & Loan. FCA grew from under $2 billion in 1980 to over $30 billion, 4 years later. In so doing, the bank took advantage of a range of questionable techniques such as selling winners and carrying losers at cost on its books; making loans to people who bought FCA properties at inflated prices with the loan proceeds; failing to document transactions properly; and generally keeping sloppy records. In 1981 and 1982, the SEC forced FCA to reverse fictitious profits from sham transactions.[9] AA, however, gave FCA clean statements throughout this period. Lincoln S&L capitalized costs, made liberal use of goodwill accounting, engaged in sham transactions, and stuffed files with loan justifications after the fact in situations where improprieties were apparent. AA gave clean statements through 1984.

Deloitte-Touche---This firm was formed in the late 1980s in a merger of Deloitte, Haskins, and Sells with Touche, Ross. The predecessor firms are referred to here as Deloitte or Touche. Deloitte was the auditor for Centrust until 1989. It allowed a substantial junk bond portfolio to be valued on the books at cost; it allowed a valuable art collection and other assets that enriched the lifestyle of Centrust's President David Paul to be carried on the books of the institution. Touche audited the Beverly Hills S&L, which was revealed in Congressional hearings as an overtly criminal enterprise.[10] After both AA and AY resigned the Lincoln account, Touche audited Lincoln and approved fraudulent transactions.

Ernst & Young---This firm was formed in the late 1980s by the merger of Ernst & Whinney (E&W) and Arthur Young (AY). Ernst & Ernst, E&W's predecessor, was the accountants for the Franklin National Bank which was the largest ever commercial bank failure at the time it occurred in 1974. The bank was headed by Michele Sindona--described by R.T. Naylor as a mafia financier and master of flight capital transactions. Sindona systematically looted Franklin through highly questionable foreign exchange shenanigans.[11] E&E, and later E&W, gave clean opinions on the Butcher banks long after the FDIC had called attention to loan shuffles and insider dealings for which Jake Butcher ultimately went to jail. The FDIC suit with respect to the Butcher banks alleges that E&W "departed markedly from professional standards."

AY was, along with C&L, the premier S&L auditor in the Texas market. Ed Grey started proceedings to prevent AY from further audits in Texas S&Ls after it was discovered that 96% of the loans of its client, Vernon S&L, were bad. The institution was declared insolvent five days after it had received a clean statement from AY.[12] AY also took over the audit of American Diversified from Touche. American Diversified had created fake profits through its dealings in financial futures, options, tax shelters and over-valued property.

KPMG Peat Marwick---Peat Marwick was relatively clean with respect to the S&L scandal--primarily because it did not have a large practice in the industry. On the other hand, along with Price Water-house, Peat is the major auditor of commercial banks. Under current conditions, Citigroup would not be allowed to fail no matter what it did for no better reason than that it is too big to fail. Another Peat commercial bank client, Penn Square, however, was involved in speculative and overtly fraudulent oil and gas participations whose failure caused tremors throughout the banking system: Chase lost over $200 million, Continental Illinois never recovered from its $1 billion loss, and Seattle National also failed as a direct result of its Penn Square losses. Peat gave Penn Square clean statements right up to the end.

PricewaterhouseCoopers--- This firm merged Price Waterhouse (PW) with Coopers and Lybrand (C&L). C&L, along with Arthur Young, was the premier firm operating in the Texas S&L market. C&L audited Empire Savings & Loan of Mesquite Texas---the first of the large Texas S&Ls to fail. Empire primarily used land flips and other phony real estate transactions to create book profits that didn't exist in the real world but were perfectly acceptable to its auditors. C&L was one of several of the big firms to be sued by the FDIC for irregularities in its audit activities.

Like Peat, PW remained relatively clean in the S&L debacle principally because it did not have a large S&L practice. It made the mistake, however, of trying to get a foothold at exactly the wrong time. In 1990, PW replaced Deloitte as the auditors for Centrust and gave it an unqualified opinion shortly before its collapse. PwC audits more money-center bank clients than any other firm. Its clients have included Continental Illinois, Chase Manhattan, Morgan Guaranty, and Chemical Bank. The accounting treatment accorded international debt alone is indicative of the lack of reality-based accounting in these banks. PwC also gained notoriety as auditor for Bank of Credit and Commerce International (BCCI). BCCI principals were engaged in criminal (albeit profitable) activities and still managed to loot the bank to the point of insolvency. PW was there all the way.

The findings of accounting firms appear to directly relate to who's paying the bills. Never does one see a major paying client publicly embarrassed by a qualified opinion. At worst, the auditors will merely resign the account. There will generally be another Big Five firm hungry enough to pick up where the previous firm left off. Even overt criminal or fraudulent behavior will not be revealed. The auditors maintain that their function does not extend to looking for, or even calling attention to, fraud. In an in-depth GAO study of eleven failed S&Ls, six were found to be so negligent that formal action was indicated. [13]

On the other hand, when accountants are offered money to find fraud they seem to have no problem finding it. A perfect example is the Lincoln S&L case. AA, AY, and Touche each audited Lincoln and were able to provide clean statements. When Kenneth Levanthal, an auditing firm specializing in real estate that is now part of Ernst&Young, was hired by the San Francisco Home Loan Bank to audit Lincoln, it had this to report:

> *Seldom in our experience...have we encountered a more egregious example of the misapplication of generally accepted accounting principles. This association was made to function as an engine designed to funnel federally insured deposits to its parent [ACC] in tax allocation payments and dividends. To do this, it had to generate reported earnings by making loans or other transfers of cash or property to facilitate sham sales of land. It created profits by making loans. Many of the loans were bad. Lincoln was manufacturing profits by giving its money away.*

This is truly amazing. When independent auditors are hired to find fraud, they seem to have very little difficulty finding it. However, when they have a client covering up the fraud, they appear to be totally blind to it. Figures don't lie, but liars figure.

When Senator DeConcini tried to play dumb to this apparent characteristic of accounting firms during the infamous five senator meeting with the San Francisco Home Loan Bank regarding Lincoln, he was immediately set straight by one of the Home Loan Board examiners.

DeConcini: Why would Arthur Young say these things...

Patriarca: They have a client...

DeConcini: You believe that they would prostitute themselves for a client?

Patriarca: Absolutely. It happens all the time.[14]

Under current procedures, there can be little doubt that bank regulation, examination, and accounting is virtually meaningless. Institutions that are, in reality, insolvent deny reality for years with the help of those who are presumably there to assure us that such developments do not occur. The longer this situation continues, the more ordinary taxpayers will pay when the bubble finally bursts. A society that tolerates this general lack of responsibility is doomed to pay the consequences. It is just a matter of time. Will we wait for the inevitable before doing something about this insane situation? A moral society would not. Ideally, appropriate reform will establish regulatory, examining and accounting procedures that limit the natural inclination to lend credibility to situations that do not justify it. This is surely possible. If it is not, however, we would be better off to eliminate the appearance of propriety, by eliminating the regulatory, examining and auditing functions altogether. If anyone were allowed to open a bank, at least potential depositors would not be under the false impression that the mere existence of regulators and auditors gives some assurance of the system's viability. The banks that would thrive under such conditions would be the ones that would be relatively sounder. They would be the banks that eschew secrecy in favor of divulging as much information as possible about their operations and their performance.

Chapter IX

Destroying the Host Organism

I see in the near future a crisis approaching which unnerves me and cause me to tremble for the safety of my country. Corporations (of banking) have been enthroned, an era of corruption in high places will follow, and the money power of the country will endeavor to prolong its reign by working upon the prejudices of the people until the wealth is aggregated in a few hands and the Republic destroyed.

-Abraham Lincoln

We have now covered each of the six key areas of special privilege enjoyed by the monetary elite. The implications are summarized below.

Money creation- In our society, only banks have the privilege of creating and distributing money. First, the Federal Reserve Bank (a private corporation) has the special privilege of creating unlimited liabilities against itself called Federal Reserve Notes, which, by virtue of legal tender laws, are accorded the status of "money." Individual banks are then allowed to create multiple dollars of liabilities against themselves for each dollar of Federal Reserve Notes that they have. Throughout history---even when this process was partially limited by gold---whomsoever has been granted this special privilege, has abused it.

Asset protection- If the Fed so chooses, it can guarantee the assets of any bank by buying the bank's assets at their time-adjusted face value. Since the Fed has an unlimited ability to do this, no bank, no matter how poorly managed, can ever fail if the Fed merely chooses to rescue it. To date, the Fed has favored taxpayer bailouts, instead. The effect is essentially the same.

Liability protection- FDIC deposit guarantees pervert the very essence of the investment process. More dollars are deposited in banks than would otherwise be the case. FDIC protection enables anyone with a banking charter to loot the system; it enables failing banks to try to speculate their way out of trouble, without regard to consequences. FDIC protection virtually guarantees that most deposits will find their way into the most speculative banks offering the highest interest rates.

Public rescue missions- Various taxpayer bailout schemes permit the banks to pay no attention to the risk of any enterprise---no matter how stupid---particularly if they all act in concert with each other. By acting together---whether it is lending to Mexico, South-East Asia, Donald Trump, or LTCM---they can virtually guarantee they will be rescued if things go wrong.

Accounting irregularities- Accounting rules allow banks, and only banks, to carry investments at acquisition cost when the current market value is lower. This unquestionably perverts the bank's true financial health. No rationale for this is plausible. Other rules are similarly perverse and distort reality. In addition, regulatory bodies and politicians intervene with their own irregularities whenever such intervention is required to protect these inherently unsound and unstable institutions from their own excesses.

Bank secrecy- Bank management is permitted to keep vital information away from both its stockholders and the general public. The Fed acts in secret and the Federal Advisory Council meets in secret with the Fed. These are some of the manifestations of the special privileges relating to secrecy.

Putting it all together: banks have the special privilege of creating and distributing money to favored borrowers; the Fed expands and contracts this privilege, at will; the Fed can also buy a bank's assets at face value, at will, thereby guaranteeing the value of the banks assets; FDIC deposit protection assures that money flows into banks, in general, and unsound banks offering above market interest rates, in particular, by removing risk considerations for potential depositors; when banks get into trouble, ordinary taxpayers pick up the tab while the banks continue to operate however they see fit; voodoo accounting enables banks and their accountants to create their own reality and to prevent the real reality from being discovered; and, for still further protection, banks are allowed to operate in greater secrecy than virtually every other segment of society.

We are talking about special privilege---plain and simple. Each of the root causes of the coming collapse of our money and banking system reflects it. The solution is to remove it or, at least, reduce it substantially. Those who recognize the truth of this summary will favor meaningful reform. Most people who are not, themselves, members of the privileged class or lackeys or dupes of the privileged class, will presumably see the merits of reforming an immoral, unstable system.

In the movie, *Trading Places*, Dan Akkroyd's character (Winthorpe), a wealthy commodities broker, and Eddie Murphy's character (Valentine), a homeless beggar, were manipulated into trading places. Specifically, the owners of the firm that employed Winthorpe made a bet about what would happen if Valentine was given Winthorpe's position and Winthorpe, himself, lost his job due to a false accusation of criminal activity. As it turned out, Valentine prospered while Winthorpe sunk even lower due to his misfortune. To underscore the central role of special privilege in our banking system, consider the following version of *Trading Places*:

> *Take a random person of average intelligence and give him a bank charter and a one-month seminar on how this charter can be used to his personal advantage without straying beyond what has been common practice in banking over the last 20 years. Simultaneously, select a random money-center bank and merely revoke its charter. To be more than fair, require that all current depositors maintain their deposit balances at current levels for the next five years.*

Here is what you can virtually count on under this scenario:

At the end of five years, the randomly chosen person (plus most of his friends and relatives) will be rich although the "bank," itself, may either be insolvent or on its way thereto. The randomly selected ex-money-center bank will consist of a junk heap of assets that will be dwarfed by its liabilities.

Such a thought experiment---perhaps more than anything else in this book---dramatizes the role of special privilege in our banking system.

PLACEBOS, NON TREATMENTS AND CURES

The political base for sweeping bank reform is unfortunately nowhere to be found. Not a single political figure, today, embraces the concept that major reform is desirable, let alone, necessary. While there have been several multi-billion dollar taxpayer bailouts within the last 10 years, not one of these events was even viewed as a banking crisis. Those in a position to define events cleverly disguised these events as bailouts of the debtors rather than bailouts of the creditors. Even during and after the last acknowledged system-wide problem---the S&L crisis---bank reform of the kind proposed here was hardly on the radar screen. In other words, even when people were generally aware that the banking infrastructure was seriously ailing, significant bank reforms were not suggested, let alone implemented. In fact, even in 1933, after 1/3 of all banks failed in a three-year period, reform came in the form of the relatively mild Glass-Steagall Act. Nonetheless, the stakes are too high, to sit back and do nothing. After all, our fundamentally unsound and immoral monetary system is maintained solely by special privilege and is virtually guaranteed to crash if it is not reformed.

Realistically, a grassroots groundswell is unlikely to occur and, even if it does, would likely fail to bring about the needed changes. What we need is a change in the power structure. This can occur in either (or both) of two ways: a future crisis (short of total collapse) demonstrates inherent problems and the current system loses general credibility; a countervailing power block recognizes that it is unnecessarily and inappropriately disadvantaged by the special privileges that the banking system enjoys.

Either of the cases, above, could move us toward reform in a heartbeat. The existence of books like *Special Privilege* will serve a useful educational role under such circumstances. Until then, all we can do is wait and consider what possibilities might unfold. While these possibilities are literally endless, an example may be instructive. Assume, for example, that a stock market meltdown of gigantic magnitude is set off for some reason---it doesn't really matter what the reason is. Selling panics have a habit of feeding upon themselves and becoming uncontrollable. Hedge funds that have made highly leveraged bets will become hopelessly insolvent as well as any banks that are exposed to these hedge funds as lenders or counter-parties. Uncertainty and panic abounds. As people sell, more and more of them decide to put their money in gold "until the dust settles." Seeing this process unfold, other people also look to get out of currencies and into gold, thereby exacerbating a stampede out of paper and electronic money. When the dust does settle, people will again become starkly aware of the folly of storing one's value in paper currency and electronic money that someone else can print or create in unlimited supplies by whim. Real bank reform ensues.

LARRY KING, LIVE: March 1, 1991

> ***Larry King:*** *Good evening and welcome to Larry King Live. My guests tonight are Will B. Fehr and Y.B. Fehr, co-authors of the book, "Destroying the Host Organism."*
>
> *Some of you viewers may have received this book, unsolicited and for free in the mail. In one of the more unique and remarkable marketing strategies that I have ever heard of, the Fehr's have, at their own expense, mailed out, totally free of charge, one million copies of their book. Later on in the show, we will include your phone calls. Will, Y.B., welcome to Larry King Live.*

Will: Thank you, Larry. It's great to be here!

Larry: I have read your book and found it fascinating. You bring up lots of things that I personally wasn't aware of. Your solution to our current banking crisis seems to entail rather extreme reforms to the system. Do you really feel it is necessary to institute such sweeping reform?

Y.B.: All of the reforms we suggest, Larry, spring quite naturally from widely recognized and widely reported observations. We have merely taken these observations to their logical conclusions. For example, current banking practice is inherently unstable because banks finance long-term assets with short-term liabilities. We, therefore, recommend that banks be required to match the maturities of their assets with those of their liabilities. If the reforms we recommend to achieve this goal appear radical, that is just testimony to how far we have wandered from sound practice.

Larry: Let me stop you right there for a minute. You believe that checking account money should not be lent out by banks at all and that 1-year CDs, for example, should only be lent for a year. Do I have that right?

Y.B.: Exactly, Larry, although the only thing we would absolutely require is that they not lend out any of the checkbook money. In our judgment, to do so is morally fraudulent, in that it creates money. Matching other maturities would be left to the banks themselves, but in the atmosphere that we would encourage, banks will, hopefully, freely choose to operate on a sound basis. Other businesses already operate on the sound principle that asset and liability maturities should be reasonably matched. It is something that a first-year business student learns early on. To operate otherwise is unsound because creditors cannot be paid off on the promised schedule. If this were all that were wrong with the system, we would be in great shape. Even though banks would not be able to meet their obligations on a timely basis, they would, at least, ultimately be able to do so.

Larry: *Do you mean that they can't do so now as the system now stands?*

Will: *Unfortunately, not. Theoretically, any bank whose assets exceed its liabilities can do so, and, theoretically every operating bank in the country is in such a position according to its accounting records. But, unfortunately, the accounting records bear very little relationship to the actual financial condition of most banks.*

Larry: *Let me see if I understand what you are saying. Are you saying that in actuality most banks have liabilities that exceed their assets? If that is so, doesn't that mean that these banks are already insolvent?*

Will: *You understand perfectly, Larry. Let me put this in everyday terms for your audience. Suppose that I had $1 million and I borrowed another $10 million. Suppose I lend $2 million to my Cousin Donald and $9 million to my Uncle Sam. As long as both debtors can repay the money that they borrowed, I will be able to pay back all of the money I borrowed. Now assume that the $10 million I borrowed is due on demand whereas the loans I made are due in 1 year. The situation would be as Y.B. described earlier wherein I cannot pay back my liabilities within the agreed upon time frame (on demand) but I can eventually meet my obligations. But now suppose, for whatever reason, Cousin Donald cannot repay me* *the $2 million---now or at any time in the foreseeable future. Now I have $10 million in liabilities and only $9 million of assets (the good loan to Uncle Sam). My real net worth at this point is minus $1 million. I can therefore, only pay back 90 cents on every dollar that I borrowed from my creditors. But if accounting gimmicks allow me to maintain that Cousin Donald is still good for the money, I can maintain that I am perfectly solvent.*

Larry: *So the whole issue turns on whether your loan to your Cousin Donald is good and, therefore, worth $2 million or is bad and, therefore worth nothing. But from what you asked us to assume in your example there is really little choice. If Donald can't pay, the loan you made to him has no value.*

Y.B.: *Quite right, Larry. It's a question of whether the loan to Donald is recorded at par---the value at the time the loan was initiated---or is recorded as being worthless (i.e. the amount someone would be willing to pay now to purchase the loan). We argue, along with every independent economist, that the current value of the loan is the only meaningful number. And you would think that anyone who had his or her head screwed on right would see it the same way. Unfortunately, in the sorry state of affairs that now exists, people from Alan Greenspan to Ted Kennedy are looking for new and ingenious ways to allow banks to maintain the fiction that the loan to Cousin Donald is still worth $2 million.*

Larry: *Wait a second. You are moving ahead too fast for me. What exactly are you saying that Alan Greenspan and Ted Kennedy, for example, are doing to obscure the true facts and what is their rationale for doing so?*

Will: *Just last month, in late February 1991, for example, in Congressional testimony, Greenspan suggested that the Fed has been looking into the feasibility of purchasing commercial loans from banks at par. While he claimed to be opposed to this expansion of Fed powers (sure!), and indicated he wasn't even sure that legal authority existed (yet) for such moves, he, nonetheless, decided to trot out the concept in public. Ted Kennedy, who was concerned about the so-called credit crunch and its effects on the New England economy, wondered why any additional authority was even necessary. Greenspan has also openly opposed carrying bank owned real estate at market value. His publicly stated rationale is that this would artificially peg values at their currently depressed levels. This argument would make no sense coming from a first year economics student. Coming from Alan Greenspan, it's simply amazing! It's equivalent to a buyer of stock on margin objecting to a margin call after a market crash because it is unfair to value the stock at its current depressed level. Greenspan's real reason for opposing market value accounting is to protect the banks and to instill (false) confidence in a system that is currently in a state of severe deterioration and has been for some time. With apologists and agents arguing for denials of reality, the situation will only get worse.*

Larry: *You have argued that those in power deny reality---which only make things worse. I find it hard to believe their sole motivation is to grant and extend special privileges to the banks.*

Y.B.: *It's a little more complex than that---but not much. Certainly some succumb to strong lobbying efforts and other cozy relationships with the banks. But there are other factors. For many, maintenance of the status quo and confidence is of paramount importance; for others, finding easy, short-term palliatives* *is preferable to finding difficult, long-term solutions. Look at the arguments, for example, regarding the expanding federal deficits. Most political leaders will now freely admit that we are mortgaging our future in order to avoid today's harsh realities. That does not stop them, however, from continuing to approve one deficit after another. We would, at least, like to get to this stage with regard to the equally obvious situation in the banking system. In other words, even if they continue to act foolishly against our long-term best interests, we would like to see more acknowledgment of the real problem as a prelude to real reform at some future point.*

Larry: *Westport, Connecticut, go ahead. You're on the air*

Caller: *Larry, congratulations for a great show. I'd like to ask the Fehr's a question. I am a banker and I wonder if they truly understand the problems involved with market value accounting. Market values cannot be easily established for loans in which there is no active market. It's not as if we are dealing with stocks or something where there are active public markets that allow us to determine market value. How do they propose to deal with valuation problems?*

Y.B.: *No one said that it will be easy, but many bankers would have us believe that it is impossible to accomplish. They take this position because it is in their best interests to do so. First of all, a bank's assets consist of loans and investments. The investment portion of a bank's portfolio is easily reflected at market value rather than at cost. Secondly, some forms of loans---like the LDC loans---do have a secondary market. These loans trade at a fraction of their par value. But the key first step is to at least get general agreement that market value is the appropriate stan-*

*dard. Procedures can be developed once we ac-
knowledge the obvious---that market value is valid
and historical cost is not. For example, (and I hesi-
tate to give a specific example, because other ap-
proaches are equally plausible) banks can be required to put up for auction loans that have a specified set of characteristics in terms of size, growth in
amount over time, non-performance status, etc. They
could then be required to either sell these loans to the
highest bidder or, alternatively, to record the loans
on their books at some discount from par (e.g. half
way between par and the highest bid). Certainly procedures can be established and refined once there is
a philosophical commitment to the concept.*

Larry: *Couldn't the procedures you suggest push
many banks into insolvency?*

Will: *Only if they are already insolvent. All we are
arguing for is recognition of reality rather than denial of reality.*

Larry: *Tulsa, Oklahoma, go ahead, you're on the air.*

Caller: *Thanks for taking my call, Larry. Great show.
I have read the Fehr's book and found it to be quite
interesting and informative. What struck me most is
how overwhelming evidence of our still deteriorating
banking system has not yet moved our political leaders toward appropriate reform. It makes an individual, concerned citizen, like myself, frustrated to see
this degree of lethargy. It stands in such stark contrast to the very bold moves we took in the Middle
East, for example, where we moved with speed and
purpose when the President deemed that our vital interests were at stake. What I'd like to ask is this:
what can we do, individually, and as a nation, to begin to move in the right direction on these matters?*

Will: *I share the caller's frustration. It is so easy to become complacent and to feel that there is no use fighting a battle where so many powerful forces are aligned against what you see as logical, common sense remedial action. Our solution to this dilemma was to write a book. I can't help but feel that as more people become aware of the situation, complacency will give way to real solutions. Perhaps, as more and more is written and as more and more concerned citizens write to their representatives in Congress, things will begin to change.*

As we see it, there are three areas that we must address: control of the money supply, deposit insurance, and regulatory and accounting reform. While these three areas are all vitally important, the issue of deposit insurance represents the best opportunity for a grass roots movement, around which average citizens can rally. Control of the money supply, is seen to be within the purview of the Fed, and regulatory and accounting rules are within the purview of all the regulators and the accounting community. It would be difficult to attack these latter issues without running into serious defensive and protective reactions on the part of these special interests. However, a grass roots movement of ordinary citizens who want to give up its own special privilege of deposit protection as part of a package to achieve broader objectives would be difficult to ignore. In effect, the general population would offer to give up its special privilege in order to eliminate all special privileges. It's like being willing to take the lead in disarming as long as it is linked to general disarmament.

Larry: *Old Bridge, N.J., you're on the air. Go ahead, please.*

Caller: *I have read the Fehr's book and am convinced that most people will share their views once they inform themselves on these issues. I want to thank the Fehr's for writing their book and ask them to comment on the importance of controlling the money supply which may not be obvious to the viewing audience unless it is specifically pointed out. Thanks.*

Y.B.: *I'm glad you made that request, caller, because clearly the lack of control of the money supply is at the core of all our problems. In our book, we provide a rather specific way to gain control of the money supply. The procedure is too involved to detail, here, so we recommend that you all read the book. Our solution admittedly involves substantial reform to current policies and institutions. It was our attempt to cover all the bases. It is also possible that somewhat less global solutions are also feasible. In any event, control of the money supply is of paramount importance. Had monetary control been achieved over the last quarter century, we would not be in our current state. Federal deposit insurance and accounting gimmickry would be dormant rather than active threats to our system. Liberal creation of bank money has always been and will always be a threat to the values and vitality of any modern society. The inescapable effects of uncontrolled and even undercontrolled money creation is inflation, high interest rates, get rich quick schemes, fraud, and, at the core, a declining morality.*

Liberal creation of money for unproductive purposes is worst of all and is particularly descriptive of bank lending over the last 15 years. It destabilizes existing productive enterprise by changing the value of the very standard of value. It encourages borrowing and speculation and discourages saving and productive investment. It produces extreme concentrations in the distribution of wealth. Worst of all, it is a sickness, like other addictive diseases, that feeds on itself and leaves a lasting mark on the society long after it has seemingly abated.

Larry: You seem to be arguing in favor of freezing the amount of money in the society. I have always been led to believe that monetary expansion was consistent with and even necessary for economic expansion and wealth creation.

Y.B.: With all due respect, Larry, that belief may be widely held, but it just doesn't stand up to inspection. I will readily admit that if monetary expansion is firmly tied to productive enterprise, there is a good chance that economic expansion will follow. It is also possible for seemingly productive enterprises to fail. And when they do fail, wealth is destroyed rather than created. Creation of new money is not a prerequisite for wealth creation. Transfer of money from bona fide savers to bona fide investors will take place at sufficient levels to finance economic expansion. When money is created for consumers to spend, inflation occurs and everyone suffers. The offsetting benefit and often the justification for it, is increased employment. If you or I were allowed to manufacture and spend our own money, it would also have the same effects. That doesn't mean it would be good. When the money supply is increased to support the redistribution of wealth, it produces somewhat less inflation, increases employment, and, as a byproduct, makes some very wealthy people even wealthier---at everyone else's expense. This 'byproduct' is the real rationale for much of this activity--- although those who justify such activity rarely mentioned it. Nor do they mention the destruction to real wealth and the sapping of true productive activity that such lending inevitably engenders. In our book we discuss this form of money creation under the titles of the Trump and Milken syndromes. It is the worst form of money creation and has little or no redeeming virtue. And, again, it would not have occurred without the inflationary money creation of the 1970s preceding it.

Larry: Atlanta, Georgia, you're on the air. Go ahead, please.

Caller: Thank you, Larry. I have not read the Fehr's book, but it seems to me that they are putting forth a very radical proposal to completely revamp our banking system and appealing to the masses for support of their agenda. Why should anyone listen to them, when the people in control see things so differently? It's easy to be an armchair general and a Monday morning quarterback. They don't have to deal with the tough real issues that our politicians and bankers have to in dealing with the largest and best economy in the world.

Y.B.: The first thing I will say is 'read the book' before you decide how radical, undesirable, or unnecessary our recommendations are. We reject the idea that we should blindly assume that the people in charge of a particular problem or issue are always doing the right thing or even trying to do the right thing from the standpoint of the general population. That kind of thinking usually leads to the perpetuation of rather than solutions to problems. Much of the problem springs from an improper view of the role and the motivation of key institutions. For example, if you see the Fed as a regulator trying to keep the banks and the money supply in check for the good of society, you may feel like the caller. If, instead, you see the Fed as an agent for the banks---and, in particular, the money-center banks that proposed, designed, and promoted the Fed to begin with, you will more likely see things as we do.

The objective fact that cannot be ignored in all of this, however, is that the Fed has not controlled the money supply--- whether or not it was trying to do so. The only room for disagreement is whether you think a regulator is doing a poor job of regulating or

*whether you think an agent of the banking elite is try-
ing to do a good job for its client. We obviously think
it is the latter, but, even if you think it's the former,
you may want to consider more effective ways to control monetary growth. Since money is unquestionably
of central importance to the economy and the society,
we feel it is reasonable to expect it to not be perverted. A similar issue applies to bank accounting
rules and the accounting profession. Is the profession
attempting to properly reflect bank performance on
behalf of society, or is it, instead, primarily motivated
by the interests of its clients? Clearly, it has been either unwilling or unable to give early warnings of
bank failures.*

Larry: *Los Angeles, you're on the air.*

Caller: *Larry, I feel that the ideas expressed by the
Fehr's are dangerous to the country. They are totally
negative on everything and everybody. None of our
institutions are sacred to them and, if their views are
given a forum on your show and elsewhere they will
undermine people's confidence in the system. That's
all I have to say.*

Larry: *Caller, can I ask you what you do for a living?*

Caller: *I am a partner in a 'Big Six' accounting firm.
I am not personally involved in bank audits, but I
know my partners who are and they would not compromise their independence to support a client's
point of view. We don't operate that way, and I resent
the implication that we do.*

Will: *Aside from the obvious conflict of interest, the
caller is stating the widely held belief that confidence
in the system is an end in itself. We totally reject that
reasoning. Having confidence in something which is*

undeserving of the confidence, in our judgment, is the worst of all possible states of affairs. Building confidence, by building effective, reliable institutions, we are very much in agreement with. We even agree with the stated underlying objectives of the institutions that we are critically examining. The Fed's objective is, supposedly, to control the money supply. We agree so much with that objective that we want to institute policies, programs, and institutions that are capable of, desirous of, and willing to achieve it.

The objective of bank accounting is to reflect, accurately and fairly, the financial conditions of banks. Here, too, we are in total agreement. The objective of federal deposit insurance is to provide a safe and secure banking system and savings environment on which the average citizen can depend. Again, of course, we agree with the objective and its importance. We just feel that the means are not only ineffective but counterproductive, as well.

Larry: *Let me ask you this. Do you see any signs that other observers are holding views similar to your own?*

Will: *Yes and no. Many people have made observations similar to those we make, but they have not always followed through with what we feel are the logical conclusions or have not supported them forcefully enough. For example, many people have come to recognize the perverse influence that federal deposit insurance had in helping to create the S&L crisis. Some academic studies have even looked into the feasibility of phasing it out over a number of years. On the other hand, even with all the evidence suggesting how detrimental it can be, politicians are afraid to touch the issue. Even those who came out initially with statements that FDIC protection should be reduced retreated from these positions as politically dangerous.*

With regard to control of the money supply, politicians are more than willing to pay lip service to the goal of monetary restraint and control. Congress has even introduced bills that are designed to make the Fed more accountable to them. But such moves have been an "on again, off again" affair since the mid 1970s with no real progress ever having been achieved. Milton Friedman has championed various concepts designed to achieve this goal. As reasonable and self-evident as most of his positions were, they were ignored for 20+ years. When they were given a three-year trial from 1979-82, they were only partially successful because banks had learned various techniques for circumventing the control. It was argued that, because of these banking gimmicks involving Eurodollar transfers and the proliferation of new financial instruments, direct control of the money supply was not possible. The attitude seemed to be that if we try to make a serious attempt to accomplish something as important as controlling the money supply, and the banks find gimmicks to circumvent those controls on behalf of their own self- interest, we should passively give in to them. Why not, instead, shut off these self-serving ploys in order to achieve beneficial public policy objectives. The Fed, however, quickly abandoned the controls that were so unpopular with the banks apparently without regard to the obvious general benefits.

These are just a few of the telling incidents that we report in our book, wherein just a superficial reading between the lines leads one to conclude that the Fed is more the agent of the banks than an independent regulator. On the issue of market versus cost accounting and some other satellite accounting issues such as goodwill accounting, there has been pressure on the accounting profession to develop more meaningful accounting rules. The profession, itself pays lip service, at least, to looking into alternatives. After years of looking into alternatives, the profession has come up empty handed. This is, however, the area most likely to produce a breakthrough.

Larry: *That's surprising, because it seems to be the area least likely to inflame the passions of the public or to be fully understood by them. Why do you think this is?*

Y.B.: *You have to recognize, Larry, where the pressure is coming from. Then it will become very clear. You might think that the Fed, as regulator of the banks, would insist on accurate reporting. If anything, however, the Fed has lined up on the other side of the issue---making apologies for the banks and coming up with empty logic why various elements of market-based accounting are inappropriate. We discussed Greenspan's position on market based accounting for real estate earlier, if you will recall. This is more consistent with a Fed role as bank agent rather than as bank regulator. Curiously, on this issue, the SEC is providing the pressure. It just so happens that the SEC is the regulator of (perhaps, instead, the agent for) the securities industry. A cynic might very well see a pattern here. The industry that the SEC regulates would benefit to some extent if the banks were weakened. Merrill Lynch and Goldman Sachs would certainly not be adverse to a shift in power away from commercial banks and toward investment banks. Therefore, the SEC might very well be comfortable championing a reasonable position that can be cloaked in public interest, but which also supports the narrow interest of its client industry.*

Larry: *This has all been very interesting. We are out of time but maybe you can come back at some time in the future. The name of the book, again, is 'Destroying the Host Organism' by the brother and sister team of Will B Fehr and Y.B. Fehr. Please stay tuned* *for the second part of the show. My guest will be Ivana Trump.*

THE O'REILLY FACTOR: March 1, 2001

Bill O'Reilly: You are about to enter a no spin zone. We'll be back in 90 seconds...

Now for the talking points memo...

O.K., When we come back from our break, we will be speaking to Y.B. Fehr, one of the authors of a new book entitled, "Special Privilege", which purports to document why we are heading, unavoidably, for a monetary crash. Stick with us---you won't want to miss this....

O.K., we're back, and I'm sitting here with Y.B. Fehr, one half of the brother/sister team that authored an intriguing book 10 years ago called "Destroying the Host Organism" and has just authored a new book entitled "Special Privilege". I've read the book and must admit, I learned things that I truthfully did not fully understand about our money and banking system. Ms. Fehr, may I call you Y.B.?

Y.B.: Please do, and may I call you Bill?

Bill: Of course; now as I said, I've read your book and confess that you put forth a seemingly compelling case for your point of view. However, I have also spoken to people who are recognized experts in these matters and they assure me that your arguments are pure sophistry. What do you say to that?

Y.B.: Well, it's hard to deal with a general allegation of sophistry other than to point out that most recog-

nized experts are part of the established power structure in one way or another and, therefore, have a vested interest in putting forth the "party line." To both you and your listeners, I would say this: don't take my word or anybody else's word. Examine the evidence yourself and be suspicious of those who marginalize the other side's point of view---not with logic and reason---but with nebulous characterizations. Such arguments amount to thinly veiled "spin" which I am glad to be protected from here in the "no spin zone."

Bill: *Fair enough, Y.B. Why don't you start by explaining exactly what your book is about?*

Y.B.: *Great. The single most important point of our book is that our monetary system WILL collapse (if it is not reformed along one of the lines we suggest). Of this we have zero doubt. Furthermore, we can tell you exactly WHY this will occur. This is quite different than merely saying the system will crash at some undefined point for some unpredictable reason. We know the reason, for sure. Ironically, the very same reason that tells us WHY we will crash prevents us from saying WHEN we will crash. We have summarized that reason in the two-word title of our book: Special Privilege.*

Special privileges for the monetary elite not only make our march towards a crash inevitable, but they also allow those who have these special privileges to deny, disguise, and put-off the consequences of reality. So, to your question "Why are we going to crash?" I answer, "special privilege;" to your question, "Why haven't we already crashed?" I again answer, "special privilege." Bill, if you will permit me a minute to put forth a limited amount of relevant background, I think I can explain myself by posing a hypothetical to you. Is that O.K.?

Bill: *Sure, go ahead. I'm intrigued.*

Y.B.: *OK, Bill. Assume that the government guaranteed from loss any money that people chose to deposit with Bill O'Reilly. Do you agree that you would be the beneficiary of a special privilege?*

Bill: *Yes, I would acknowledge that.*

Y.B.: *That is special privilege #1. It corresponds to an actual special privilege of banks. OK, Let's assume the government did that for you and, say, 99 other people. Suppose, further, that for every paper dollar that you keep in the O'Reilly bank vaults (or any of the other 99 banks in the cartel) you are allowed to lend up to $9, at interest, to other people simply by opening up checking accounts for these borrowers. Each paper dollar in your vaults supports $10 in checking account balances. In other words, Bill, you have been allowed to create $9 out of thin air and lend it out at interest. This is special privilege #2: the money creating privilege. It, too, is a special privilege of our actual banking system. This system will, of course, collapse if enough people want to get cash from you (which isn't there). That's what used to happen every twenty years or so throughout the 19th and early 20th centuries. To be absolutely clear, Bill---from day 1---the O'Reilly Bank is incapable of fulfilling its legal obligation to depositors. The O'Reilly Bank can only survive if people do not present their legitimate claims for cash redemption. This is no different than any other Ponzi Scheme.*

Bill: *Well wait a second here. Are you saying that the O'Reilly Bank (which is your proxy for all banks) is nothing more than an elaborate scam from the git-go?*

Y.B.: *Well, clearly it is never capable of meeting its legal obligations. If you consider that to be a scam (as I do), then it is a scam (albeit, a legally condoned one). Others feel that as long as we have confidence in the system and keep our money in the banks, everything is fine and we all benefit from it. But let me go on. Since all money is created by the banking system and since most dollars have initially been lent into the system, it is hard to fathom how all of those borrowers can manage to pay both the interest and principal on their loans unless still more money is lent into the system. In other words, more and more money is needed just for current borrowers to be able to pay interest and principal on existing loans. This on-going process is why we used to deal in millions of dollars; then, we dealt in billions of dollars; and more recently, we have become used to trillions. Since we can't predict when the crash will occur, we may be using quadrillions before it comes. In any event, to keep this system afloat, the Fed can and does create money, without limit, whenever it must--- and that will be often just to keep things afloat.*

Bill: *Well isn't that good? The Fed acts as a lender of last resort to make sure we always have enough money?*

Y.B.: *Not in my view. It merely guarantees that the Fed will pump more and more money into a system that will always need more and that ultimately our money will be worthless. Anytime anyone has been given the special privilege of creating money out of nothing in the past, they have always abused it. It's human nature.*

Bill: *I think I see, now. If the only money in the system must be lent into it, there will never be enough to pay the banks principal and interest unless the Fed creates it for them.*

Y.B.: Exactly. The money creators will always need to "feed the monster." Since the Fed can do this at no expense, without limit, and to the benefit of its clients at everyone else's expense, why wouldn't it do so? Now, let's go a step further, Bill. As president of the O'Reilly Bank, you can choose to lend money to whomever you wish. Let's say that some types of loans benefit from arbitrary accounting rules while others don't. Which loans do you think you will make?

Bill: Well, I'd like to believe I would make loans to the borrowers that actually had the best chance for success.

Y.B.: Okay, fair enough. But, all other things being equal, I assume you would lend to the entities with the more favorable accounting treatment. Let me ask you this: let's assume that for some loans you get to keep the profits if the loans work out but other people will shoulder any losses if the loans do not work out. I presume you will favor such loans over those where you have to absorb your own losses.

Bill: Well, of course.

Y.B.: That's exactly what most actual bankers do in these circumstances. First of all, some loans can be manipulated and disguised to look profitable even when they don't work out---these loans tend to get a disproportionate amount of the action. Also, by making loans in the same area as all other banks guarantees that when things go wrong, taxpayers will bail you out. So accounting rules allow you to defy reality (special privilege #3) and taxpayers rescue you when things go wrong (special privilege #4). Add to this the fact that you are allowed to operate in relative secrecy (special privilege #5)---even from your own

222

stockholders---and you begin to get a picture of the perverse special privileges that both guarantee the crash and put it off, at one and the same time. And we haven't even considered the icing on the cake: when all else fails, the Fed can---without restriction or limit---buy the assets of any bank at any price with money it creates out of thin air (special privilege #6)!

Bill: *Well, how do we deal with all this?*

Y.B.: *There are several different possible solutions--- it all depends on which aspect of this perverse situation one thinks is the worst part. All of the alternatives would remove the special privileges from the banking cartel. Some favor a concept called social credit that takes the money-creation privilege away from private banks and gives it to the government. Essentially, the social credit school argues in favor of having the government spend money into existence rather than having banks lend it into existence. Another school believes that the worst aspect of the system is that our currency is a fiat currency that is issued rather than a commodity that has intrinsic value, in and of itself. Some in this camp favor a return to the gold standard; others in this camp believe we should merely remove the special privileges of the banking cartel by allowing anyone to open a bank and requiring them to fully disclose their activities. As different as these solutions are, each substantially improves upon the current system. My solution, however, is to freeze the monetary base by taking the money-creation privilege away from everyone. This goal can effectively be accomplished by simultaneously paying down the national debt by issuing Treasury certificates (i.e. money) while simultaneously increasing the fractional reserve ratio of banks- -until the reserve ratio is ultimately pegged at 100%. This solution eliminates the national debt, saves billions in annual interest, removes special privileges* *from the banking system, and establishes a stable, immutable, monetary unit. Leading academic monetary experts such as Irving Fisher of Yale and Frank Graham of Princeton put forth a version of this solution during the banking crisis of the 1930s*

Bill: *Well, I'd have to give some thought to those proposals before I could have an opinion one way or another. On a related subject, though, it really angers me when Alan Greenspan fails to recognize we are going into recession and then fails to lower interest rates as early as he should. Now, it looks like we're going into a recession, no matter what---just because he failed to act. It also galls me that he isn't answerable to anyone. Where am I wrong?*

Y.B.: *First of all Bill, let me tell you where you are right. You're right to question why we have a system where the entire economic and financial well being of our society hinges on the decision of one unaccountable man, acting in secret. Where you're wrong is in not pushing to change this system. There is ample evidence that Greenspan is not being up front with us on a number of issues. You have to ask why.*

For example, Greenspan has been saying for years how important it is to pay down the national debt. Yet, on 1/25/01, in testimony before Congress, he essentially took the position that unless we do something about it, right now, we will have to pay down the debt too quickly and have large surpluses left over that would have to be invested in private assets, which would be a bad turn of events. Even superficial examination of the facts, however, reveals that Greenspan had to distort the statistics to allow him to reach his new conclusion. First, he assumed that the social security budget surplus would be used to pay down the national debt. There is zero justification for this assumption. It has never been done before, so why now? Greenspan manufactured this "fact" to "support" the conclusion that we no longer need to concern ourselves with what he has always maintained was of vital importance. Second, he ignored the fact that the numbers he relied on assumed that the entire unified budget would be used to pay off the debt and/or acquire private assets. If it is not so used, the surpluses will be 25% lower. A more complete analysis can be found on the FAME website.[1]

Why did Greenspan change his mind? The answer is that the Fed---and therefore Greenspan---never favored paying off the national debt. That was only part of its typical misdirection. After all, the national debt transfers $50 billion per year from ordinary citizens to banks---the Fed's clients. The banks own about $1 trillion of the debt without doing any work for it. They just used their special privilege to create money out of thin air to acquire it. Furthermore, the Fed holds another ½ trillion of the debt that they use to manipulate the economy. That manipulation has resulted in a 92% devaluation of the dollar in 60 years---and yet, through misdirection that can only be described as masterful, the Fed has convinced everybody that it is not only responsible enough, but rather too responsible in its efforts to combat inflation!

So Bill, even with your ire over the Fed's behavior, they still have you eating out of their hand. You react to them just as they want you to: as if they were the parent and you were the child. Your question boils down to, "Why won't mom and dad let me have the car? I've been responsible and besides, if they don't give me the car I run the risk of having my social life fall behind the other kids." Your more proper reaction should be, "Why is this stranger now offering me this candy I've been begging for? Why does this stranger have control over the candy supply to begin with?"

Bill, if anybody in your listening audience believes Greenspan and these other politicians (yes, I con-

sider Greenspan a politician---a shameless one at that!) that our debt will now be paid down by two trillion over the next decade even with the planned tax cut, I will make an offer they can't refuse: I will give them 3-1 odds that the national debt won't be reduced by even 1 penny over the next decade.

Bill: *Well, this has been a lively and interesting discussion. We'll have to have you back on "The Factor" soon. For now, I'll let you have the last word.*

Y.B.: *Thank you so much for having me on your show, Bill. All I'd like to say to your listeners is this: please read our book, Special Privilege, and then decide for yourself whether significant reform is needed in our monetary system. Trust your own minds and hearts. Listen, respectfully, with an open mind, to all opinions on all sides, but then form your own conclusions. Be particularly suspicious of vested interests that imply they know these things better than you, and that you, therefore, should just let them do what they know is best.*

DESTROYING THE HOST ORGANISM

Hopefully, some day soon, ordinary citizens will recognize the perverse effects of special privilege on our monetary system. Over the last quarter century, our banking system lent money to one risky project after another. When many of these risky projects went bad, the losses were "socialized." Favorable accounting gimmicks permitted banks to pretend everything was fine. In other words, those who benefit when things went well were not the ones who suffered the consequences when things went badly. This completely perverts the investment process and guarantees bad investment decisions. It is called moral hazard. When moral hazard is confined to a relatively small area, it is possible to avoid devastating results. Unfortunately, the situation with our monetary system is not confined.

The entire financial infrastructure is at risk to moral hazard. At present, a financial collapse of grave and lasting consequences is virtually guaranteed unless we set about, purposefully, to re-instill morality and remove the obscene special privilege that characterizes our financial system.

Will we continue to shore up a status quo in which one's fate largely rests on how close he is to the money-creating process? How close he is to the money-creating special privilege? Wide disparities in wealth, power, and privilege have, historically, been associated with societies that are in decline or heading toward revolution. Such conditions are most evident in unjust and exploitative societies where special privilege massively redistributes wealth from the weak to the powerful. Disparities are appropriate when they reflect differences in ability and effort. In fact, as long as the vast majority of members in a society are moving in the right direction, everything is usually fine. After all, even the relatively affluent tend to be unhappy when their situation is deteriorating; and even the abject poor are generally happy as long as their condition is improving. More than almost anything else, current disparities reflect the degree of access one has to newly created money. Inequities reflect the banking system's very uneven and unfair distribution of newly created money.

Over the last decade, the M-3 money supply grew from about $4.1 trillion to about $7.1 trillion. In other words, banks have created and very unevenly distributed about $3 trillion. Take away this capability of banks and we will have gone a long way toward a more equitable and just society. Continuing current trends enables the creators of money to destroy wealth. The primary borrowers over the last two decades have not been the producers of wealth---but rather the acquisitors of wealth. They borrow and buy up the existing wealth of the country and sap our productive capacity in the process. The creators of money will not willingly give up their special privilege and will not see the destructive consequences of their acts. They feed off the process and are nourished by it. Like all parasites, they will remain blithely unaware---until it is too late---that their actions are destroying the host organism.

List of Additional Resources

Books

Money, Whence It Came, Where It Went by John Kenneth Galbraith, published in 1975, provides an excellent history of money and money matters.

The Mystery of Banking by Murray Rothbard, published in 1983, provides an excellent introduction to the concept of money and the perversions of fractional reserve banking.

The Case Against the Fed by Murray Rothbard, published in 1994, is an irreverent look at the all-powerful Federal Reserve.

Paper Aristocracy by Howard Katz provides an interesting overview of the money creation special privilege and its implications.

Websites

http://www.fame.org is the home page for the Foundation for the Advancement of Monetary Education. This website is devoted, primarily, to the immorality of fiat currency.

http://www.visi.com/~mts// is the home page for Money Talk$ Journal. It offers an interesting populist slant to the money issue.

http://www.norfed.com/ is the home page for NORFED (National Organization for the Repeal of the Federal Reserve Act and Internal Revenue Service. Some of the articles on the Federal Reserve link are of interest.

http://www.devvy.com/money0.html contains links to interesting articles on money.

http://landru.i-link-2.net/monques/ has many links to other sites of interest.

http://www.themoneymasters.com/ offers an excellent video on monetary history and suggests bank reform in conformance with the ideas in *Special Privilege*.

http://www.geocities.com/Athens/Rhodes/4061/scring.htm has links to many sites that support the concept of Social Credit discussed briefly in Chapters 6 and 9.

ENDNOTES

Introduction: Tick, tock...tick,tock

[1] John Kenneth Galbraith, *Money: Whence It Came, Where It Went*, Boston, Houghton Mifflin Company, 1975, 18

[2] Email correspondence with Edward Goertzen

[3] William Greider, *Secrets of the Temple*, New York, Simon and Schuster, 1987, 433

[4] Galbraith, op. cit., 15

Chapter 1: Early Casualties

[1] The cost of the S&L bailout has been written about in many books, magazine articles, etc. estimates have ranged from $140 billion to $1 trillion. Part of the wide difference has to do with whether interest expense is included in the cost since most of the money was borrowed (i.e. created out of thin air by the banking system---and then lent to us at interest.) $300-$500 billion is used as a reasonable mid-point of these estimates.

[2] Penny Lernoux, *In Banks We Trust*, Garden City, NY, Anchor Press- Doubleday, 1984, 134

[3] Raymond B. Vickers, *Panic in Paradise, Florida's Banking Crash of 1926*, University of Alabama Press, 1994, 12

[4] William Black, *The Incidence and Cost of Fraud and Insider Abuse*, Washington, DC: National Commission on Financial Institution Reform, Recovery and Enforcement, Staff Report No. 13, 1993, 9

[5] GAO, "Thrift Failures: Costly Failures Resulted From Regulatory Violations" GAO/AFMD-89-92, June1989, 21

[6] "The Bulletproof Thrift Villains," *U.S. News and World Report*, July 23, 1990, 18

[7] The story of the back room meeting is covered in several sources (while many participants denied what went on and/or the extent of their participation.) See for example, Kathleen Day, *S&L Hell*, NY, W.W. Norton & Company, 1993, 66

[8] "The Bad Guys of the S&L Fiasco," *U.S. News and World Report*, June 18, 1990, 92

[9] Ayn Rand, *Atlas Shrugged*, NY, Random House, 1957, 387

[10] FDIC, "Savings Institutions Report, Deposits FDIC-Insured Savings Institutions United States and Other Areas," *Historical Statistics on Banking*, http://www2.fdic.gov/hsob/hsobRpt.asp

[11] "Banks: Is Big Trouble Brewing," *Business Week*, July 16, 1990, quoting Lowell Bryan, partner, McKinsey & Company, 146

Chapter 3: The Recurring Nightmare

[1] Michael Jackman, *Business and Economic Quotations*, NY, MacMillan Publishing Co., 1984, 11

[2] Ibid., 11

[3] John Kenneth Galbraith, *Money, Whence It Came, Where It Went*, Boston, Houghton Mifflin Company, 1975, 38, quoting from Harry Miller *Banking Theories in the U.S. Before 1860*, 21

[4] Ibid., 18

[5] Gerald D. Nash, Ed., *Issues in American Economic History,* Boston, D.C. Heath and Company, 1964, 209, from *The Age of Jackson*, 115-131, by Arthur Schlesinger, Jr., Little Brown and Company

[6] George Seldes, *The Great Quotations*, NY, Lyle Stuart, 1966, 355

[7] Gerald D. Nash, op. cit. 218

[8] Ibid., 211

[9] Ibid., 213

[10] Ibid., 216

[11] Michael Jackman, op. cit., 13

[12] Gilbert C. Fite and Jim E. Reese, *An Economic History of the United States,* Boston, Houghton Mifflin Company, 1965, 257

[13] Ibid., 330

[14] http://www.buyandhold.com/bh/en/education/history/2000/121799.html

[15] Wilbur Aldrich, *Money and Credit*, NY, The Grafton Press, 1903, 187

Chapter 4: Building False Confidence

[1] Milton Friedman and Anna Jacobson Schwartz, *The Monetary History of the United States*, Princeton, Princeton University Press, 1963, Appendix A, 708

[2] Lawrence S. Ritter, Ed., *Money and Economic Activity*, 2nd Ed., Boston, Houghton Mifflin Company, 1961, 294-95, from *100% Money*, Irving Fisher, New Haven, The City Printing Company, 1945

[3] Maxwell Newton, *The Fed*, New York, New York Times Books Co., 1983, 212

[4] Milton Friedman, op. cit., 232

[5] Charles P. Kindleberger, *The World in Depression 1929-1939*, Berkeley, University of California Press, 1943, 113, from "Federal Reserve System, Banking and Monetary Statistics"

[6] Milton Friedman, op. cit., Appendix A, 708

[7] Adam Smith, *Paper Money*, NY, Summit Books, 1981, 12, speech before the Committee on Banking, Housing, and Urban Affairs, United States, March 14, 1980

[8] "Burns Cites Limits on Fed Powers," *The New York Times*, October 1, 1979, D1, quoting from speech entitled "The Anguish of Central Banking"

[9] Marjorie Deane and Robert Pringle, *The Central Banks*, NY, Viking, 1995, from the Foreword by Paul A. Volcker

[10] William Greider, *Secrets of the Temple*, New York, Simon and Schuster, 1987, 481

[11] Ibid., 144

[12] Lawrence S. Ritter, Ed., *Money and Economic Activity*, 2nd Ed., Boston, Houghton Mifflin Company, 1961, 83, from "Continuous Borrowing Through 'Short-Term' Bank Loans," Federal Reserve Bank of Cleveland, September, 1956, pp 6-13

[13] Ibid., 84

[14] Greider, op. cit., 190

[15] "Why the Fed Bent on Speculative Loans," *Business Week*, May 19, 1980, 32

[16] http://www.fame.org/NotableQuotes.asp quoting from St. Louis Federal Reserve Bank, Review, Nov. 1975, p.22

[17] James Ring Adams, *The Big Fix: Inside the S&L Scandal: How an Unholy Alliance of Politics and Money Destroyed America's Banking System*, NY, Wiley, 1990, 49

[18] Ritter, op. cit., 297

Chapter 5: "Nothing to Fear, But..."

[1] On the following day, March 3rd, banks in 8 western states were closed and the *New York Times* reported it on page 9. Finally, on March 4th, it finally reported bank closures (in New York and Illinois) as a page-one story.

[2] James Ring Adams, *The Big Fix: Inside the S&L Scandal*, NY, John Wiley & Sons, Inc., 1990, 18

[3] George G. Kaufman and George J. Bentson, *Risk and Solvency Regulation of Depository Institutions: Past Policies and Current Options*, Monographed Series in Finance and Economics, 17

[4] George G. Kaufman, "Implications of Large Bank Problems and Insolvencies for the Banking System and Economic Policy," Staff Memorandum 85-3, Federal Reserve Bank of Chicago

[5] "Greenspan on Deposit Insurance," *The New York Times*, October 4, 1990, D2

[6] Martin Mayer, *The Greatest Ever Bank Robbery*, New York, Charles Scribner's Sons, 1990, 263

Chapter 6: Dollars and Sense

[1] Dr. Lawrence Parks, *The Fight for Honest Monetary Weights and Measures*, Six Essays, a White Paper, Jersey City, Palisades Business Press, 2-3

[2] Board of Governors of the Federal Reserve System, *Private-sector refinancing of the large hedge fund, Long-Term Capital Management,* October 1, 1998, before the Committee on Banking and Financial Services, The U.S. House of Representatives, http://www.federalreserve.gov/boarddocs/testimony/1998

[3] http://www.fame.org/PDF/RonPaulInterview.pdf, from J. Taylor's "Gold and Technology Stocks," May 11, 2000

Chapter 7: Heads I Win, Tails You Lose

[1] Adam Smith, "Unconventional Wisdom: How Our Banks got in Trouble," *Esquire*, Jan. 1983, 51

[2] James Dale Davidson and William Rees-Moog, *Blood in the Streets*, New York, Summit Books, 1987, 117

[3] William Quirk, "The Big Bank Bailout," *The New Republic*, February 21, 1983, 43

[4] William Greider, *Secrets of the Temple*, New York, Simon and Schuster, 1987, 433

[5] Martin Mayer, *The Money Bazaars*, NY, E.P. Dutton, Inc, 1984, 374

[6] "Fed Urges Caution on Reserves," *The New York Times*, January 22, 1988, D1

[7] Jeffrey Sachs, "Robbin' Hood," *The New Republic*, March 13, 1989, 19

[8] "Road to New Debt Policy: Fed-Treasury Tug of War," *The New York Times*, March 10, 1989, D2

[9] "Debt Policy Shift Set," *The New York Times*, March 11, 1989, I 35

[10] "Third World Debt Woes," *The New York Times*, September 23, 1989, I1

[11] Riva Atlas, "Dollars for Donald", *Forbes*, September 14, 1992

[12] "Trump Jumps the Gun a Bit On Success of His Bonds," *New York Times*, June 18, 1993, D1

[13] "Mother of All Stings", Graham Strachan, Truth In Media, October 21, 1998, http://www.truthinmedia.org/Bulletins/tim98-10-7.html

Chapter 8: Who's Watching the Watchdogs

[1] "Who Should Regulate the Banks?" *Bank Stock Quarterly*, April, 1976, 20

[2] Dr. Lawrence Parks, http://www.fame.org/HTM/Why2_FOR HTM CONVERSION.htm

[3] Stephen Pizzo, Mary Fricker, and Paul Muolo, *Inside Job: the Looting of America's Savings and Loans*, NY, McGraw-Hill, 1989, 276

[4] Dr. Carol Schwartz Greenwald, *Banks Are Dangerous to Your Wealth,* Englewood Cliffs, 1980, 217

[5] James Ring Adams, *The Big Fix: Inside the S&L Scandal: How an Unholy Alliance of Politics and Money Destroyed America's Banking System,* NY, Wiley, 1990, 89

[6] Kitty Calavita, Henry Pontell, Robert H. Tillman, *Big Money Crime*, Berkeley, University of California Press, 1997, 94, *from* House Committee on Banking, Finance and Urban Affairs, "Savings and Loan Policies in the late 1970s and 1980s," hearing before the Committee, 101 Congress, 2nd session, 1990, 1 and 3

[7] The New York Times, Sept 14,1990, D2

[8] See for example, Michael M. Lewis, *Liar's Poker*, NY, Penguin Books, 1990

[9] Martin Mayer, *The Greatest Ever Bank Robbery*, New York, Charles Scribner's Sons, 1990, 111-113

[10] Ibid., 294

[11] R. T. Naylor, *Hot Money and The Politics of Debt*, NY, Simon and Schuster, 1987, 51

[12] Martin Mayer, op. cit., 11

[13] Kitty Calavita, et al, op. cit., 73

[14] Martin Mayer, op. cit., 200

Chapter 9: Destroying the Host Organism

[1] Vincent R. LoCascio, "Why Did Mr. Greenspan Change His Mind? An Analysis of his Testimony of 1/25/2001 before the Committee on the Budget, United States Senate, http://fame.org/HTM/LoCascio Greenspan4 rev 02 01 01.htm

INDEX

Printed in the United States
1106000006B/58-75